Advance Praise

"The Antifragile Organization *is a must-read for leaders navigating the complexities of today's business world. Janka and Jörg offer a clear, actionable roadmap to surviving and thriving amid disruption. Their deep insights, supported by compelling case studies, make this book an invaluable guide for anyone looking to build a resilient and innovative organization."*

Ricardo Vargas

Former Chairman of the Project Management Institute and Former Director for Project Management and Infrastructure at the United Nations

---

"*In* The Antifragile Organization, *Janka Krings-Klebe and Jörg Schreiner lay out a powerful blueprint for how companies can do more than just withstand disruptions — they can emerge stronger because of them. This resonates deeply with my own experience leading GE Appliances through periods of intense transformation. To thrive today, organizations must go beyond resilience and embrace antifragility — where challenges become catalysts for reinvention.*

"*The authors offer compelling examples of companies like Haier and Netflix that have mastered the art of adaptation. Their focus on decentralization and empowering teams to move quickly is exactly how we've approached innovation at GE Appliances. This approach has allowed us to stay agile, respond to the market faster, and keep user need at the centre of everything we do.*

"*This book is essential reading for any leader who is serious about breaking free from legacy thinking. If you want your organization to continuously evolve and thrive, you need to stop being afraid of disruption and start seeing it as the opportunity it is.* The Antifragile Organization *perfectly captures that shift."*

Kevin Nolan

President & CEO, GE Appliances, a Haier company

"The Antifragile Organization *is such an exciting read. Janka Krings-Klebe and Jörg Schreiner present the book with the utmost reverence, vast experience and deep passion for organizational transformations. Their thorough research and framework bring to bear the essence of the modern organization's mindset. The concept of antifragile organization embodies the new rising paradigm, the new order affirming alignment, autonomy, decentralized self-organizing structures, holism, interconnectedness and emergence. The authors offer not only a fresh narrative and metaphors so needed for navigating this unfolding liminal space but also inspire us to approach it with the right attitude. Their message is clear: We can do hard things. We are capable of assimilating shocks into our individual and organizational structures allowing them to transform us intellectually, emotionally and spiritually. After each disruption, we are resilient enough to bravely bounce forward, instead of automatically bouncing back. 'Antifragile Organization' is also a beautiful tribute to all the leaders and trailblazers out there who dare to cultivate human creative potential, human innate need to learn, evolve, make autonomous decisions, operate and coop-erate in environments in constant flux. The concept of antifragile bridges the emerging future with the wisdom of ancient stoic philosophy. We can almost hear Marcus Aurelius's voice echo in our heads: 'The impediment to action advances action. What stands in the way becomes the way.'"*

Ewa Pasternak
Co-Founder and Director Quantum Management Centre

「《悲剧的诞生》中说，"因为你抛弃了酒神，梦神也就抛弃了你"。每个人都追逐梦神，但梦神是动态的。达到了"梦神"的境界后，却路径依赖，只是不断完善原来的工作，那就是脆弱的。而"永远自我颠覆"的酒神精神则代表了反脆弱。《反脆弱组织》倡导要打破封闭的科层制组织，因为反脆弱组织也需要持续的进化，只有自主人、自组织、自进化迭代的开放生态组织才能做到。

「而人工智能时代为这种组织创造了条件。世间万物都可以装上芯片和AI相连，"数百万人共同工作"，所有国家、所有产品和行业之间的界限将被消除，变成一个巨大的智能交互生态。因此，我提出"产品会被场景替代，行业将被生态'复'盖"。」

张瑞敏
海尔创始人、海尔集团董事局名誉主席

"*In* The Birth of Tragedy, *Nietzsche says, 'Because you had deserted Dionysus, you were in turn deserted by Apollo.' Everyone pursues Apollo, the god of dreams, but the Apollonian state is dynamic. Once you reach the state of the 'Apollonian,' you risk becoming path-dependent, merely refining your past work — exactly what is fragile. In contrast, the Dionysian spirit, which 'perpetually subverts itself,' represents antifragility.*

"*The Antifragile Organization advocates breaking down closed, hierarchical structures of traditional bureaucracy, because antifragile organizations require continuous evolution. Only an open ecosystem organization built by autonomous individuals, capable of self-organization and self-evolution, can achieve this.*

"*The era of artificial intelligence has now created the conditions for such organizations to exist. Everything in the world can be equipped with chips and connected to AI, enabling 'millions of people to work together.' All boundaries between nations, products and industries will dissolve, evolving into a vast, intelligent and interactive ecosystem. Therefore, I propose that 'products will be replaced by scenarios, and industries will be 'enveloped' by ecosystems.'*"

Zhang Ruimin
Founder of Haier and Chairman Emeritus
of the Board of Directors of Haier Group

Published by
LID Publishing
An imprint of LID Business Media Ltd.
LABS House, 15–19 Bloomsbury Way,
London, WC1A 2TH, UK

info@lidpublishing.com
www.lidpublishing.com

A member of:

BPR ✺

businesspublishersroundtable.com

ISBN: 978-1-915951-87-8
ISBN: 978-1-915951-88-5 (ebook)

THE ANTIFRAGILE ORGANIZATION

FROM **HIERARCHIES** TO **ECOSYSTEMS**

JANKA KRINGS-KLEBE & **JÖRG SCHREINER**

LID

MADRID | MEXICO CITY | LONDON
BUENOS AIRES | BOGOTA | SHANGHAI

Contents

In *The Antifragile Organization — From Hierarchies to Ecosystems*, readers are invited on a strategic tour de force on how to prepare organizations for today's era of relentless change.

In a business landscape where traditional models of predictability and control are becoming obsolete, *The Antifragile Organization* introduces the powerful concept of antifragility. Borrowing from the antifragility of natural ecosystems, the book explores how businesses cannot only withstand, but prosper from, the shocks and stresses of the modern market. With a wealth of real-world examples from companies like Haier, Netflix, Amazon and many more, it illustrates how embracing disruption can be a source of competitive advantage and sustained growth.

Each chapter methodically builds upon the last, delving into the principles and practices that constitute antifragile organizations. From redefining adaptability in a disruptive era to constructing dynamic business systems and ecosystems, the book offers a comprehensive compendium of strategies for navigating and leading in an environment where change is the only constant.

The book's practical approach is punctuated by reflective questions, encouraging readers to critically assess their organizations and apply the rich insights offered. *The Antifragile Organization* is both a reading experience and an interactive toolkit for business leaders seeking to pioneer new paths. Embrace the lessons of *The Antifragile Organization* and transform your organization into a beacon of strength, innovation and sustainable success.

Foreword

by Bill Fischer

"We have met the enemy,
and he is us."

– Walt Kelly

"We have met the enemy, and he is us."[1] This epithet was originally meant as an indictment of an intransigent American wartime government, 50 years ago, unable to extract itself from Vietnam and forfeiting its continued relevance in the ensuing confusion. Far from being dated, however, this adage still perfectly fits the dilemma of anyone trapped within a large, complex organization that appears insensitive to the change-drama it is caught up in, or befuddled by unfamiliar new demands emerging within its markets. It is as relevant today as it was originally, and for the same reasons. Look closer, and you will see that it is also an indictment of all of us who are stakeholders in these recalcitrant organizations; unable, unwilling or uninterested in making the necessary momentous changes in our actions, our business models or our organizations that the times demand. Increasingly, it seems, as Janka Krings-Klebe and Jörg Schreiner admit so plaintively in the opening words of this book, "We are losing control." Yet, even this acknowledgment, and the realization of all that is at stake, is insufficient to induce the necessary lifesaving managerial choices that are called for.

Look around us, in our everyday lives as managers, competitors, customers and admirers of once-great organizations now lost in the confusion of contemporary market change. Have you not wondered, 'What's wrong with them?' or, even, 'What's wrong with us?' This is not a new dilemma, as Kodak, Nokia, Blockbuster and others remind us, but the urgency it calls for is exploding as the pace of technical and social change around us accelerates. For a hundred years, at least, the practice of management has been about mastering uncertainty: transitory surprises in familiar domains such as demand, supply, labour and capital. Today, increasingly, successful leadership is about confronting the unknown — technologies we have never considered; customer experiences that are increasingly multidimensional, calling for knowledge we have never before accessed; new business models that change the markets we serve, the ways we price, the partners we engage. There is a big difference between the *uncertain*, which we are veterans of, and the *unknown*, which we are unprepared for. It is the *unknown* which will dominate our future.

No wonder the term *disruption* has become so popular for describing myriad industries: from automotive to space flight, from journalism to alt-dairy, from taxis to Uber to flying cars. Unforeseen change is the dominant theme emerging in all of these fields, and so many more. What they have in common is that technological upheavals and business model surprises have resulted in severe market displacements and rearrangements of once-familiar industry landscapes. However, we do ourselves a huge disservice by being distracted by the technologies, rather than the leadership failures at the heart of this self-inflicted chaos. In industry after industry, we have met the enemy, and he is truly us. It has been our organizations, our legacy thinking and our leadership-by-intimidation that has held us back. The result is that we are all too often the victims, hostages and even the perpetrators of a lack of the responsiveness necessary to sustain our position in the industries we have led in the past. This is where we discover that, in the face of the unknown, not only are we unprepared for the surprises around us, but there are no reliable signposts into a future we have never seen. The managerial question 'What do we do now?' becomes critical.

What makes this book so valuable is that the authors recognize that we are in need of new paradigms, new thoughts and new directions for the practice of management. Richard Straub, President of the Global Peter Drucker Forum, has put it succinctly: "The practice of management is still largely based in its industrial age roots — the discipline has not adapted to this new age."[2] Krings-Klebe and Schreiner argue persuasively in this book that the path to the future should go well beyond mere resiliency, where a return to the *status quo ante* would be considered an acceptable response to unanticipated big external changes. Instead, ambitious organizations, mindful of sustaining their continued relevance as a supplier, employer and community player, must strive for growth out of surprise. Adopting the ideas of statistician and risk analyst Nassim Nicholas Taleb regarding antifragility, the authors set out to consider what an antifragile organization, one that 'gains from disorder,' would look like, and what managerial choices would be required to make it work. Along the way, they consider a host of organizations that are now doing just this. These are pioneering companies such as Amazon, Bosch, Klöckner & Co, BBVA Google, Netflix, Henkel, Tata Steel, Alibaba, Buurtzorg and Haier, an organization I have admired for more than a decade. They represent a wide range of industry contexts, geographies and business models — from emerging to mature, from products to services, from simple to complex.

They are all thriving in the midst of disruption, despite many of them being in mature sectors where everything is changing around them. Rather than resisting change, they are, in the words of philosopher Alan Watts, "joining the dance." This is an idea that is particularly attractive in multi-business businesses, which are transforming into multi-opportunity businesses.

'Joining the dance' is an apt metaphor for what we need going into the unknown, and what this book offers us. At its core, it is about recognizing the new opportunities inherent in radical change, and then having the courage to make managerial choices that raise the likelihood of benefitting from being in the middle of such change. It prizes agile non-linearity over management's historical preference for being linear whenever possible. It seeks to add ideas, rather than reduce them, even in market maturity. It calls for more leaders within an organization, rather than more managers. It rejects the notion of going it alone as an organizational player in a fast-moving industry, and sees ecosystem participation as the inevitable future. It celebrates diversity, in all of its manifest variety, as being an essential advantage for seeing further, faster, despite having never been in the future. All of this makes abundant sense, calls for a massive rethinking of our organizational and leadership paradigms, and asks us to reconsider who we are and what we do. It provokes us to not only reinvent our organization, but ourselves as well.

Not a spoiler, but a heads-up: late in the book, you will be reminded that antifragility cannot be achieved through a one-size-fits-all approach. This book is about changing everything, anything, and as you read further, and respond to the authors' prompts to consider your own organization in light of what you are reading, remember that this is also an invitation to reawaken your own imagination to create the future you would hope for. Legacy thinking has gotten you, and/or your industry, into the doldrums you are currently experiencing. There is no reason to think that this will change going forward. It is you who must change.

Krings-Klebe and Schreiner offer a rich palate of choices and illustrations to draw from and help you anticipate many of their adoptability challenges. Use this as a launching pad, but do not be limited by what you read here. Our future will depend upon to what extent our leaders are explorers, and that means considering what testable hypotheses result from your reading of this book, and how best to pursue them.

Big change is not for the faint-hearted. Better to join the dance yourself than to be run over by it.

Bill Fischer
Co-author of *Reinventing Giants, How Chinese Global Competitor Haier Has Changed The Way Big Companies Transform*
Emeritus Professor of Innovation Management, IMD
Senior Lecturer, Sloan School of Management, MIT

Introduction

Charting the Unknown

*"In the midst of chaos,
there is also opportunity."*

– Sun Tzu

We are losing control. In today's business world, shock after shock ripples through organizations, leaving leaders in a state of perpetual emergency management. The pace of change, exacerbated by the density and interconnectedness of our global market landscape, where a local event can trigger major global repercussions, exceeds our abilities to see and plan ahead. Hard-won best practices that have guided businesses for decades are no longer viable in the face of rapid technological advancements, global competition, shifting consumer demands and the escalating pace of innovation. Worse yet, established management and leadership practices seem to lock companies deeper into a state of never-ending crisis. How to escape this trap? How can leaders end this perpetual, doom-loop crisis mode?

Nature offers an appropriate model for this age of disruption. It is the notion of *antifragility*. Just as the natural world's ecosystems adapt and thrive amid uncertainty and fluctuating conditions, so too must businesses. Like a body that strengthens its defenses with each infection it fights, organizations can learn and evolve through adversity.

Yet, most organizations have never learnt how to do this.

As long-time organizational coaches, with decades of professional experience in international industries, we have worked for renowned multinational corporations, such as Bosch. We are passionate about sharing our knowledge to help executives and teams accelerate their learning curves and effectively guide their organizations through complex transformations. Executives leave our certification courses for Digital Transformation at TÜV Nord with much deeper understanding and sharpened strategic focus. At the University of Applied Sciences Burgenland, we established an MBA program on Agile Management, and provide lectures for the Steinbeis School of International Business and Entrepreneurship. Applications for our master classes have tripled in the last year. Even after successful completion, our clients and alumni remain hungry for more inspiration and deeper insights. They have asked for a connecting framework that can provide clear orientation and act as a strategic guide to move into the highly complex challenges of organizational transformation.

With this book, we answer their call. We believe it will be of great value to all leaders and managers who want to increase the adaptive and innovative capacity of their businesses. After 20 years of research and leading transformation projects in the field, it is a compendium of successful transformation strategies, reflecting our own experience and complemented by the most useful thinking we have found.

This, then, is our call to action for leaders, entrepreneurs and changemakers. Join us in exploring and building antifragile organizations. For those who master antifragility, the rewards are immense. Let this book guide you through its principles and surprising ways to implement them. In four chapters, we explore the path to antifragility:

1. The opening chapter, **Thriving in a World of Disruption**, builds a foundation for understanding the importance of adaptability in a rapidly changing business environment. It introduces the concept of antifragility in companies and explains the power of business ecosystems in a hyper-dynamic world.

2. The second chapter, **Understanding Antifragility in Business**, derives the principles and values of antifragile organizations from numerous case studies. It highlights how aligning organizational values and principles with the concepts of antifragility creates a culture that is highly adaptive and innovative.

3. In the third chapter, **How Antifragile Organizations Work**, we dive deep into the operational fabric of such enterprises. We explore how they manage their business processes and organizational structures, as well as how they lead, align and empower their workforce. The chapter takes a look at how antifragile organizations leverage digital technology as an enabler for new practices of distributed leadership and management, elevating innovation, adaptation and entrepreneurship to the next level.

4. The final chapter, **Building Antifragile Organizations**, is a comprehensive guide for transforming organizations into dynamic and antifragile ecosystems. It highlights customer-centric and collaborative transformation strategies, and how to implement them through a highly effective organizational learning loop. This chapter will equip readers with the actionable steps, strategies and knowledge they need to transform their organizations.

We hope that the book imparts valuable knowledge and inspires action. Ideally, it contributes to more organizations becoming anti-fragile, and leading the world toward a brighter future. Take this journey with us and transform your organization into a beacon of innovation and strength, ready to thrive upon the myriad opportunities that uncertainty brings.

Janka Krings-Klebe & **Jörg Schreiner**
January 2025

Chapter 1

Thriving in a World of Disruption

In the crucible of change and uncertainty, organizations must find new ways to thrive and stay relevant.

"The only way to make sense out of change is to plunge into it, move with it, and join the dance."

– Alan Watts

As we stand on the brink of a world in constant flux, navigating the complex business landscape has become a daunting challenge. Traditional strategies for survival and growth are no longer sufficient in the face of relentless change and disruption. Speed and rapid adaptation have become critical for survival. Chasing these traits is not sufficient — organizations need to become fast and adaptive down to their very foundations. In this first chapter, we explain the concept of antifragile organizations and why they matter in an era of hyper-dynamic change.

1.1

Adaptability in a Disruptive Era

The 4th Industrial Revolution, broadly defined as the rapid technological progress of the 21st century, has brought significant changes and challenges to organizations across all industries. They face a dynamic and complex business environment that is characterized by uncertainty, volatility, unpredictability and hypercompetition. Technological advances and market effects are mutually reinforcing. Competition is intensifying as global digital interconnectivity reduces traditional barriers to market entry, making rapid innovation imperative for survival.

Business environments have always changed, with new technologies, competitors and market conditions constantly emerging. Companies have followed suit, adapting to these changes, and for decades a slow and steady pace of adaptation was sufficient to survive. But now, change is coming at them dizzyingly much faster. They are increasingly at risk of falling behind their competitors, losing market share and ultimately failing. Their ability to respond is being stretched to the limit as the pace of market change accelerates in tandem with exponential technological challenges.

Organizations were not built for this new age of disruption. They have long benefited from the strategic paradigms of the 20th century, where profitability and market share depended mostly on efficiency and control, and much less on the speed of adaptation. They did not need to be the fastest, just faster than their slowest competitor. In this environment, high rates of adaptation were unnecessary, and would have meant sacrificing efficiency and control.

In the 21st century, uncertainty is the new normal. Sudden and unexpected challenges are multiplying at a dramatic rate. Globalization and interconnectivity have led to an explosion in the number of competitors and services available, creating a whole new dimension of interaction density. Rapid and unpredictable changes in market conditions, customer preferences and tech innovation are the hallmarks of this hyper-dynamic environment. Today's customers expect ever more personalized, convenient and innovative products and services. Businesses must anticipate and respond quickly to their needs. In addition, competition forces them into new technologies and business models. All this change requires a whole new set of strategic paradigms. Organizations have to adopt a strategic approach that enables them to respond quickly to changes. They need to adapt rapidly to a constantly evolving environment.

The answer to hypercompetition is hyperadaptability. Antifragility is the key to achieving this. To thrive in an ever-changing world, organizations must evolve and adapt together with their environment. This approach allows them to not only withstand shocks and disruptions, but to grow stronger and more capable with each ensuing challenge.

1.2

Antifragility in Business

Fragile, Robust and Antifragile

The concept of antifragility was first introduced by Nassim Taleb, in his book *Antifragile: Things that Gain from Disorder*.[3] Taleb's work focused on understanding the nature of systems and their ability to adapt and grow stronger in the face of volatility, uncertainty and chaos. Thus, antifragility goes beyond the conventional strategies that imply the ability to withstand shocks and return to a previous state, unharmed but also not improved.

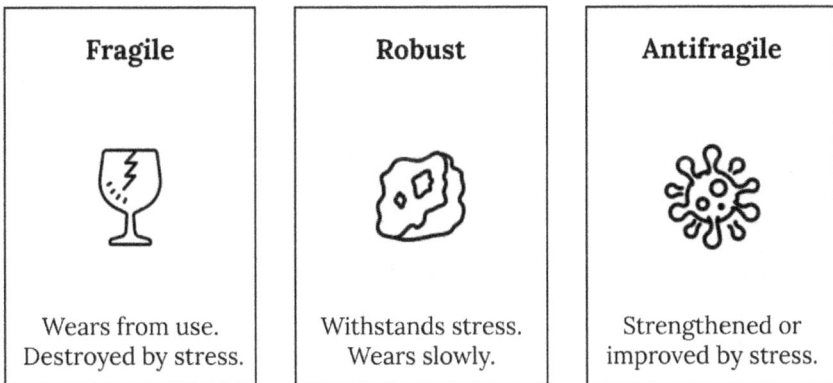

Fragile	Robust	Antifragile
Wears from use. Destroyed by stress.	Withstands stress. Wears slowly.	Strengthened or improved by stress.

Figure 1.1
Fragile, Robust and Antifragile Systems

Fragile systems (Figure 1.1) or entities are those that are easily affected by disruption, shocks or stressors. They tend to break down, malfunction or suffer significant damage when exposed to adversity. In a business context, fragile organizations require a very stable environment. They have difficulty adapting to market changes or disruptions, which can lead to their decline or all-out failure.

Robust systems or entities are able to withstand shocks, disruptions and stressors without immediately faltering or breaking. They maintain their functionality and stability. However, robust systems are still subject to ageing and wear, which means that over time they may eventually degrade in performance, or break at some point. Robust organizations can withstand market changes and disruptions without these significantly impacting their performance in the short term, but they do not necessarily improve or grow as a result of these challenges, and their resilience may diminish over time.

In contrast, **antifragile systems** or entities go beyond robustness. They actually benefit from shocks, disruptions and stressors. Rather than simply withstanding them, antifragile systems have the ability to learn, adapt and become stronger as a result of the attacks. These organizations are able to use market changes and disruptions to drive innovation, adapt their strategies, and ultimately improve their performance and competitiveness. Taleb's idea was inspired by the observation that many natural systems, such as biological organisms and ecosystems, have evolved to thrive in constantly changing and unpredictable environments.[3] These systems have built-in mechanisms that allow them to quickly adapt and learn, and as a result emerge stronger from adversity and stress.

For Taleb, antifragility is an essential quality for systems that seek to survive and flourish in a complex and uncertain world. His ideas have been widely adopted and applied across various disciplines, including economics, finance, engineering and business management.

In the context of business, antifragility refers to the ability of an organization and its ecosystem to capitalize on disruptions, challenges and changes in the market landscape. An antifragile business ecosystem is one that continually explores its markets to quickly innovate and develop solutions to new situations and problems as they arise. This emphasis on innovation and adaptation extends beyond product development to all aspects of the business, including its processes, business models and organizational structures. It helps each part learn from every move it makes, whether they are successful or failures, continuously strengthening the wider organization's ability to innovate and adapt.

It is an old concept, dating back to management legends Peter Drucker and Joseph Schumpeter. Both noted that companies are inherently designed to adapt to change, and that their capacity to fail and recover is precisely what makes them so valuable. Businesses must continually prove their right to survival, making them the most adaptable institutions. Drucker suggested that the key strength of a business lies in its ability to make and manage change, with the capacity to face and recover from losses being its most compelling feature. Schumpeter's concept of *creative destruction* adds to this. In certain cases, he argued, some components of a business must fail in order to strengthen the system as a whole. Shocks and stress factors determine which pieces survive and which do not. Schumpeter's theory describes how continuous innovation and entrepreneurship dismantle old structures and processes to make way for new and more effective ones.[4,5]

The conclusion is clear: Antifragile organizations are able to replace non-performing elements before they start dragging the whole organization down. Constant renewal allows antifragile organizations to adapt and evolve, ensuring that only effective components remain and thrive. Yet today, management systems largely ignore these ideas. They prioritize stability, protecting old ways of creating value, instead of paving the way for new ones.

Navigating Volatility: Nokia's Tale

Maintaining the status quo and making incremental improvements sufficed for companies in a stable business landscape, where future outcomes could be well predicted by looking at past performance. However, today's world, fuelled by rapid technological advancements, changing consumer preferences and fierce global competition, demands continuous evolution and rapid innovation. The pressure to maintain a competitive advantage necessitates strategic alignment between an organization's internal resources and capabilities and the external environment's demands.

The fall of Nokia, once the world's largest seller of mobile phones, serves as a powerful reminder of what happens when organizations fail to adapt. Despite its early and formidable lead, Nokia did not respond swiftly enough to the rise of smartphones and touchscreen technology, unlike competitors Apple and Samsung. Nokia's Strategic Fit faltered as it remained invested in its outdated mobile phone business, unable to foresee the disruption smartphones would cause. The company's market share declined significantly, demonstrating its inability to adapt to changing market dynamics, despite its resources and strong brand.[6]

The Adaptation Imperative

Innovation, adaptation and Strategic Fit are essential for gaining a competitive advantage and rapidly aligning with changing market conditions. Unfortunately, organizations that have operated in a stable environment for an extended period easily become complacent and rigid, losing their ability to adapt to sudden changes in a timely manner. A prolonged absence of exposure to shocks and stressors results in a relative rigidity that ultimately renders an organization fragile and vulnerable.

To mitigate this risk, they must sustain the drive for exploration, innovation and agility that characterized their early days. This must be deeply embedded in their decision-making processes and cultural DNA. It is imperative that they achieve constant alignment of their resources and capabilities with evolving market demands, responding to market changes proactively, capitalizing on emerging opportunities and maintaining relevance in an increasingly competitive landscape.

In light of the Nokia case and insights from John Johnson and Adrian Gheorghe,[7] recognized for their work in risk analysis frameworks, organizations should undertake a comprehensive examination of their products, services, business processes, structures, leadership and governance systems, with the aim of identifying and addressing any gaps in their adaptability.

To better understand adaptability, it is helpful to look at one of the most potent structures that exemplify and facilitate this trait: business ecosystems. These can provide valuable insights into how to cultivate the innovative power of adaptability, and how to effectively integrate their lessons into one's own strategic approach.

1.3

Business Ecosystems

In nature, an ecosystem is a complex network of living organisms and their physical environment, functioning as a cohesive unit. Ranging from small ponds to expansive rainforests, ecosystems actively benefit from variety and an intricate web of interactions, characterized by myriad separate feedback loops and adaptive responses to changing circumstances. Their dynamic nature helps ensure continuous evolution, showcasing antifragility — the power of remarkable adaptability under varying conditions.[8]

Ecosystems are not limited to nature; they also exist in the world of business. A business ecosystem is a network of organizations and individuals that collaborate within a shared environment to create and deliver value. These ecosystems include suppliers, manufacturers, distributors, customers, competitors and regulators, as well as complementary products and services. Each participant impacts and is impacted by the actions of others, creating a constantly evolving landscape. The diversity and redundancy within business ecosystems, their capacity for adaptive learning, the distributed nature of risk, collaborative innovation and resource flexibility all contribute to their adaptability.[9]

Collaboration with diverse partners allows organizations to drive innovation by pooling together knowledge, expertise and resources. This collaborative approach to innovation accelerates the development process and allows for rapid testing and implementation of new ideas.

As a result, companies can meet evolving customer needs and create value in unique ways. Engaging with different stakeholders within the ecosystem also helps them identify emerging trends, develop new products and services, and explore new business models.[10]

In summary, organizations that want to succeed in hyper-dynamic environments clearly benefit from working in business ecosystems. This requires developing new organizational capabilities, which traditional management paradigms are unfortunately not equipped to provide. In the next chapter, we will see how organizations must completely rethink their foundational principles to develop these capabilities.

1.4

Conclusion

In today's rapidly changing environments, traditional approaches to business, rooted in the certainties of the 20th century, are no longer sufficient. Organizations must transcend the limitations of traditional management paradigms. The concept of antifragility challenges them to completely rethink their setup. By emulating the antifragility of eco-systems in nature, they cannot only survive, but grow stronger in an age characterized by accelerating change. As we progress deeper into this challenging era, the imperative is clear: embrace uncertainty as a source of opportunity.

1.5

Reflection

Reflect on these questions to critically assess your organization's position within its environment and identify areas for improvement.

- What are the key trends, challenges and opportunities in your business environment?

- How do these factors impact your organization?

- What is your current strategy for remaining relevant in the face of rapid change?

- How viable is this strategy over the long term?

- How well equipped is your organization for rapid adaptation?

- How well is it performing in collaborating with other organizations?

Chapter 2

Understanding Antifragility in Business

Companies that embrace the values of antifragility can turn tough challenges into opportunities for growth and innovation.

"In the middle of difficulty lies opportunity."

– Albert Einstein

Organizations that quickly adapt to and capitalize on market changes gain a competitive advantage. Antifragile organizations stand out for their fine-tuned responsiveness and ability to maintain efficiency while proactively seizing emerging opportunities. They are excellent at recognizing early signs of new opportunities and acting upon them decisively, enabled by a specific set of organizational capabilities that promote continuous experimentation, adaptation and learning. Early engagement with new opportunities enables them to out-learn and outpace their competitors. They continuously evolve their strategies and operations, and develop business capabilities ahead of the mainstream.

This chapter analyses and explains the principles that underpin antifragile organizations. By adopting a systematic approach to continuous experimentation and establishing a framework for rapid learning and adaptation, they demonstrate unparalleled agility in navigating change and thriving in dynamic environments. Where others shy away from uncertainty, they see opportunity.

2.1

Antifragile Response Patterns

Consider the smartphone revolution, a significant disruption that transformed the tech industry and changed the way businesses operate, consumers interact and people everywhere engage with one another. This shift provides the perfect backdrop to examine and understand the two typical patterns of how most organizations respond to disruptions.

The first reaction pattern is displayed by companies that prioritize stability over evolution, demonstrating what we might characterize as *robustness*. These organizations, such as Blackberry, had built an impressive legacy in their domain, making them sturdy and reliable in the face of predictable challenges. Blackberry was a pioneer in secure, business-focused mobile communication, and at its zenith dominated the nascent smartphone market. However, as consumer preferences shifted toward more versatile devices — with touch interfaces and rich app ecosystems, epitomized by Apple's iPhone and later Android devices — Blackberry found itself in a challenging predicament. The company adhered to its original design and market strategy, pointing to the robustness of its services, but this rigidity severely limited its pace of innovation relative to up-and-coming competitors. It quickly became clear that ruggedness was not a top concern for consumers, and Blackberry faded away. In an era of rapid change, robustness alone has proved to be insufficient. A dogged commitment to the status quo slows innovation and leaves companies vulnerable to emerging trends and market shifts.

The second typical response pattern is evident when organizations have the capacity to absorb shocks, adapt and then recover, thus returning to their previous state. An apt illustration of this is Microsoft's journey during the smartphone revolution. Initially, the software giant fumbled with its Windows Phone platform, unable to compete effectively with the more consumer-friendly iOS and Android ecosystems. However, the company's response set it apart from those who faltered entirely, such as Blackberry. Recognizing the need to adapt, Microsoft refocused its efforts on its strong software suite, which was a linchpin for businesses, providing essential access to contacts, calendar data and email.

During the mobile revolution, access to data on smartphones became vital for users. Microsoft's mobile apps provided access to essential data on their phones, which increased overall usefulness. Without these capabilities, even the most advanced smartphone hardware had limited utility for business purposes. This move enhanced Microsoft's position as a top IT service provider and revitalized its market standing.

Microsoft's journey exemplifies the *resilience* paradigm — the capacity to endure significant disruption and bounce back, albeit without substantial transformation as a direct result. While resilience is an essential trait in the unpredictable markets of today, it is inherently reactive. Recovery to a previous pre-stressor state often means that organizations are always one step behind, trying to keep up with market leaders who are proactively defining the pace of change.

The third and most dynamic category of organizations exhibits response patterns that can be described as *antifragile*. Unlike resilience, which means recovering to a pre-stressor state, antifragile organizations use disruptions as catalysts for development, enhancing their strength and operational effectiveness.[11] Amazon provides a compelling case study in this context, showing an impressive track record of recognizing important trends and transforming them into profitable business ventures. This is demonstrated by their development of the Kindle in response to the emerging e-reader market, as well as the launch of Amazon Web Services (AWS), which took advantage of the rapid growth of cloud computing. Each move was not only a response to emerging technological advancements, but it also preempted and shaped future market conditions. By doing so, Amazon has not merely adapted to change, it has thrived by continuously creating and dominating new market niches. As we've seen with Amazon, antifragile organizations are distinguished by their proactive, specific, actionable strategies and behaviours that enable them to capitalize on market changes to fuel their growth.[12]

Classifying Organizational Responses to Disruption

As the above examples illustrate, organizational responses to stressors can be clustered into three broad categories, shown in Figure 2.1: *robustness*, *resilience* and *antifragility*. Those demonstrating robustness tend to resist and withstand shocks and disruptions up to a certain degree. They show minimal to no adaptation and typically resist change, which may degrade their viability over time. Such organizations are focused on maintaining a stable status quo.

On the other hand, organizations showing resilience are able to withstand shocks, recover and bounce back to their pre-stressor state. They can respond to change, but this is limited and temporary, aiming to recover to the previous state as soon as possible.

Finally, antifragile organizations not only withstand shocks but also improve and grow stronger as a result. They adapt and evolve to a more capable state.

Understanding these distinct concepts enables organizations to evaluate their current status and devise strategies based on the response patterns demanded by their market environment. These patterns may require robustness, resilience or antifragility. As we will explore further, organizations in today's fast-changing environment must aim for antifragility, to take advantage of the potential opportunities that arise amid continuous disruption and uncertainty.

	Robustness	**Resilience**	**Antifragility**
Basic Definition	Resists and withstands shocks and disruptions up to a certain degree of force	Recovers and bounces back from disruptions to pre-stressor state	Improves and grows stronger from shocks and disruptions
Response to Stressors	Resists change and maintains current state	Returns to intended state as soon as possible	Adapts and evolves to a more capable state
Adaptability	Minimal to no adaptation; system is designed to resist change	Limited and temporary adaptation; system aims to recover to its pre-stressor state	High level of adaptation; system evolves in response to stressors
Attitude to Change	Resists change, degrades over time	Seeks equilibrium	Seeks opportunity
Flexibility	Minimal, degrades over time	Limited, tied to necessities of its intended state	Limited only by the need to preserve its own integrity
Investment, Stake	Focus on former stakes	Focus on former and current stakes	Focus on current and future stakes

Figure 2.1
Comparison of Organizational Response Patterns

2.2

Increasing the Level of Antifragility

The need for antifragile responses in today's business world is undeniable. To stay relevant in the market, it is no longer sufficient to be robust like Blackberry, which stood its ground but faded, nor resilient like Microsoft, which recovered but trailed the pacesetters for an extended period of time. The new survival imperative pivots on the principles of antifragility — the ability to rapidly and effectively respond to new opportunities or threats, and continuously adapt business capabilities to meet changing market demands. This agility and adaptability allows companies to thrive in situations that would negatively impact more rigid or less adaptable organizations. The fact that so few companies exhibit antifragile response patterns is an indication that there might be more to it than a simple managerial decision to 'henceforth implement antifragile strategies.'

In fact, the implementation of such strategies requires dynamic capabilities that are out of reach for traditional organizational setups. They must operate according to a completely different set of principles in order to successfully implement antifragile strategies.

In the following sections, we will explore the principles of antifragile organizations, all of which contribute to their adaptability and enable them to thrive in dynamic environments.

Adaptability

Adaptability means to timely adjust and evolve in response to external or internal stimuli, especially changes in the organizational environment, emerging threats, opportunities or business needs.

Adaptability is the foundational principle of antifragile organizations. It defines an organization's ability to respond to internal and external changes in a timely and effective manner. Changes in the environment, emerging threats, opportunities or evolving business needs trigger adjustments that result in better alignment with the new conditions. In environments that remain stable over a longer period, the pressure to adapt approaches zero. In stable contexts, adaptability brings no discernible advantage, as the existing state of affairs already meets the organization's needs and aligns with external conditions. In stable markets, adaptability was therefore long viewed as a reactive task, limited to specific areas of the business and occurring rarely, with the primary goal of preserving the status quo and mitigating negative impacts.

However, in highly dynamic markets with rapidly changing trends and customer needs, the pressure to adapt is high. In these situations, the ability to adapt at market speed is what differentiates a company. The dynamic of such markets triggers a perpetual cycle of innovation and adaptation in which companies must constantly evolve to stay relevant.

To illustrate adaptability in action, let us examine how highly competitive companies like Haier have embraced these principles. The Haier Group, a Chinese-based global leader in appliance manufacturing, demonstrates outstanding adaptability through its innovative approach to organizational structure and customer-centric innovation. The catalyst for this shift was a recognition that to stay competitive, the company needed to become more responsive to customer needs, encourage innovation and empower employees to make decisions more efficiently. Legacy management practices were becoming a hindrance to quick decision-making and responsiveness. Therefore, Haier created a more dynamic and flexible management system that could rapidly adapt to market changes and better satisfy customer demands. A pivotal move in this transformation was the creation of the *RenDanHeYi* management model, which has been widely recognized as a cornerstone of Haier's success. This model, thoroughly examined in *Reinventing Giants* — the first comprehensive book about Haier's transformation, authored by Bill Fischer, Umberto Lago and Fang Liu[13] — fosters employee entrepreneurship, creating an environment that supports innovation and swift adaptation to market demands. The concept of *Zero Distance* — closing the gap between the company, its employees and its customers — helps ensure that employees' initiatives directly involve user input, to increase value and drive innovation.[13, 14]

This unique approach resulted in a network of thousands of autonomous teams or micro-enterprises. Each micro-enterprise is self-managed, with its own profit and loss responsibility, and acts as an independent unit within the company. The micro-enterprises are encouraged to identify and fulfil customer needs efficiently and effectively. This network makes Haier much more aware of shifting customer needs, market changes and upcoming business opportunities. Autonomy and a decentralized structure enable it to act quickly and seamlessly adapt to these changes. Haier's journey demonstrates the transformative power of adaptability by embedding it into the core of its operations. The company's greater adaptability has led to a multitude of innovative approaches to meeting the nuanced needs of its diverse customer base. For example, by acknowledging the unique lifestyle of rural customers, Haier introduced a versatile washing machine that could not only clean clothes but also wash potatoes. This practical and multifunctional solution was developed based on direct feedback from this subset of users.[15]

Banco Bilbao Vizcaya Argentaria (BBVA) is an example of adaptability in the financial sector. The Spanish bank, one of the world's largest financial institutions, acknowledged the profound effects that technological changes have on the economy, societal structure and the financial industry as a whole. Facing these changes, BBVA underwent a technological and organizational transformation. Similar to Haier, it formed multidisciplinary teams and equipped them with agile methodologies to quickly meet emerging customer needs. The first agile teams started the development of a new mobile banking application, aiming to enhance the customer experience. By addressing personal account management needs and offering value-added services through new technologies like artificial intelligence (AI), it gained a competitive advantage. However, these innovative services required much faster collaboration between departments, which ultimately led to a radical restructuring of BBVA's organizational structure.

The company moved away from traditional functional silos toward a flexible and transparent team-based model, with specific roles and responsibilities. The prioritization of projects based on strategic alignment further improved transparency, efficiency and resource allocation. The use of new technologies enabled BBVA to understand and serve its customers' needs, trends and future requirements more effectively.[16, 17] Its *Data Science Centre of Excellence* was a critical component in this transformation, providing strategic insights that inform decision-making across the organization. By analysing vast amounts of data, the centre helped BBVA identify trends, anticipate market changes and develop strategies that aligned with its long-term goals. The data-driven approach enabled it to remain agile and responsive to the evolving needs of its customers and the ever-changing financial landscape. This was exemplified by the data centre's development of *Commerce360*, a service that provided commercial insights to small and medium-sized companies.[18]

The examples of Haier and BBVA demonstrate how adaptability can catalyse innovation, enabling companies to seize new opportunities and overcome challenges more effectively. Adaptability nurtures a dynamic environment at the core of antifragile organizations, where successes and failures provide essential feedback, shaping strategies in a continual, real-time process.

Supercompensation

Supercompensation is the ability to absorb shocks and stressors in a way that they ultimately push organizational performance and abilities to new levels.

The principle of supercompensation describes the ability to recover from stress or damage in a way that enhances the performance or capabilities beyond the original state. Supercompensation is essential for enabling an organization to handle stressors more effectively. By enhancing performance and capabilities beyond the level of stress they are subjected to, it is better equipped to cope with subsequent stressors, helping it recover more quickly and perform at a higher level when faced with similar challenges in the future.

This concept is often discussed in the context of biological systems, where the body can adapt and improve in response to stressors, such as exercise or injury. Supercompensation is a well-known term in sports. After periods of intense training or competition that push their bodies to the limit, athletes often find that they adapt and become stronger, especially when this period is followed by a regeneration process that results in adaptations.[19]

Organizations can undergo similar stressors that challenge them to their core. Instead of leading to breakdown or failure, these pressures can trigger the process of supercompensation, where the organization not only recovers but also grows stronger and more capable. In this context, stress may be perceived as a threat to a company's survival, but it can also be a catalyst for innovation, learning and the development of new capabilities. Over time, with frequent exposure to stress, organizations can recover from setbacks faster and become stronger, increasingly adaptable and more capable of thriving in dynamic market environments. This could involve adopting new strategies, innovating or enhancing operational efficiencies.

The absence of stressors in an organization would likely lead to a state of stagnation, or even decline in performance and capabilities. This is because stressors, whether they are external challenges or internal pressures, serve as catalysts for adaptation and improvement. Without them, an organization may not experience the necessary push to innovate, adapt or improve its processes and capabilities. It would not undergo the cycle of training (introducing new challenges or demands), recovery (allowing for adaptation and regeneration) and supercompensation (enhanced performance and capabilities as a result of the recovery process).

Netflix and Amazon demonstrate how organizations can successfully use supercompensation, enhancing their capabilities and nurturing innovation. In the early 2000s, Netflix faced a significant challenge. The rise of streaming services and the increasing demand for instant access to content posed a threat to its DVD rental business model. The company was operating in a market that was rapidly changing, with consumers moving toward digital content consumption. Recognizing the need to adapt, Netflix made the strategic decision to shift its business model from DVD rentals to streaming.

This was a bold move that required a significant investment in technology and content production. The company knew that this transition would lead to short-term challenges, including a loss of customers and revenue. Netflix's transition to streaming was indeed challenging. It had to manage both the complexities of digital content delivery and the transition of its customer base, while adapting to new regulatory environments. It absorbed the shocks of the transition and used the experience to strengthen its core capabilities. The company invested heavily in content production, technology and customer service, all while maintaining a focus on innovation and customer satisfaction. This investment allowed Netflix to compete effectively with other streaming services and differentiate itself in the market. The outcome was a long-term advantage that transformed the company into a global leader in streaming services. Its ability to absorb the shocks of the transition and use the experience to improve its offerings led to a significant increase in customer satisfaction and loyalty.

Today, Netflix has millions of subscribers worldwide and continues to innovate and expand its services. Its shift to streaming is a prime example of supercompensation in action. By deliberately changing its framework conditions and absorbing the shocks of the transition, Net-flix was able to emerge stronger and more capable than before.[20, 21]

Amazon's venture into cloud computing, initiated by the need to address server capacity challenges during peak shopping periods, also showcases the transformative power of supercompensation. Amazon Web Services (AWS) evolved far beyond its initial purpose. By turning its internal solution into a marketable service, Amazon transformed a former limitation into an opportunity, launching AWS as a powerhouse in cloud computing. This move not only compensated for the initial lack but also significantly enhanced Amazon's strategic position and revenue streams. The move into cloud computing represents a substantial expansion beyond Amazon's e-commerce roots. The company capitalized on its technological infrastructure to deliver reliable and cost-effective cloud computing services, encompassing applications like web hosting, data analytics, AI and machine learning.[12]

The success of AWS is not solely grounded in its technological competencies. Amazon nurtured a comprehensive ecosystem around AWS, comprising consumers, independent software vendors, systems integrators and public sector partners. This ecosystem has experienced rapid growth, driven by synergistic interactions among its constituent parts. For example, independent software vendors are attracted to AWS's comprehensive range of services, which provide a stable, scalable platform for their applications. These apps attract additional customers to AWS, stimulating its growth. At the same time, the business extends extensive support to systems integrators, who offer value-added services to AWS customers, expanding its reach and reinforcing the ecosystem. Amazon's venture into cloud computing, coupled with the creation of a thriving ecosystem around AWS, has been pivotal in the company's continuous innovation and rapid expansion into a wide range of industries.

The principle of supercompensation, as demonstrated by Netflix and Amazon, emphasizes an important insight for businesses operating in dynamic markets: Challenges and stressors, when used strategically, can lead to significant improvements in operations and innovation.

Accountability

Accountability ensures that all members of an organizational entity are invested in its success, benefit from their contributions and feel an ownership of their actions.

The principle of accountability establishes a clear link between decisions, their implementation and the outcomes, whether positive or negative. The stronger this link, and the more significant the personal consequences of decisions are for decision-makers, the more incentive they have to make good decisions, for both the short term and the longer term.

Family-run businesses in Germany are a prime example of this. These make up a great part of the *Mittelstand* — the small and medium sized businesses — which account for roughly 50% of Germany's GDP. A family business can only be passed on to the next generation if it is healthy. Only then can it generate profits and secure personal income for both the new and the old generations. Family businesses are therefore constantly adapting and repositioning themselves for both short-term opportunities and long-term developments. Decisions are always made based on a comprehensive view of long-term opportunities and risks. As such, responsibility and sustainability are in the DNA of German family businesses.[22, 23]

In contrast, we see a disconnect between accountability and sustainability in non-owner-managed businesses, especially in the majority of corporations. There, accountability is often perceived as attainable only by managing performance of teams and individuals through goals and incentives, close monitoring and managerial interventions. Despite the best intentions, this usually results in a framework of control and supervision that disempowers the front lines. Accountability in these companies flows top-down, with decisions made in the boardroom and then cascaded to frontline teams. In dynamic environments, the trailing and reactive control model proves to be too slow and ineffective.

Boeing is a clear example of the dangers of this disconnect. Decisions to centralize and physically separate management from production, to prioritize financial over engineering expertise and to outsource critical activities led to a series of outcomes that jeopardized the company's reputation and safety standards. As decision-making became more removed from the engineering and production realities on the ground, the accountability loop was not just stretched, but broken, leading to catastrophic failures and a badly tarnished reputation. The consequences included regulatory fines, compromised product quality, sustained bad press, and ultimately a loss of trust and standing in the industry and with the flying public.[24]

In the long run, closing the accountability loop is vital for any organization. It becomes even more critical in dynamic environments, because response times to avoid critical failures become much shorter. Antifragile organizations need to avoid decision-making bottlenecks, which are responsible for much of the organizational lag. The majority of their decisions need to be made at the front end, where teams are directly engaged with customers and markets. This is what Peter Drucker has been arguing about for decades. Those closest to the front lines of business, where actual value is created and customer interactions occur, are best positioned to make informed, effective decisions.[25] These frontline teams have better situational awareness and more contextual understanding than those in the boardroom. Passing decisions on to higher, but more detached, levels of authority creates significant disconnects. First, it delays making a decision and taking productive action. Those remote decision-makers need to rely on complicated, time-consuming management systems to obtain the necessary situational awareness and contextual information. This alone is bad enough in dynamic environments, where threats and opportunities come and go quickly, and do not wait for long, drawn-out decision-making processes. Additionally, this detachment interrupts the feedback loop, severing the connection between decision-making and facing the consequences. Remote decision-makers experience the impact of their choices only much later, if at all.[26]

In fast-changing environments, prompt decision-making, swift implementation and immediate learning from outcomes are essential. Decision-makers must derive insights from their actions, often via experiential learning, rather than overly relying on analytical techniques to comprehend unexpected situations.

Accountability aligns personal goals with organizational purpose, building a sense of ownership and commitment. This alignment helps ensure that every decision and action reflects a personal commitment to the organization's success, improving overall adaptability and performance.

Nucor Corporation and Patagonia are good examples of how deeply embedded accountability both enhances responsiveness and fortifies organizational success.

Nucor, one of the largest steel producers in the United States, exemplifies how innovative management practices can enhance accountability. Established in the 1950s, the company has grown to prominence through a management philosophy that places strong emphasis on decentralized operations and employee empowerment. Nucor's distinctive pay-for-performance system and decentralized management structure links rewards directly to individual, team and company performance. This helps ensure short- and long-term accountability for results, along with deep involvement in decision-making. Employees have a direct and substantial stake in the company's success. This direct link helps ensure that they are accountable for their decisions and actions, and share risks and rewards. Nucor's promotion system is based on earned peer trust, skilled performance and a track record of coordination and consultation in making important decisions. Because power in the company *trickles up*, employees develop a deep sense of accountability, knowing that no one but themselves can be blamed for bad decisions and poor execution. This involvement has been shown to enhance the organization's overall performance.[27, 28]

In a different industry context, Patagonia, a leader in the outdoor apparel industry, incorporates environmental and social impact into every aspect of its decision-making process. Founded in 1973, Patagonia has consistently prioritized environmental stewardship, which directly influences its accountability structure. This commitment is intricately linked to its corporate identity and shapes how the company conducts business. For example, ethical concerns prompted a shift in the climbing equipment it sold, from steel pitons that were hammered into rocks to aluminium chocks that could be wedged into natural cracks.

The case demonstrates the extent of accountability embedded in Patagonia's operations. Moral responsibility for the environmental impact of the company's actions falls upon its leaders and employees, a model that extends accountability to the broader community and the planet. Employees share this passion for preserving the environment for future generations, and act accordingly, out of moral obligation and to the best of their knowledge. Patagonia's culture builds this sense of obligation, making decisions with a thorough understanding of their long-term consequences. The company's innovative ownership model, which directs profits toward environmental causes, reinforces this commitment and helps ensure that business goals align with sustainability efforts. This close alignment has strengthened Patagonia's dedication to environmental stewardship and positively influenced its brand perception and customer engagement, creating a powerful example of how business success and environmental responsibility can grow together.[29, 30]

German *Mittelstand*, Nucor and Patagonia show that when individuals are deeply engaged in both the processes and results of their actions, they intrinsically feel a strong sense of accountability, far surpassing the influence of any extrinsic managerial control system. This active involvement keeps employees committed to the consequences of their decisions. Such alignment is vital to push decision-making authority to the front lines of organizations. This human-centred approach can empower a significant portion of the workforce, laying the foundation for autonomy.

Autonomy

> **Autonomy is the ability and degree to which organizational entities are authorized to make their own decisions and manage their own affairs, with minimal oversight from other parts of the organization.**

Autonomy is a key enabler for antifragile organizations. It provides the structural and operational flexibility necessary for a company to remain responsive and adaptable in highly competitive markets. In this context, autonomy refers to the ability of various components within a business — individual employees, teams or entire departments — to make decisions and act independently, guided by the overarching purpose of the organization. Autonomy reduces the dependencies between different parts, allowing each team to manage its own tasks and make decisions without requiring constant coordination or approval from a central authority.

This is why teams at Haier are fully responsible for profit and loss, and their products must prove themselves in the marketplace. Haier encourages each team or micro-enterprise to innovate based on the specific needs of their customers, resulting in highly customized and innovative products. This approach is a core part of the *RenDanHeYi* model we described earlier, which facilitates direct engagement with users and rapid response to market demands.[31, 32] In this construct, no middle management or board member has the authority to decide on product launches. Instead, it is the customers who determine whether a product meets their expectations and whether it succeeds or fails. One example is at GE Appliances, a Haier company, where a team identified a market opportunity for an indoor wood-pellet food smoker. CEO Kevin Nolan initially had strong reservations about the project. Nevertheless, the team's autonomy and decision-making authority enabled them to proceed with their idea. Convinced they could fulfil an unmet customer need with an innovative solution, they collaborated with barbecue experts, incorporated feedback from their customer base, and ultimately launched the product successfully.[33, 34]

However, autonomy does not mean there are no rules, standards or guardrails. Granting autonomy to all units could lead to chaos if there is no accountability for overall alignment with the company's purpose. While Haier's micro-enterprises operate with significant autonomy, the organization recognizes the critical need for alignment to avoid fragmentation and help ensure coherence with overall strategic goals and purpose. Haier's introduction of *Ecosystem Micro-Communities* (EMCs) exemplifies a strategic approach to maintaining this balance. These communities cultivate a shared purpose among autonomous units by aligning them around specific consumer needs and market opportunities. Such alignment is essential, as it allows individual micro-enterprises to innovate and grow within a synergistic framework that directs their efforts toward collective goals. It also helps ensure that their independent actions contribute positively to Haier's overarching mission.[35, 36]

Steelmaker Nucor also demonstrates the principle of autonomy through its unique operational model. Similar to Haier's network of micro-enterprises, Nucor features a network of autonomous mini-mills, each acting as an independent entity responsible for its own profit and loss. This decentralization minimizes bureaucratic overheads, enhancing operational efficiency and responsiveness to market dynamics. The mini-mills have substantial autonomy in critical business decisions, including sourcing inputs, developing new products, hiring their own staff and adapting production processes, without the need to wait for directives from corporate headquarters. This local autonomy increases the company's overall flexibility and strengthens the accountability at the mini-mill level, mitigating the risk of strategic failures. By entrusting employees with decision-making authority and cultivating a culture of innovation, Nucor helps ensure that creative solutions and strategic adjustments emerge organically from those closest to operational challenges and market opportunities. This empowerment is rooted in a deep belief in the ability of individuals to self-manage, supported by a framework of trust and capability development programs. As previously discussed, accountability is essential in aligning the mini-mills' efforts with the company's overarching strategic goals. Equipped with a high degree of internal flexibility and adaptability, Nucor continuously explores new markets, develops innovative steel products and adopts advanced manufacturing technologies. This proactive stance mitigates risks associated with market volatility and allows Nucor to rapidly capitalize on growth opportunities in their early stages.[27, 37]

To summarize, autonomy is a powerful enabler for adaptability, responsiveness and innovation within antifragile organizations. However, with great power comes great responsibility: The limits of autonomy are determined by the degree of responsibility one is prepared to take on. This old truth has big implications. Autonomy necessitates certain prerequisites — accountability, alignment with a shared purpose and preparation through gradually growing into roles with greater power. As demonstrated by Haier and Nucor, when applied wisely, autonomy can significantly enhance the antifragile capabilities of a business. It paves the way for greater organizational diversity and opens the door for a multi-opportunity business.

Diversity

Diversity means deliberately building a wide range and variety of options, enhancing the strategic flexibility and responsiveness of an organization.

Diversity, whether in terms of products, markets, strategies, organizational capabilities or people, creates a broader set of options for how a company can respond to various situations. For example, when market demand shifts away from one product, having multiple options available allows a company to pivot more easily. It helps protect organizations from the significant risk of becoming locked into a single path of action. Similarly, a diverse workforce brings a wider array of ideas, skills and perspectives to problem-solving, opening up a broader set of strategic options. Greater diversity naturally leads to increased flexibility, which enhances an organization's ability to act and gives it more room to manoeuvre. Thus, diversity is a key strategic advantage in dynamic and fast-changing markets.

To achieve diversity in business, traditionally managed companies tend to pursue a linear response, where the outcome scales predictably with inputs. This strategy allows for rapid expansion into new markets, access to a broader range of technologies and the integration of varied customer bases. However, it usually misses the opportunity to improve broader organizational capabilities. Merger and acquisition programs aim to integrate a new business into the existing organizational management framework, standardizing and trimming down their existing capabilities, reducing diversity for the sake of corporate efficiency. This leads to a lack of organic growth and innovation within the core business, as resources are focused on integrating acquired entities rather than stimulating the buildup of internal innovation capabilities.

Bosch, a global leader in engineering and electronics, provides a compelling case study of these challenges. Historically dependent on the automotive sector, Bosch has made numerous attempts to diversify its business through innovations and strategic acquisitions.

Despite efforts to branch into consumer goods, building technology and industrial automation, the dominance of its automotive division has often impeded the growth of these diversified sectors. Notably, Bosch's ventures into sectors like solar energy systems and packaging technology eventually failed. Before being acquired by Bosch, these companies were in a good position. After the merger, they soon suffered from the limitations of a management framework primarily designed for automotive operations, which impeded their growth options and ultimately lead to a divestment of Bosch's acquisitions in the solar and packaging sector. This shows the linear and often restrictive nature of traditional diversification strategies, where new ventures must conform to or function effectively within the regulatory and operational framework originally developed for a different business sector. Such rigidity stifles innovation and growth in areas that require more tailored management practices and greater autonomy to thrive.

To avoid this inflexibility, antifragile organizations deliberately expand their range of organizational capabilities and available response patterns by valuing diversity over efficiency. This allows them to learn and super-compensate, further bolstering the ability to adapt and evolve in response to changing circumstances while preserving organizational integrity.

Going back to Haier, it demonstrates how diversity sets the stage for a multi-opportunity business. Each micro-enterprise at Haier is in charge of finding a promising market opportunity and developing its own product strategy. Together, the collection of micro-enterprises form an ecosystem that is highly adaptable and antifragile to market disruption. There are always micro-enterprises in the incubation stage, others that are exploring new market niches, and many more in various stages of profitability. Not every one will survive in the market, and this is considered perfectly normal. Haier's organizational ability to learn, innovate and quickly adapt allows for the development of diverse solutions catering to a broad spectrum of products. The multi-team 'swarming' ability is central to Haier's strategic advantage. It enables the company to explore and seize multiple market opportunities simultaneously, much faster and more comprehensively than its competitors. Their rapid development cycles allow Haier to also capitalize on short-term opportunities and local niches. During the COVID-19 crisis, this flexibility transformed pandemic-related issues into business opportunities. An example of Haier's effectiveness is their rapid handling of the urgent need for virus eradication from apparel. The company achieved this by swiftly introducing a new machine equipped with a specialized program designed to kill the infectious disease.[32, 38]

Another example is W.L. Gore & Associates, widely known for its revolutionary waterproof, breathable Gore-Tex fabrics. The company operates under a unique organizational model characterized by a lack of traditional hierarchical structures. Instead of a conventional top-down approach, Gore adopts what they call a *lattice* organization, where there are no fixed chains of command or predetermined communication channels. Employees are grouped into small, self-managed teams, whose members are encouraged to make commitments to projects that resonate with their skills and interests. Their autonomy extends to allowing teams to choose their own projects and recruit members based on their needs, which fosters a strong sense of ownership and accountability. Gore's product diversification is vast, spanning multiple sectors that include electronics, medical devices, pharmaceuticals and consumer products. Each benefits from Gore's core fluoropolymer product technology but adapts and innovates independently, according to market demands. This diversification is supported by the company's culture of experimentation, enabled by the autonomy of its teams. This structure and approach allows Gore to be highly responsive to changes and challenges. As teams operate independently, they can pivot and adapt without the constraints of a rigid corporate framework, turning potential threats into opportunities for innovation. Gore's model exemplifies how diversified operations and capabilities, coupled with empowered employees, can create an antifragile organization.[39]

Diversity serves as a fundamental principle for antifragile organizations, enhancing their adaptability in rapidly changing markets. By diversifying products, markets, strategies, capabilities, solutions and team structures, companies like Haier and Gore demonstrate that a diverse, multi-opportunity approach, when combined with high degrees of team autonomy, greatly improves their dynamic adaptation and innovation capabilities.

Redundancy

> **Redundancy means deliberately creating and sustaining organizational entities that are kept as a reserve force, able to immediately respond to, mitigate or compensate for failures or shortcomings in critical operations.**

The principle of redundancy fortifies an organization's capacity to act in uncertain environments, under stress, or when primary systems fail. Unlike redundancy in engineering, which often focuses solely on fail-safe mechanisms, organizational redundancy involves creating overlapping capabilities where multiple elements can perform the same function. Erwin Danneels, a researcher and strategist known for his work on dynamic capabilities, highlights the strategic role of *slack resources*, which he defines as excess resources that enable organizations to respond to internal and external pressures adaptively.[40] This concept of redundancy protects the organization from failure if one part underperforms. Beyond that, it also provides the flexibility to act quickly on upcoming opportunities, and to adapt and innovate by testing new solutions without compromising the overall integrity of operations.

In traditional settings, redundancy is frequently seen as an inefficient increase in operational costs, as it involves investing in duplicate resources or systems that do not contribute directly to revenue. Redundancy is typically reserved for critical parts of a system where a failure would immediately incur high costs. For example, in the pharmaceutical industry, redundancy is essential and often mandatory, especially in areas such as drug manufacturing and quality control.[41] The stakes are high because any system failure can lead to significant public health risks, regulatory penalties and financial losses. However, in efficiency-driven companies, resources are always scarce, and usually dedicated to a single purpose. This makes it difficult and time-consuming to excavate and rewire existing assets, capabilities and structures for a new business opportunity.[26]

In contrast to traditional models, antifragile organizations prioritize flexibility and speed over efficiency. They build and sustain redundant resources, as these can provide a strategic edge in a dynamic environment. This strategic redundancy helps ensure continuity during disruptions, while also providing the capacity to scale up operations or pivot to new opportunities without lengthy delays or restructuring. Their business processes and management systems are designed to reconfigure assets and capabilities dynamically. Resources are not fixed in their roles but can be combined in various configurations to meet specific needs or to seize new market opportunities, increasing overall flexibility and response speed.

On top of that, these organizational systems no longer need to work as closed systems. Instead, they are able to further expand their adaptability and reach by integrating into broader networks of partners. This open network approach allows them to access and mobilize external resources, assets and capabilities, effectively growing their opportunities without proportionately increasing their own resource base. By leveraging these external partnerships, antifragile organizations can enhance their capacity for innovation and scale in a nonlinear way.

Again, Haier provides an excellent example of this open network approach. The company's micro-enterprises are not obligated to contract only with predefined internal functions. Teams have full autonomy for all contracting, budgeting and recruitment decisions of their micro-enterprise. This allows each to independently allocate resources, tailor its support services and choose value-creation partners according to its specific needs and conditions. In fact, micro-enterprises are actively encouraged to collaborate with external partners for value-creation or services, and to take advantage of external financing. To facilitate easy contracting, Haier established a support platform that is open to all kinds of internal and external value-creation partners and suppliers. This facilitates external partners joining the network and cooperating with micro-enterprises. It even encourages competition between internal and external entities in bidding for services; micro-enterprises are not obliged to acquire them from internal providers. Instead, they can also source capabilities from external partners. This approach makes it impossible to hide behind red tape or create unnecessary internal bureaucracy. Internal services have to perform at market level. This significantly reduces technical and organizational debt within the company.

In such an open and competitive system, Haier's micro-enterprises can quickly scale operations up or down while remaining fully flexible in the allocation of assets to multiple business opportunities. Micro-enterprises can dynamically engage with a broad spectrum of external resources and capabilities, instead of relying on fixed internal procedures and scarce resources. Haier achieves strategic redundancy through diversification of its partnerships and resources, so the organization can swiftly respond to changes and opportunities without being constrained by traditional bureaucratic limitations.[13, 42]

Buurtzorg, a pioneering Dutch home healthcare organization, provides another relevant example, demonstrating the power of redundancy in a very different industry. Buurtzorg is achieving remarkable results, including a 30% increase in patient satisfaction and significant reduction in overhead costs. Increased nurse engagement and motivation are driving innovative approaches to patient care. Instead of a hierarchical structure, Buurtzorg uses self-organized teams of caregivers who take responsibility for patient care. Their autonomy is considerable, ranging from patient scheduling to making critical decisions regarding care and treatment. It includes management of all operational aspects and collaboration with other healthcare entities within their geographical purview. Unlike traditional healthcare models that depend on strict role assignments and hierarchical command chains, Buurtzorg's teams are composed of nurses who are cross-trained to handle a wide array of patient care tasks, as well as fulfilling certain managerial roles. This allows each team member to step in for another at any time, providing continuous and seamless care. Nurses rotate roles and responsibilities within the teams, which means that each is prepared to take over various functions as needed. This system is particularly effective in emergency or high-demand situations where care must not be disrupted. The redundancy built into this model helps ensure that patient care is adaptable, and not dependent on any single individual. This 24/7 capability across all teams enhances Buurtzorg's responsiveness and reliability, key aspects that distinguish its care model in the healthcare industry. The flexibility of role assignment and each nurse's broad range of skills allows the company to maintain a lean organizational structure while maximizing its operational efficacy. This approach enhances patient satisfaction through consistent and holistic care, while increasing job satisfaction among nurses who value the trust and responsibility given to them. Allowing nurses to collectively self-manage their schedules and responsibilities creates a strong team dynamic and supportive work environment. This strategic redundancy covers immediate operational needs and contributes to long-term sustainability by building a workforce capable of adapting to the evolving healthcare landscape.[43, 44]

Antifragile organizations achieve strategic redundancy by designing management systems that facilitate dynamic interactions between internal and external capabilities. Both Haier and Buurtzorg exemplify how this approach enables organizations to respond swiftly and effectively to changes, allowing them to rapidly adapt and innovate. This strategic integration of redundancy into their business operating systems enhances their responsiveness while driving continuous improvement, positioning both organizations to thrive in unpredictable environments.

Continuous Learning and Evolution

Continuous learning and evolution is the ongoing process of gaining insight and understanding through internal and external interactions, and improving strategies, abilities and actions based on the knowledge gained.

An antifragile organization is characterized by its ability to improve and grow. It recognizes the importance of continuous learning and evolution for maintaining relevance, efficiency and effectiveness in dynamic and complex environments. This involves acquiring new knowledge, capabilities or insights through direct experience, experimentation and observation. According to Edgar Schein's adaptive coping cycle of observation, learning, unlearning and relearning, organizations need to not only acquire but critically evaluate and update their knowledge and practices in response to changing conditions.[45] Based on the insights gained from learning, individuals or systems adjust their strategies, capabilities and actions to better achieve their goals or adapt to change. This involves refining existing methods, developing new approaches or modifying behaviours. Learning and evolution is not a one-time event, but a continuous cycle. It requires a commitment to regular reflection, adaptation and improvement. This cycle is driven by curiosity, the desire to improve and the ability to recognize and respond to changes. By continuously learning and improving, companies can develop new ideas, products or services that meet changing needs or exploit new opportunities.

In traditional organizations, structural rigidity and cultural norms often create significant barriers to continuous learning and evolution. A mere fraction of the resources is allocated to learning, adaptation and innovation. Furthermore, these resources are often isolated from operational realities, so they become detached from the actual work of the business. These organizations tend to prioritize stability, predictability and control over the flexibility and adaptability needed to enable learning from new experiences and failures. This mindset significantly impedes their ability to innovate and adapt in response to changing market dynamics. It still regards failure as inherently negative — something to be avoided — rather than a learning opportunity. Such a risk-averse approach discourages experimentation and innovation. It conditions employees and managers to play it safe rather than pursue new ideas that could potentially fail, even if that means missing out on groundbreaking opportunities. The fear of potential consequences can discourage employees from taking calculated risks or suggesting innovative solutions. Change is also met with trepidation, as the dominant cultural patterns tend to view it as a disruption of the established order rather than an upside opportunity. As a result, the overall stance remains largely passive, with the organization merely responding to changes brought about by the external environment rather than of proactively shaping them.

In contrast, antifragile organizations are designed with a unique structure and culture that inherently fosters continuous learning and evolution. As discussed earlier, in environments where conditions remain stable, adaptation — and by extension, learning — is not typically required. However, in dynamic environments where conditions frequently change, the need to explore, learn and adapt becomes essential to maintain relevance. Antifragile organizations understand that stability is the exception rather than the norm in today's business landscape. They recognize that continuous change requires building the capabilities for a continuous adaptive response, and thus, they build systems and cultivate a culture that anticipates and embraces change rather than resists it. These organizations structure themselves to be adaptable by decentralizing decision-making and flattening hierarchies, which promotes faster response times and greater flexibility. This structural adaptability facilitates rapid learning and application of lessons learnt across the organization, valuing exploration, curiosity and questioning of the status quo. This cultural orientation encourages employees to continually seek out learning opportunities and innovative solutions. Antifragile organizations build extensive learning and adaptation cycles. They systematically leverage interactions with their environment as learning opportunities, using customer feedback, market trends and competitive moves as inputs to drive ongoing organizational adjustment and innovation. By integrating continuous feedback loops into all activities, from customer interactions to internal projects, these companies ensure that learning is immediate and actionable. Real-time feedback helps to quickly identify and address gaps, align strategies with current realities and continuously improve processes.

The concept of continuous learning and evolution in antifragile organizations is emergent by nature. It involves every level of the organization. It is not confined to specific departments or leadership levels, but part of the daily experience for all employees. This widespread integration means that learning happens in a way that is deeply ingrained in operations and the organizational culture, affecting everything from the most basic processes to complex strategic decisions. Employees are active participants in generating, sharing and applying what they learn. The learning processes are not wholly predefined, but develop organically in response to the organization's needs and external pressures. This aspect of emergence is essential because it allows the business to adapt to unexpected changes or new challenges more fluidly. Learning outcomes and insights can arise from any interaction within or outside the organization, leading to innovations and adaptations that were not initially anticipated. By learning more and faster, these organizations are better able to respond dynamically to complex environments and generate more innovation. At this point, agile methods, with their fixed product iteration and learning cycles, while useful as a first step to maintaining synchronization, are only an intermediate step to unlock their complete dynamic potential. Organizations need to evolve beyond these fixed-length cycles. Adaptation and innovation need to move beyond being scheduled events and become naturally integrated into every aspect of organizational life. By making learning an emergent, deeply integrated and ongoing capability, organizations can achieve a state of perpetual adaptability, where learning and innovation are as fluid and responsive as the changing environments in which they operate.

Nucor exemplifies continuous learning and evolution through its commitment to constant improvement. The foundation of the company's learning culture is its routine operational meetings, which occur frequently — often weekly — and include cross-location visits and peer exchanges. These meetings serve as platforms for thorough performance evaluations, where teams identify challenges and collaboratively develop solutions. Nucor also actively engages with a broad network of stakeholders, including customers, suppliers and external technical experts. With this inclusive approach, learning extends beyond internal operations, incorporating external insights that help refine strategies and align operations with market demands and technological trends. The result is a highly adaptive organization that navigates the volatility of the steel market with ease, consistently outperforming competitors. Nucor's model embodies a robust capacity for continuous improvement and innovation, leveraging an ongoing cycle of learning, feedback and strategic adaptation to transform market challenges into opportunities for growth and competitive advantage.[27, 28]

The Morning Star Company serves as another example of a continuous learning and evolution culture, from a quite different industry. The California-based company is a leading producer in the vegetable processing sector, renowned for its innovative approaches to business operations and management. Renowned for its commitment to self-management and continuous improvement, the company can rapidly respond to industry changes and enhance its production processes. Morning Star uses a systematic bimonthly cycle of action, feedback, learning and adaptation to drive iterative growth. This model helps ensure that each part in the cycle contributes effectively to the business's development. What distinguishes Morning Star is the speed with which it implements changes based on these insights. The organizational structure is expressly designed to support swift incorporation of new learnings, allowing immediate or next-cycle adjustments. Successful initiatives are rapidly scaled, while struggling ones are quickly adjusted, increasing overall effectiveness and contextual knowledge within the organization.[46]

Antifragile organizations demonstrate the principle of continuous learning and evolution by creating environments that embrace dynamic change and nurture cultures inherently designed for continuous and emergent learning. By deeply integrating learning cycles and capabilities into their operations, companies like Nucor and Morning Star ensure that adaptation and innovation are ongoing and responsive to their ever-changing environments.

Collective Intelligence

Collective intelligence leverages the wisdom and insights
of large numbers of individuals to support decision-making,
innovation and organizational learning.

The principle of collective intelligence represents an organization's ability to access and use the diverse knowledge, skills and experiences of its members. This collective capability enables organizations to solve problems, make decisions and achieve goals more effectively. In a dynamic and complex business environment, leveraging collective intelligence is a critical driver of innovation, adaptability and sustained success. It encourages a decentralized approach where ideas and information can flow freely across all levels, harnessing diverse perspectives that lead to more holistic decision-making, enhanced innovation and superior organizational learning.[47, 48]

In traditional organizational settings, the flow of information and decision-making authority is tightly controlled and often centralized at the upper echelons of the hierarchy. As we have discussed, this concentrated control leads to decisions that are often disconnected from the operational realities and the nuanced insights that frontline employees and diverse teams can provide. Hoarding information as a source of power or advantage in the cutthroat game of managerial competition stifles collective intelligence. It creates power imbalances and fosters an environment where decision-making relies on the limited perspectives of a few individuals at the top. The resulting intransparency hinders collaboration and communication across different parts of the organization, impeding learning and diminishing the organization's capacity for collective problem-solving. This slows its response to market changes and reduces overall agility.

In contrast, antifragile organizations excel by utilizing collective intelligence to respond swiftly and effectively to changes. By pooling knowledge and insights from across the organization, these entities help ensure the quick dissemination of critical information, enabling real-time adaptation to emerging challenges and opportunities. The distributed nature of decision-making in antifragile organizations leads to choices enriched by diverse perspectives, reflecting the complexities of the external environment and increasing the likelihood of effectiveness. Collective intelligence makes these organizations more responsive, adaptable and innovative — all essential traits for thriving in an uncertain world.

The banking giant BBVA provides an excellent example of how this can be practically implemented and the benefits it can bring. BBVA's *New Approaches to Work* initiative, launched in 2008, aimed to rethink banking beyond old conventions and meet the needs of the 21st century customer. The program is based on three interrelated considerations: the work environment, the adoption and use of new technologies and people management, all with the goal of encouraging collaboration and collective intelligence within the organization.[49] For example, the agile project management methodology *Scrum* is used to expedite project initiation and coordination. Every quarter, the bank launches numerous innovation projects with a strict timeline: teams are formed within three days, prototypes are ready in six weeks, and the product reaches the customer within nine months.

As part of its *New Approaches to Work* initiative, BBVA conducted an ethnographic study to understand the functional and emotional needs of its employees. This included workshops and in-depth confidential interviews, and was instrumental in understanding their attitudes toward technology adoption and change readiness. This helped the company create profiles based on people's starting point with the digital transformation process, an essential step to ensure the inclusiveness of the new on-the-job experience and promote collaborative work.

The power of collective intelligence was a key aspect of BBVA's transformation. They recognized that by drawing on the talent and capabilities of all their people, they could develop a form of collective intelligence to adapt to the new environment, resulting in enhanced productivity, agility, innovation capabilities and motivation.

Furthermore, BBVA's digital transformation journey reflects the broader changes in the financial industry and society at large. Technological advances and shifting consumer preferences are transforming the way business is done, creating a new environment that poses significant challenges for the financial industry. The increased use of the internet and social media, the availability of more information and options, and rising customer demands for convenience and simplicity are driving a shift toward digitalization.[50] BBVA recognized these trends and harnessed its collective intelligence to meet emerging needs, embracing digitalization to offer more customized services and develop new business models. Leveraging digital technology, BBVA has been able to further enhance its collective intelligence. It connected closely with its clients and placed that bond at the centre of its Innovation Cycle.

Google, while under the lead of its founders, is another prime example of these principles in action. During this era, the tech juggernaut had a unique ability to connect talented individuals for moonshot innovation projects, illustrating the power of collective intelligence. Its organizational system was able to create an environment that encouraged collaboration and cross-functional teamwork. It facilitated interaction across different functions and projects, promoting innovation and teamwork. Despite its size, the company maintained a flat structure with few hierarchical layers and great employee autonomy, cultivating an environment where open communication and idea sharing were the norms. From its open and inclusive culture that encourages every employee to contribute ideas, to its deployment of cross-functional teams for tackling complex projects, Google exemplified how diverse perspectives can lead to groundbreaking innovations.

Notably, its suite of collaboration tools facilitated brainstorming and teamwork, so that insights and expertise could flow freely across the organization. The company's innovative management practices, such as the *20% time* policy — which allowed employees to take one day a week to work on side projects or learn additional skills — empowered them to explore new ideas outside their primary job functions, leading to products like Gmail. This autonomy, within a culture of continuous feedback and learning, enabled Google to adapt and evolve rapidly, maintaining its edge in the hypercompetitive IT sector.[51, 52]

Google's response to the COVID-19 pandemic, particularly the development within weeks of an exposure notification system in collaboration with Apple, is a significant example of its ability to harness collective intelligence through a networked structure. This required the rapid establishment of cross-functional teams from both companies to work together seamlessly, alongside health authorities and researchers, to create a system that balanced public health needs with privacy concerns.[53] This demonstrates the effectiveness of a networked structure in utilizing collective intelligence for cross-company collaboration. It shows how Google's organizational design enabled it to adapt and evolve rapidly in response to challenges.

In conclusion, both BBVA and Google have effectively utilized collective intelligence to improve decision-making and drive innovation. This has contributed significantly to their sustained growth and ability to adapt to rapid change, demonstrating the critical role of these strategies in building antifragile organizations.

Summary of the Principles of Antifragile Organizations

As we have illustrated, each of these principles contributes to an organization's adaptability, and ultimately its antifragility. Figure 2.2 provides a comprehensive overview. The principles are not prescriptive rules, but rather strategic levers that can be adjusted according to an organization's context and the specific challenges it faces. Their implementation in different companies gives an indication of the unique organizational paths toward antifragility. Each principle contributes independently to creating a more adaptable, and ultimately antifragile, organization. Their effectiveness is maximized when they are understood and applied within the specific context of the organization.

When discussing the principles of antifragile organizations, it should be noted that implementation levels vary. Antifragility is not a fixed strategy but an evolving one, uniquely adjusted over time. Above all, this means companies do not need to start implementing all principles simultaneously to progress toward antifragility. Each, given its unique circumstances, market position and strategic objectives, will prioritize different principles. A tech startup like Airbnb, during its early stages, might focus on *Continuous Learning and Evolution* for enhanced innovation and adaptability regarding its diverse stakeholder needs. Conversely, an established bank like Handelsbanken might concentrate on *Autonomy* and *Accountability* to build loyal customers and maintain steady growth amid economic shifts.

Principle	Definition
Adaptability	The ability to timely adjust and evolve in response to external or internal stimuli, especially changes in the organizational environment, emerging threats, opportunities or business needs.
Super Compensation	The ability of absorbing shocks and stressors in such a way that it ultimately pushes organizational performance and abilities to new levels.
Accountability	The means of ensuring all members of an organizational entity are invested in its success, profit from contributions and can be held accountable for their actions.
Autonomy	The ability and degree to which organizational entities are authorized to make their own decisions and manage their own affairs with minimal oversight from other parts of the organization.
Diversity	Deliberately building a wide range and variety of options, enhancing the strategic flexibility and responsiveness of an organization.
Redundancy	Deliberately creating and sustaining organizational entities that are kept as a reserve force, able to immediately respond, mitigate or compensate for failures or shortcomings in critical operations.
Continuous Learning and Evolution	The ongoing process of learning from internal and external interactions, and improving strategies, abilities and actions based on gained insights.
Collective Intelligence	Leveraging the intelligence and insights of large numbers of individuals to support decision-making, innovation and organizational learning.

Figure 2.2
Principles of Antifragile Organizations

The different approaches show that customization of the principles is key. Each organization may start with a different focus based on its immediate needs, and further develop according to its long-term strategy, context and opportunities. Importantly, the implementation of even a few principles can significantly enhance an organization's adaptability. The journey to antifragility is not strictly linear or comprehensive; it often involves selective implementation, phased evolution and continuous adaptation. However, the key aspect to highlight is that the adoption of even a handful of these principles can profoundly enhance an organization's capabilities, underscoring the power and potential of the antifragile framework.

Over time, as implementation of these principles deepens inside an organization, they interact and mutually reinforce each other, further boosting the antifragile capabilities. For example, *Diversity* is often bolstered by *Accountability*, *Autonomy* and *Redundancy*. As organizations evolve, the integration of more principles strengthens their ability to flourish amid uncertainty and disruptions. The deep interconnectedness of these principles and their collective impact is illustrated in the next section.

2.3

Interconnectedness of Principles

It is important to recognize the interrelated nature of the principles (Figure 2.3). They do not exist in isolation — they inform, complement and reinforce each other, influencing every decision an organization makes and every response it generates. Not all interactions are equally important, and some are more critical than others in driving the organization's antifragility. We will highlight the most relevant and strongest connections among these principles.

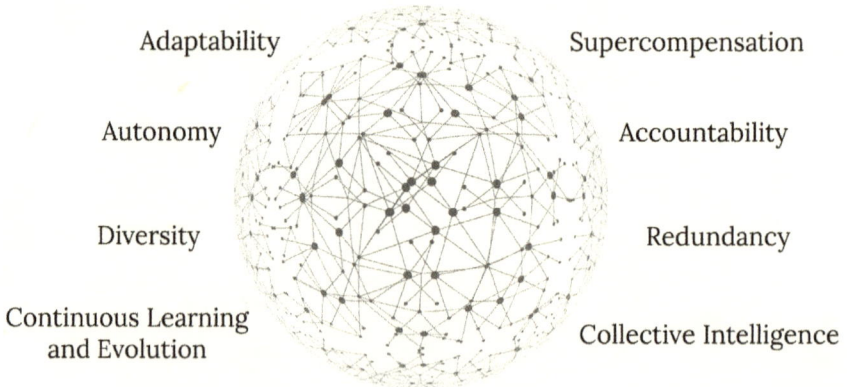

Figure 2.3
Interconnectedness of Principles

Adaptability and **Supercompensation** can contribute to organizational success independently, but in synergy they are particularly powerful in ensuring that enterprises are able to continually evolve and improve through change. *Adaptability* fuels *Supercompensation* as the stress created by *Adaptability* efforts forces the organization to develop new strengths, thereby enhancing overall performance.

On the other hand, the improvements and capabilities developed through *Supercompensation* make an organization more adaptable. Having increased its baseline capabilities, the enterprise can respond more effectively to future changes. Enhanced capabilities, improved structures and refined processes all contribute to an increased state of readiness and a more flexible ability to respond. This creates a virtuous cycle in which each act of adaptation potentially leads to new strengths, and those strengths facilitate better adaptation.

Accountability serves as a central hub in the network of principles, ensuring that *Autonomy* does not lead to disarray and that *Adaptability* results in effective change. It grounds *Collective Intelligence* and *Continuous Learning and Evolution* in responsible and outcome-focused practices. *Accountability* ensures that while teams and individuals have the freedom to act autonomously, their actions remain aligned with organizational goals. Along with *Adaptability*, it cultivates an environment where changes are not only responsive but also well-considered and aligned with long-term goals. Additionally, in interaction with *Collective Intelligence* and *Continuous Learning and Evolution*, *Accountability* establishes a framework where insights and lessons are responsibly acquired and applied to make informed decisions and drive continuous improvement and strategic evolution.

While **Autonomy**, **Diversity** and **Redundancy** can individually drive significant impacts within an organization, their synergistic application amplifies their collective effectiveness. These principles are strongly interconnected, mutually strengthen each other and enhance the effectiveness, response time and adaptive capacity of an organization. *Autonomy* empowers individual teams to operate with self-direction, optimizing responsiveness and agility. *Diversity* adds onto autonomy, broadening the spectrum of capabilities and alternatives for action beyond the organization's boundaries, and increasing the strategic adaptability. Adding *Redundancy* to the equation allows for flexible resources that are fluidly redeployed to address emerging needs or seize market opportunities as they arise. Together, these principles pave the way for network-style organizations that interact with their environment in a more dynamic and flexible manner. This promotes an ecosystem where innovation can occur anywhere, ensuring that businesses can adapt quickly and remain competitive in dynamic markets.

Continuous Learning and Evolution and **Collective Intelligence** are inherently interconnected and work best in synergy. They amplify each other's impact and that of other principles, enhancing their overall effectiveness. This profoundly impacts an organization's adaptability, innovation and growth. Together, *Continuous Learning and Evolution* and *Collective Intelligence* create a dynamic environment where learning is accelerated, and knowledge is maximized across the organization. This enhances its internal capabilities and strengthens its external competitiveness by ensuring that new opportunities and insights not only lead to rapid and effective adaptations, but further strengthen the organization's knowledge and decision base.

The total impact of these principles, when combined, exceeds the individual contributions of each, forging an antifragile organization. Adopting even a handful of these principles can set off a chain reaction that exponentially increases the organization's capabilities. This interconnectedness means that the whole can be far more powerful than the sum of its parts. Businesses aiming to cultivate antifragility should understand the interconnectedness of these principles. The point is not to selectively adopt just a few. The true strength lies in embracing the synergies, nurturing a dynamic, adaptable organizational system that can thrive amid the unpredictability of market forces.

However, adopting new principles is difficult. All organizations have a certain working set of core principles and values that guide all of their actions. These principles have proven their value. They have evolved over time, creating a specific organizational culture and a decision-making framework that has enabled success. Changing the foundation of success is therefore not an easy task. It is best done gradually

— organizations must unlearn old principles and values that are holding them back and replace them with more future-oriented ones. This takes time, patience and perseverance.

Sound like bad news? There is good news, too: No organization is an island. Organizational culture naturally evolves over time. Through new generations of employees, and the cultural environment in which businesses operate, there will always be an influx of new ideas and values. These will influence the organizational culture and can be used to deliberately strengthen the adoption of new principles and values. Let's take a closer look at this relationship.

Organizational principles form the foundation for the way an organization operates, makes decisions and responds to various situations. The extent of their adoption varies over time. They have a significant impact on workplace culture, shaping the attitudes, behaviours and collective identity of its members.[54] The tangible, observable behaviours and reactions — the organizational response patterns — result from adherence to these underlying principles. Real-life outcomes serve as practical lessons that further reinforce or weaken certain principles and values, depending on success. Thus, the adopted set of organizational principles is never static. It continuously evolves over time based on internal shifts, such as growth or restructuring, and external influences, like market trends or societal changes. These adaptations can even shape new or modified principles and response patterns in a cyclical process of continuous learning and evolution.

All attempts to consciously adopt antifragile principles need to first develop a good understanding of the principles and values that underlie organizational actions, learn to influence the organizational learning cycle, and then strengthen the progression toward antifragile organizational principles.

Pursuing antifragility, while demanding, yields substantial benefits. It significantly enhances an organization's operational aspects, rendering it more customer-oriented, faster, competitive, innovative and adaptive. Furthermore, the potential economic gains can be significant, as demonstrated in the next section.

2.4

Economic Performance

The principles of antifragile organizations are compellingly demonstrated in the economic performance of companies across a range of sectors. Haier Smart Home is a prime example, having consolidated its leading position in the major appliances market in 2023, marking its 15th year with that distinction, according to research firm Euromonitor.[55] Despite a turbulent industry environment, Haier Smart Home achieved 7.3% year-on-year revenue growth and 13.3% year-on-year net profit growth in 2023, per its annual report.[56] The company's commitment to digital transformation across all business processes has led to increased operational efficiency, and its adaptability in overseas markets, with 9.5% growth despite industry challenges, reflects its antifragile nature.

In 2023, BBVA received the best score in the Dow Jones Sustainability Index for the fourth consecutive year. It achieved impressive customer growth in 2023, adding more than 11 million new clients globally — more than double the 2018 rate. The bank's digital transformation, in alignment with the principles of antifragile organizations, is clearly manifest. More than two thirds of customers engaged with the bank via mobile platforms in 2023, up from 35% in 2017, with digital channels accounting for a remarkable 80% of the group's total sales.[57]

Steel producer Nucor embodies the principles of antifragile organizations through its decentralized structure. This approach has yielded profit margins that surpass the industry average by around 6% over the past five years, indicative of the company's economic robustness.[58]

In the healthcare sector, Buurtzorg's commitment to principles such as autonomy, accountability and redundancy has yielded in measurable advantages. The firm has held overhead costs to 8%, significantly lower than the Dutch average of 25%. In addition, it boasts patient satisfaction rates 30% higher than similar organizations.[44]

Over at Amazon Web Services (AWS), the company posted impressive revenues of 90 billion US dollars from its cloud services in 2023, continuing a growth trajectory set in motion in 2013. AWS's consistent success speaks to its steadfast adherence to the principles of antifragile organizations, particularly continuous learning, iteration and adaptability.[59]

These companies demonstrate how adopting antifragile principles can lead to sustainable success across industries, even in the face of volatility and uncertainty. However, the full potential of these principles is realized when they are aligned with and supported by the organization's core values. With such alignment, the principles are not just stated, but deeply integrated in the organizational culture, driving behaviour and decision-making at every level.

2.5

Organizational Values for Antifragility

While organizational principles serve as guidelines that shape decision-making, it is the organizational values that determine whether outcomes are considered desirable or not. Values encompass fundamental beliefs and attitudes. They define what is important within the company and often reflect its culture and ethical stance.[54] They guide how the organization and its employees behave and interact with each other, their customers and the broader community. Together, values and principles work in unison to provide a guiding framework for the enterprise. Values offer the *Why* (underlying beliefs and attitudes that inspire and guide behaviour), while principles provide the *What* (specific guidelines for action). This interplay shapes the organization's culture, propelling its performance and influencing its ability to achieve strategic goals.

The essential role of an organization's culture, composed of values and principles, as a primary driver of performance has been highlighted in the seminal work of Edgar Schein,[54] Mary Jo Hatch[60] and Mary Parker Follett,[61] each renowned for their pioneering insights into organizational culture and dynamics. Their research suggested that aligning organizational practices with values and principles fosters a robust and adaptive culture. This perspective is further supported by recent studies from Kim Cameron and Robert Quinn,[62] known for their work on organizational effectiveness and the Competing Values Framework; Daniel Denison,[63] a specialist in linking corporate culture with performance; and Charles O'Reilly and colleagues,[64] who have extensively studied organizational innovation and leadership. They all agree that organizations with a strong alignment between their values, norms, practices and principles navigate the dynamic and often volatile business environment more effectively. Building on this foundational research, the key values that underpin antifragility can be derived from organizations that have successfully implemented, at least partly, the principles of antifragility, such as Haier, Netflix and Alphabet. From there, we can identify the following key values of antifragility:

Embracing Opportunities Rather Than Seeking Certainties

This value is about the importance of being adaptive, prepared and open to seizing emerging opportunities, even in the absence of certainty. Adaptability is key in this context, emphasizing the organization's ability to respond flexibly to market shifts and continuously evolve in response to changing circumstances. It induces learning and adaptations that enable the organization to not just return to its baseline but to exceed it, creating a new threshold of capability and performance after each challenge. Embracing this value facilitates innovation, helping a business venture into new markets, explore unconventional strategies and be at the forefront of change. A compelling example is Netflix, which has demonstrated agility and openness to innovation by identifying and capitalizing on opportunities in the digital streaming space and continuously evolving its business model to meet changing consumer preferences and technological advances.

Fostering Emergence Over Prediction

Antifragile organizations acknowledge the inherent unpredictability of the business landscape. Instead of trying to predict future outcomes, they cultivate an environment that embraces the spontaneous emergence of innovative solutions. This approach recognizes that unpredictability is fertile ground for growth and adaptation. By embracing emergence, these organizations are better positioned to take advantage of unexpected changes, challenges or new opportunities. For example, Haier's culture promotes continuous innovation and adaptation to market trends, demonstrating the antifragile trait of growing stronger through stress and unpredictability.

Valuing Diversity Over Optimization

Valuing a diversity of perspectives primes organizations to better handle the uncertainty inherent in business environments. When an organization harnesses the power of diverse experiences, insights and ideas, it boosts its collective problem-solving capacity, enhances creativity and promotes a more comprehensive understanding of varied business challenges and opportunities. Diversity also builds a sounder decision-making process by helping to avoid groupthink and bringing in a wider range of strategies to deal with uncertainty. A case in point is Patagonia's commitment to diversity, equity and inclusion. It fosters a wide range of perspectives that fuel innovation and help the company nimbly navigate business uncertainties.[30] Its diverse workforce and inclusive culture amplify its capacity to adapt and evolve, enhancing its antifragility in the face of market unpredictability and change.

Prioritizing Practical Effectiveness Over Ideals

Antifragile organizations value practical effectiveness over strict adherence to ideals. They recognize the importance of flexibility in decision-making and the ability to pivot strategies based on situational demands. This approach allows them to maintain a fine balance between following preestablished standards and adapting to real-time changes, thereby enhancing their efficiency and adaptability. Amazon's data-driven, customer-centric approach exemplifies this, demonstrating a focus on achieving practical effectiveness that ultimately enhances customer satisfaction and drives growth.

Promoting Integration Over Demarcation

In an antifragile organization, emphasis is placed on integration and collaboration rather than strict departmental boundaries. This means encouraging the free flow of knowledge, ideas and resources across teams, and valuing diverse perspectives. Such an environment encourages cross-pollination of ideas, promotes innovation and enhances the organization's ability to adapt to change. This might seem counterintuitive to a conventional command-and-control structure, but in the context of antifragility, it enhances resilience and flexibility. For instance, the global tech conglomerate Alphabet, Google's corporate parent, embodies this value in its organizational structure. As described earlier, it encourages employees to work collaboratively across different projects, cultivating an ecosystem of shared knowledge and innovative thinking. This integrated approach has bolstered the company's resilience and fuelled its growth and adaptability in the face of uncertainty.

Emphasizing Induction Over Deduction

Antifragile organizations prioritize induction, which involves forming conclusions based on specific observations and patterns, over deduction, which relies on deriving conclusions from broad, established premises or general rules. With this focus on learning from real-world experiences, they become considerably more adaptive and customer-centric. By prioritizing inductive reasoning, they base strategies on empirical evidence rather than generalized, top-down theories. This fosters continuous and localized learning, where insights from daily operations and customer interactions directly inform decisions. This inductive approach enhances agility, helping companies swiftly respond to changes. For instance, Netflix adapts its content strategy based on real-time viewer data, allowing it to innovate and meet local audience demands. Emphasizing induction strengthens connections with customers and markets, leading to more relevant, effective solutions.

Each of these values corresponds with the principles of antifragile organizations, providing a pathway to incorporate antifragility into the heart of an organization. Figure 2.4 provides a summary of these key antifragile values and their practical applications.

Embrace Opportunities over Certainties Emphasize seizing opportunities arising from uncertainty and change, rather than relying on certainty and control.	**Value Diversity over Optimization** Cultivate innovation and adaptability through diverse perspectives, experiences, and skills instead of over-optimizing for specific situations.
Foster Emergence over Prediction Encourage emergent properties and solutions from diverse components' interactions, as opposed to solely depending on top-down predictions and planning.	**Prioritize Effectiveness over Ideals** Focus on practical, outcome-driven solutions that address real-world challenges, rather than rigidly adhering to abstract ideals or theoretical models.
Promote Integration over Demarcation Advocate for collaboration, communication, and information sharing across boundaries, instead of maintaining strict separation between departments or functions.	**Emphasize Induction over Deduction** Prioritize observation and learning from real-world experiences for decision-making and strategy, rather than solely relying on top-down, deductive reasoning.

Figure 2.4
Antifragile Values

2.6

Implications for the Organizational Setup

Now that we understand the values that drive antifragility, we can consider the broader implications for an organization's governance, business processes, structures, operations, and the broader organizational fabric.

Regarding governance, traditional models are gradually replaced by a more collaborative approach to decision-making. Antifragile organizations facilitate decision-making closer to the source of information, emerging needs and opportunities. Leadership in these structures becomes contextual, adapting to the challenge or project at hand. This is not about sticking to titles and job descriptions, but efficiently mobilizing teams and resources that have the best contextual understanding, together with the capabilities necessary to make and implement effective decisions.

When we look at business processes, we see traditional linear paths of predetermined actions being replaced by more complex, adaptive, contextualized and emergent responses. Antifragile organizations view processes as interconnected networks, optimized for rapid feedback, adaptation and continuous expansion of capabilities, rather than narrowly optimizing the use of resources for a few prioritized business operations.

The structural aspects of organizations highlight the vulnerabilities of centralized entities. Antifragility promotes decentralized structures that distribute risk, authority and innovation potential. In addition, breaking down silos leads to a richer flow of information and a comprehensive approach to problem-solving. By embracing and integrating a multitude of different views, organizations can derive a more comprehensive contextual understanding, and collaboratively draw on and act upon the breadth and depth of their internal expertise.

Operationally, agility is front and centre. Operations in antifragile organizations are designed to pivot in response to both external changes and internal innovations, increasing overall adaptability. Interestingly, the inherent redundancy in organizational systems now acts as a catalyst for adaptability rather than an undesirable inefficiency. In the antifragile context, redundant resources and capabilities act as critical fallback mechanisms, ensuring continuity in the face of unforeseen disruptions.

In summary, antifragility does not just touch upon isolated facets of an organization. It permeates its very core, from governance and structures to operational practices. As we delve deeper into this, we will see how this concept challenges and overturns conventional organizational wisdom.

2.7

Reflection

The following questions can help you reflect on and analyse organizational approaches and evaluate strategies in the face of disruption and uncertainty. The goal of this reflection is to provide a straightforward examination of an organization's current state and identify potential avenues for improvement.

- **Examine the current state**: How does the organization react to stressors and uncertainties? Does it break, withstand or grow stronger?

- **Explore cultural shifts**: How ingrained are old assumptions in the organizational culture? How readily does the organization resist or push back against changes? What steps can we take to cultivate a culture of innovation, adaptability and learning within our organization?

- **Investigate structural changes**: What could drive existing structures to develop an urgent need for collaboration and sharing of information? To what extent can decentralization and redundancy be incorporated into the business model?

- **Identify growth avenues**: What overarching customer needs can help you identify and act on growth and innovation opportunities in dynamic markets?

- **Evaluate business areas**: Which areas could benefit from added optionality and flexibility?

Chapter 3

How Antifragile Organizations Work

A vibrant web of interconnectivity sparks
ingenuity and fuels sustainable progress.

"Unity, not uniformity, must be our aim. We attain unity only through variety. Differences must be integrated, not annihilated, nor absorbed."

– Mary Parker Follett

Building on the fundamental concept of antifragility, we move from understanding its implications for organizational design to a more focused exploration of how antifragile organizations work in practice. The principles of antifragile organizations lead to a radical departure from conventional designs and practices. This is reinforced by the challenges of the modern business world, which are characterized by relentless technological advances, rapidly changing customer behaviour and unpredictable market dynamics.

In this chapter, our goal is to disclose the key elements of antifragile organizations, and how they can create capabilities that are far more advanced than those of traditional organizations.

3.1

Strategizing for a Dynamic Market Landscape

For decades, corporate strategy was synonymous with long-term vision, reflecting an era of relative stability and predictability. In essence, such strategy formulated extensive and detailed plans for the future. Strategic decisions were made at the top of organizations and trickled down, with a steady focus on making incremental progress over long periods of time. Strategic investment horizons often spanned decades. But today, as global business dynamics have undergone rapid change, the rigidity of such strategic frameworks has been exposed. Rapid technological advances and changing market conditions are challenging this traditional concept of corporate strategy as a long-term, stable plan.

Today's businesses face an environment where adaptability is essential, requiring a strategic approach that can swiftly respond to dynamic changes. Against this backdrop, traditional adherence to static strategic planning has proven inadequate. Modern strategies must be much more flexible, able to adapt to unforeseen disruptions in technology and market dynamics.

Antifragile organizations represent a paradigm shift from those traditional setups that relied on stability and predictability. These organizations successfully integrate decentralized product strategies within a cohesive corporate framework that fuels both innovation and efficient strategic alignment. The strategic approaches of organizations we discussed in Chapter 2 reveal that decentralization does not imply a lack of overall direction. Rather, it enhances responsiveness and creativity, anchored in a clear corporate purpose.

Antifragile organizations implement agile methodologies in their corporate strategy processes, as exemplified by Zeiss Digital, a subsidiary of Carl Zeiss AG specializing in digital innovation and software development, and BBVA. Zeiss Digital utilizes a *Best Practice Framework* and incorporates agile methods to reassess strategic priorities and projects every four months, with reallocation of resources and changes in team membership and expertise. The strategic project plan and documentation of progress is shared transparently across the company, enabling each employee to contribute or use it for orientation in their own work. This allows for a rapid response to changes and opportunities.[65] Likewise, BBVA's transition to agile working transformed its approach to both project management and strategic decision-making. All strategies and implementation plans are synchronized through a common frame of agile time boxes. On a strategic level, the bank implemented the *Single Development Agenda* to prioritize projects worldwide and see that they support strategic goals. This shift allows BBVA to respond dynamically to market changes, harnessing agile principles to recalibrate their strategies in a timely manner.[66]

Similarly important, business strategy must place customer needs in the centre, as exemplified by Haier's micro-enterprise structure, where small units independently serve specific customers and their needs. This is a direct consequence of the *Zero Distance* philosophy described earlier. The micro-enterprises, though autonomous, operate within the strategic framework set by corporate headquarters. Their significant but strategically targeted autonomy not only encourages customer-centric innovations but also helps ensure that each unit's efforts are cohesive and contribute to the company's overall success. Rapid development cycles allow them to capitalize on short-term opportunities and local niches. This is a big strategic advantage compared to traditional strategy planning cycles, which take much longer to develop solutions, and are therefore limited to pursuing only longer-lasting opportunities with less-customizable, but highly scalable solutions. In highly dynamic markets such as the smart home industry, Haier's strategy has proven its superiority.[67]

All of these examples show how strategy and organizational capabilities need to fit together, and how they emerge to a large extent in response to needs and opportunities in the business environment.

The concept of *Strategic Fit* — where an organization's strategy is in harmony with its capabilities — gains importance as we navigate an increasingly dynamic market landscape. In fast-moving markets, the Strategic Fit of an organization needs to be reevaluated much more often, with significant consequences for its capabilities.

Figure 3.1 visualizes the non-linear progression of Strategic Fit as a function of time. It illustrates how, given today's accelerating business dynamics, markets inevitably become hyper-dynamic. And, as a consequence, how an organization's capabilities need to evolve from basic to advanced, and ultimately to antifragile. It is important to note that organizational capabilities always need to be developed first, so the business can execute advanced strategies without getting stuck. The process of capability development serves as the foundation upon which it can adjust its strategic direction, leading to long-term success. What sets antifragile companies apart is the proactive and rapid development, adaptation and continuous realignment of their organizational capabilities.

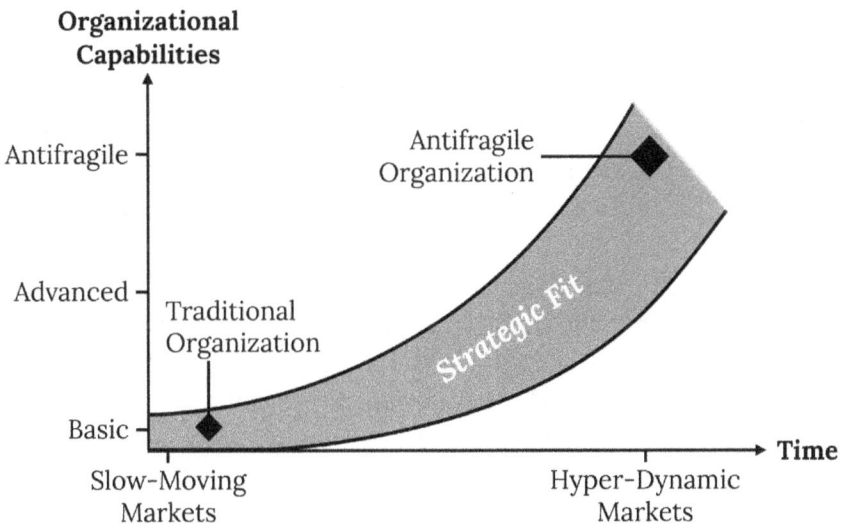

Figure 3.1
Progression of Strategic Fit

Multi-Opportunity Strategy

The mandate for today's business strategies is clear: They must be flexible and responsive to rapidly changing landscapes, yet remain firmly aligned with an organization's fundamental purpose and capabilities. To deal with the uncertainty of changes, diversification is a necessity. The integration of diverse revenue streams and market presence reduces dependency on the success of a single business opportunity.

Traditional, centralized approaches to strategy may not fully uncover and exploit all relevant opportunities. Implementing a centralized strategy is similar to sending out a single exploration team to map a huge expanse of unknown terrain. There is a high likelihood that it will struggle or even fail. When success hinges on the effort of a single team, the consequences of failure are dire, leaving the organization without an immediate backup plan and prone to setbacks. Investment-heavy, complex, long-term innovation projects are particularly vulnerable to such risks.[67]

Now, consider an alternative approach. Imagine dispatching multiple autonomous teams, each tasked with exploring a specific area of the terrain — in business terms, a distinct market segment. They operate independently, innovating and adapting to specific challenges, learning quickly and adjusting their business proposals based on real-time customer feedback. As the teams cooperate and support each other, their shared approach enables a broader, more comprehensive understanding of the terrain as a whole. However, the expectation is not that all teams will necessarily succeed. Indeed, some will commit errors, encounter insurmountable obstacles or fail altogether. Yet, in this approach, the overall progress is not halted by the failure of one or several teams. The organization can pivot based on the insights gained from unsuccessful attempts, while successful teams continue their work unimpeded. The whole organization continuously learns from failures and successes alike, and adjusts future efforts accordingly.[67]

Companies like Haier, Amazon, Nucor, BBVA and Google demonstrate that such a diversification strategy, when managed within a cohesive strategic framework, can turn potential challenges into catalysts for growth. This multi-opportunity approach allows them to actually benefit from market volatility and uncertainty, strengthening their position over time.

Enhanced abilities to act

Emerging
Opportunities

**Organizational
Capabilities**

Captured
Opportunities

Enhanced abilities to sense

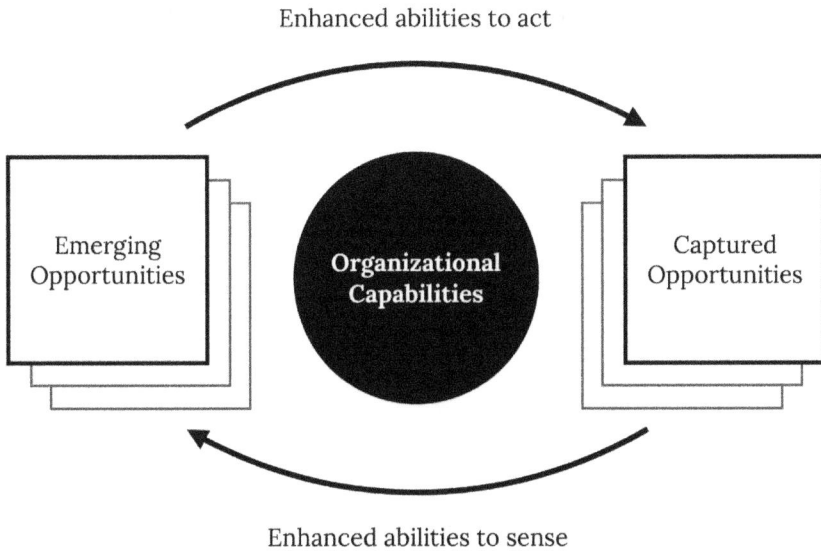

Figure 3.2
Multi-Opportunity Strategy

A multi-opportunity strategy requires organizations to rapidly and effectively act on emerging opportunities, and to sense new ones in their early stages (Figure 3.2). Antifragile organizations thus need to continually enhance their capabilities in these two important dimensions — sensing new opportunities and acting on them. The enterprise as a whole needs to enhance its receptiveness to external inputs and continuously recalibrate its capabilities according to emerging opportunities.

In conclusion, the movement of markets into higher dynamism, coupled with increased levels of uncertainty, requires organizations to implement agile strategies and diversify their sources of revenue. This leads to the concept of decentralized multi-opportunity development, which immediately leverages the required organizational capabilities to sense emerging opportunities, and to rapidly and effectively act on them. The following sections will examine the two dimensions of organizational capabilities in greater depth.

3.2

Customer Needs Govern Decisions

Customer needs are the guiding star for organizations, providing a clear focus for aligning efforts with tangible goals and valuable outcomes. Incorporating customer insights into decision-making and strategic planning can amplify the appeal and effectiveness of products and services, while strengthening an organization's foundation. This process of aligning efforts is triggered with each new stake, threat and opportunity. The more efficient the alignment process, the better a business is able to act on changed circumstances.

In a dynamic environment, the alignment process needs to achieve several important characteristics. It must be possible to perform it very quickly, at any time. Additionally, it needs to support a deep understanding of customer and other stakeholder needs, coupled with clarity about the scope of their involvement in different decisions. Thus, alignment processes must no longer cover only single decisions, but support building a comprehensive understanding of adjacent, and mutually dependent, decisions.

Dynamic market environments present particularly complex alignment challenges that require exceptional organizational flexibility and agility, to avoid missteps in a rapidly evolving marketplace. The key challenge is to skillfully recalibrate the alignment process to help ensure that: stakeholder interests are sufficiently aligned; the scope of engagement is defined; alignment is achieved at a pace that keeps the organization agile and competitive without overburdening it. This is where digital technology and business analytics can play an important role in accurately monitoring an organization's potential for increased and accelerated change.

Amazon is an excellent example of a company that prioritizes customer-centricity. The company uses advanced algorithms and real-time data analytics to gain insights and fully understand consumer behaviour and preferences. By cultivating a learning environment based on feedback, it can adjust its strategies to meet the evolving needs of its customers. Amazon founder Jeff Bezos' *Day One* philosophy[68] prioritizes continuous innovation and customer obsession, which motivates employees to always strive for better customer value and constantly adapt offerings to meet changing needs.[12]

BBVA integrates customer scenarios into its service delivery using data and technology to personalize interactions and provide customized solutions. The bank's focus on the customer is evident not only in its personalized services but also in its strong financial performance. As highlighted in Section 2.4, the bank more than doubled its customer growth rate and saw a significant increase in digital engagement, validating the economic benefits of a customer-centric approach. Through data science analysis of daily finances, BBVA offers actionable insights that cater to individualized customer profiles and promote financial well-being.[69] The system detects anomalies or significant events in a customer's banking activity, alerting them to irregularities such as unexpected bills or unusual transfers. This proactive approach helps customers anticipate financial challenges and correct potential errors. A clear manifestation of BBVA's customer-centric philosophy is its *Transparent, Clear, and Responsible Communication* approach.[70] This initiative emphasizes transparency and clarity in the relationship between the bank and its customers. Its goal is to increase trust and facilitate informed financial decisions. In addition, BBVA's *Global Wealth Client Program* offers customized financial services, ensuring that clients receive specialized advice to meet their financial and non-financial needs.

Along similar lines, Haier's commitment to *Zero Distance* has led to several transformations, most notably the emergence of *Goodaymart*, a direct offshoot of the company's feedback-based approach.[13, 71] Instead of a traditional product-centric view, Haier is delving deeply into understanding complete user scenarios. One example is their *Internet of Food* initiative, which studied user patterns related to food storage, consumption and purchasing to help provide comprehensive solutions.[72] *Zero Distance* surpasses mere user-centricity by connecting as directly as possible to customers, and closely monitoring product usage to identify and satisfy individual needs. This helps facilitate a deep and continuous alignment with customer habits, preferences and lifestyle changes.

In addition, Haier's *Smart Home Ecosystem* analyses user behaviour in the home environment to keep its offerings relevant to their evolving lifestyles. This nuanced approach to understanding user scenarios, supported by the *Zero Distance* strategy, reflects the company's forward-looking vision.[67] Competitors, such as Bosch Siemens Household Appliances are working to offer similarly comprehensive customer experiences, bringing together partners from the food, chemical and textile industries to orchestrate the necessary cross-industry value chains.

Amazon, BBVA and Haier demonstrate the significance of an alignment process that is not fixed but dynamic, in response to changing market conditions and customer requirements. These organizations have deeply integrated customer-centricity into their DNA. It is shaping their entire operational philosophy and paving the way for relentless innovation. By positioning insights about customers at the core of their business, these companies not only adapted to customer needs but have redefined the way they innovate.

Successful implementations of customer-centricity are characterized by several key concepts. First, innovations stem directly from a thorough comprehension of customer needs, guaranteeing their novelty and relevance. Second, the continual feedback loop with customers serves as a perpetual engine for improvement, with each new insight catalysing further innovation. Third, personalization and customization efforts further enhance both product development and service delivery. Co-creation with customers represents a fourth, noteworthy step forward in this evolution, welcoming customers into the heart of the innovation process. Such collaborative efforts often lead to solutions that are not only approved by the customer, but are also co-designed, resulting in a strong sense of ownership and alignment with users, creating fierce brand loyalty. In such a setting, anticipating future needs becomes second nature. Organizations that integrate customer-centricity this deeply into their operations are well equipped to anticipate and adapt to future market trends, putting them ahead of the innovation game. The result is strong brand loyalty and advocacy that goes beyond traditional marketing. Customers become brand champions, motivated by their authentic satisfaction and engagement with products and services that consistently meet or surpass their expectations.

Traditional innovation processes place several organizational and strategic filters between identifying changed customer preferences and decisively acting on these insights. Removing the red tape creates fluid business models, business processes and strategies that are dynamically evolving together with new needs.

Antifragile organizations view innovation as a natural result of their customer-centric approach, not as an isolated function or an afterthought meant to prolong the profitability of established operations. Innovation emerges as an organic and integral component of the organization's ongoing evolution within a rapidly changing business environment.

3.3

Innovate or Die

The previous discussion revealed the benefits of deep integration of customer-centricity and the role it plays in fostering innovation and continuous adaptation. In today's rapidly evolving business landscape, driven by relentless globalization and digitalization, antifragile organizations view market changes not as threats, but as rich opportunities for innovation and growth. In these companies, innovation permeates every level. It is not relegated to a specific department but is woven into the very essence of their business operations. This establishes innovation as a core, dynamic capability that is central to the organization's adaptability. The organization is constantly adapting to meet challenges and actively use them to create innovative solutions.

Traditionally, innovation has been the exclusive domain of Research and Development (R&D), sales and marketing departments. This siloed approach is grounded in the Tayloristic division of labour. It allocates the responsibility for generating new ideas to specific groups within an organization. Employees outside these departments are generally not expected, or even encouraged, to contribute to new business opportunities. Their role in innovation is often confined to making incremental improvements in operations through established *Continuous Improvement Process* (CIP) procedures. This restriction fails to utilize the full intellectual potential of the workforce, drastically limiting the scope of innovation. There is usually no transparent, straightforward or accessible process for developing new product ideas outside formally delineated innovation units.

Additionally, innovation decisions often are made far away from the frontlines, where value is being delivered to customers.

Such rigidly bureaucratic innovation pipelines were manageable in past market conditions, where changes occurred over longer periods, allowing organizations ample time to adapt. However, in today's hyper-dynamic environment, this slow-moving approach can be a distinct disadvantage. Companies must use their collective intelligence comprehensively, allowing them to quickly seize new opportunities. An inability to rapidly act on innovations across the organizational spectrum means potential market opportunities may be missed, and companies then find themselves lagging behind more agile competitors.

The Innovation Cycle: A Perpetual Loop

Before we take a closer look at how antifragile organizations enable continuous innovation, it is essential to understand the general challenge of innovation that applies to any organization: The *Innovation Cycle*. As shown in Figure 3.3, this consists of four key stages that guide a business through the journey from opportunity identification to sustained profitability. It is in their ability to cyclically and smoothly navigate these phases that antifragile organizations differentiate themselves, skillfully avoiding the efficiency trap that limits many traditional companies in their innovation efforts.

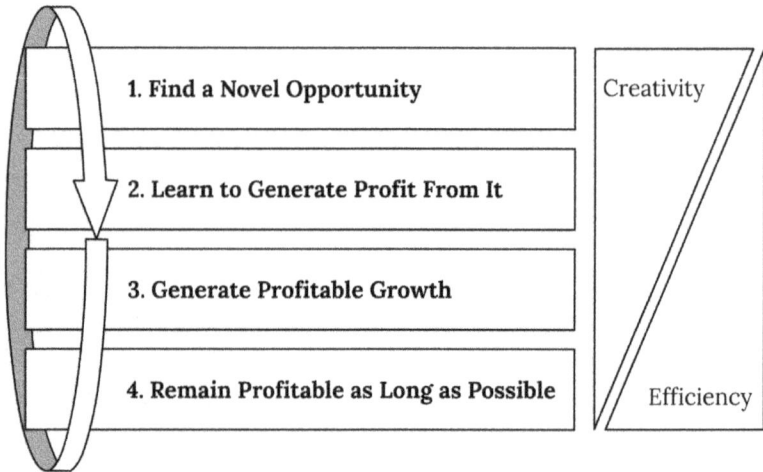

1. Find a Novel Opportunity	Creativity
2. Learn to Generate Profit From It	
3. Generate Profitable Growth	
4. Remain Profitable as Long as Possible	Efficiency

Figure 3.3
The Innovation Cycle

Stage 1: Find a Novel Opportunity
The cycle begins with the identification of emerging opportunities and challenges. This can be anything from the recognition of unmet customer needs to the development of entirely new market niches.

Stage 2: Learn to Generate Profit From It
Once a promising opportunity is identified, the organization shifts its focus to developing a profitable business model around this new prospect.

Profitability of the business model is the prerequisite for economic sustainability and growth, so this stage has to be mastered before continuing.

Stage 3: Generate Profitable Growth

With a profitable business model in place, the focus shifts to scaling that success. It is in this stage that the business model is tested for its sustainability and long-term growth potential. Here, competitors and imitators are sure to take notice and try to grab a piece of the market.

Stage 4: Remain Profitable for as Long as Possible

Finally, the goal is to optimize business processes and structures to sustain profitability over an extended period of time, in the face of competition that is eating away at market share. This ultimately leads to a loss of profitability and triggers the need to find new sources of revenue. And so, the cycle starts all over again.

It is often during the transition between Stages 3 and 4 that organizations fall into an efficiency trap, over-optimizing processes for existing business operations at the expense of overall organizational flexibility, stifling future innovation potential. The hunt for higher efficiency optimizes certain value chains to deliver more of the same output, at lower cost. Unfortunately, this focus on optimizing current operations and products results in a loss of capabilities to develop novel products or technologies from scratch. The organizational structure, people skills and resources become too rigid and narrowly focused on supporting the dominant line of business. Innovation or exploration activities do not fit well with this logic. They do not contribute directly to value creation, cost money and resources, and can even disrupt the efficiency of profitable business operations. The relentless logic of efficiency will treat such activities like any other disruption: It will largely push innovation and exploration activities aside, separating them from profitable business operations. It will support only those innovation activities that promise to prolong or increase the profitability of incumbent business operations. This is why moonshot innovation initiatives are so hard to establish inside highly successful businesses. And it is even worse when the business was successful over a long period of time. When innovations are not fully compatible with this dominant (i.e., most profitable) business operation, they are seen as risky, costly and an unnecessary drain of resources.

At this stage, the whole organization is typically designed and streamlined to support the dominant business. Innovation is then reduced to incrementally and carefully enhancing the delivered value for customers in long-established product lines. Radical new business ideas are not welcomed at this point, as they would divert resources from the dominant revenue producer. Their implementation would be costly and reduce financial performance indicators in short-term reporting periods. The decline of Nokia after the introduction of the Apple iPhone is a strong reminder of this innovation dilemma. Nokia's own research had foreseen the need to reengineer its business model, but that was not enough to alter the company's course of action.[73]

In contrast, antifragile organizations excel at seamlessly transitioning from Stage 4 back to Stage 1, fostering a continuous cycle of innovation. They are constructed to promote cross-functional collaboration and agility, which enables them to iteratively navigate through the innovation stages. They help ensure that radical new ideas receive the necessary attention and resources. As a result, these organizations remain in perpetual startup mode, constantly vigilant for new operational and market opportunities.

Netflix – Navigating the Innovation Cycle

As noted, Netflix's journey from a DVD rental service to a dominant streaming platform exemplifies its mastery of the Innovation Cycle.[74] Initially, Netflix disrupted the traditional video rental industry by addressing customer frustration over late fees, a common drawback with traditional rental stores. It waived overdue fees, allowing customers to return movies whenever they were finished with them. This shift not only pioneered a new business model but also revolutionized how movie rentals were accessed, signifying their passage through Stage 1 of the Innovation Cycle. The subsequent success of Netflix's subscription-based model highlighted their effective transition to Stage 2, establishing a profitable business framework.

Nonetheless, the advent of online streaming technology could have spelled the end for a company built around a DVD-based model.

Instead of yielding to this existential threat, Netflix embraced continuous innovation by investing in a proprietary streaming platform, effectively revisiting Stages 1 and 2 of the Innovation Cycle with this new technology. This strategic pivot not only made their later move to Stage 3 successful by ensuring additional growth potential, it prepared them for intensifying competition in the digital space.

As streaming rivals like Amazon Prime and Disney+ entered the market, Netflix again showcased its foresight by diversifying into original content production — creating its own movies and television series — a move that required revisiting all stages of the Innovation Cycle within this new, complementary business model. This strategy allowed Netflix to cater to diverse viewer preferences and regional markets, reinforcing its position during Stage 4. Despite a heavily commoditized market, the company maintained profitability and even increased subscription fees multiple times, demonstrating its ability to continuously adapt and expand in the face of industry disruptions and new technologies.

Throughout its evolution, Netflix has consistently prioritized perpetual innovation, grounded in adaptability and customer-centricity. This has enabled it to not just survive, but thrive, repeatedly progressing from Stage 4 back to Stage 1, consistently adapting and expanding in response to industry disruptions and emerging technologies.

Haier's Innovation Ecosystem

As another case study, Haier exemplifies how cross-functional teams and open innovation platforms are critical to achieving high levels of innovation. Haier employs autonomous teams that bring together experts from R&D, marketing, manufacturing and other functions. This multidisciplinary team composition facilitates a seamless integration of varied perspectives and expertise, transforming creative concepts into market-ready innovations, swiftly and effectively. The autonomy granted to these teams further accelerates the innovation process, ensuring that ideas are quickly realized as tangible products. In addition to cross-functional teams, Haier has expanded its approach to innovation by transitioning previously isolated R&D efforts into a comprehensive open innovation platform. This platform, *Haier Innovation Ecosystem* (HOPE), brings together a wide array of external experts, academic institutions and global companies. Participants act as partners and force multipliers, addressing emerging customer needs across various markets.[26]

HOPE is instrumental in breaking down traditional corporate boundaries to foster a collaborative environment for innovation. It plays a pivotal role in identifying and understanding consumer demands by engaging directly with users. The platform utilizes methods such as network big data analysis to identify consumer patterns, gathering their direct feedback on sales and after-sales service channels. Additionally, it facilitates conducting surveys, and analyses third-party data to identify broader market trends. This extensive data integration allows Haier to delve deeply into both explicit and implicit consumer needs, significantly speeding up product and business Innovation Cycles. By integrating these diverse methods, the company gains a nuanced understanding of consumer needs and wants, helping its innovation teams develop solutions that meet and exceed customer expectations.[75, 76]

Innovation in Antifragile Organizations

Antifragile organizations integrate innovation deeply into their operational and strategic frameworks. Customer-centric innovation is key, continuously fuelled by early engagement with their clientele (see Section 3.2). At GE Appliances, product teams operate with autonomy, developing and launching products based on direct market feedback without upper management approval, making customer acceptance the yardstick of success.[34] Similarly, Pixar Animation Studios uses audience screenings to directly gauge viewer reactions, making adjustments to their films based on this feedback. This ensures that the market plays a decisive role in shaping the final product.[77, 78]

When it comes to innovation, antifragile organizations do not stick to one particular method. They employ various approaches to foster creativity and initiative across all levels of the organization.

- As discussed, employees at Google are encouraged to spend 20% of their work time on projects that interest them but are not necessarily part of their regular duties. This has led to the creation of major products such as Gmail and Google Maps. Similarly, the manufacturing conglomerate 3M allows employees to use 15% of their paid time to develop their own creative projects.

- Adobe provides employees with their well-known and often imitated *Innovation Kickbox,* an actual cardboard box containing tools, guidelines and resources needed to develop new ideas, including a modest budget to validate concepts. This tool empowers employees to take charge of their innovations, from idea through to prototype.

- Amazon has institutionalized the *Working Backwards* process, where employees who have a new idea start by writing an internal press release and a FAQ document. The fictionalized press release describes the finished product in a way that is compelling to the end-user, focusing on the customer problem it solves. If the idea is approved, it moves to the next stages of development, and the employee receives funding and resources to execute. This helps ensure that innovation projects deliver value for customers from the outset, prioritizing ideas that genuinely enhance the customer experience.

- Haier offers a full ecosystem of support that includes venture financing, technical and manufacturing resources, as well as comprehensive market access. This encourages entrepreneurial behaviour within the organization and empowers employees to take ownership of their projects, from inception to market.[75]

Despite differences in execution, all these approaches share fundamental commonalities. Each method places a strong emphasis on empowering employees to take initiative. Antifragile organizations tap into the creative potential across their workforce, granting people autonomy to pursue projects that solve problems they are passionate about. Transparent and accessible innovation processes foster a culture where everyone is encouraged and feels psychologically safe expressing new ideas and taking risks. In Pixar's *Braintrust* meetings, for example, candid feedback is exchanged in an atmosphere where creative risks are not just encouraged but expected, empowering employees to push boundaries without fear of failure.[77, 78]

These approaches help see to it that necessary resources — whether time, tools, funding or support — are available to large parts of the workforce. Their flexible, short-notice allocation allows employees in all functions to experiment and develop ideas without the immediate pressure of profitability, and unburdened with resource constraints. Slack resources provide the necessary space, freedom and flexibility to quickly explore, experiment and engage in collaborative activities. Employees can then innovate without fear of being criticized for lack of productivity, and without lengthy lead times for approval of resources. A recent study by Yan Zhang, a researcher specializing in organizational innovation, and his colleagues in the financial industry highlights the significance of slack resources in fostering innovation, revealing that companies equipped with such resources tend to demonstrate higher levels of innovation.[79]

The combination of operational flexibility, psychological safety, innovation time and availability of slack resources creates an environment conducive to innovation, allowing businesses to quickly respond to challenges and achieve creative breakthroughs that will keep them ahead in a dynamic market.

Conclusion

The exploration of antifragile organizations highlights a critical insight: innovation is not a peripheral activity but lies at the core of sustained business success. Antifragile organizations excel by harnessing the collective intelligence of all employees, encouraging everyone to participate in the innovation process. This widespread engagement is key, as it creates diverse perspectives and skills to continuously redefine and adapt to the business landscape.

The engine that drives innovation into tangible outcomes is the organization's system of business processes and operations. These operational aspects, when designed dynamically, not only translate innovative ideas into reality, but also help ensure that the organization can adapt quickly to evolving market demands, thereby embodying the essence of antifragility in its daily functions. This dynamic system of operations forms the backbone of antifragile organizations, and we will explore it next.

3.4

Dynamic Business Processes and Operations

The discourse so far has highlighted the need for agility in strategy, customer-centricity and innovation, as imperatives for antifragile organizations in a volatile market environment. While these elements are critical, the machinery that puts the concepts into daily practice is the organization's business processes and operations. An antifragile organization not only thinks differently, it operates differently.

Operational Diversity

The limitations of traditional management are becoming increasingly apparent. Known in the past for their efficiency in running highly homogenized business activities, traditional management systems are struggling to keep up with the challenges of today's business world. This is mainly due to their rigid, monolithic structure and sluggish response to changes in their environment.

At the heart of these challenges is the inherent tendency of the classical system toward uniformity. Once championed for offering economies of scale and predictability through its simple, same-type, interchangeable operational models — whether in products, business models or human capital — such a uniform approach now poses risks. In today's constantly changing environment, where adaptability is imperative, this drive for uniformity can turn out to be a significant handicap. Uniform management practices often have a narrow perspective that disregards the complexities of the real world, delaying timely identification and response to important changes in the organizational environment. Consequently, internal uniformity can lead to oversimplified solutions and mental models. While these were useful for many specific standardized business needs of the past, they are not suited to addressing ever-morphing future needs. Creating a new match would require adapting the available solutions. However, initiating this adaptation is often delayed due to the unknown risks involved, and the immediate cost increase. Furthermore, the implementation of new solutions demands time and resources that are scarce, and mainly intended to further increase efficiency, not flexibility.

Examining the misfortunes of once-successful industrial giants like Nokia and Kodak reveals this pattern of uniformity in traditional operations. It limits the potential for growth and innovation by confining businesses to a single level of operational maturity for a few highly standardized product lines. This 'single maturity, uniform operations' approach is highly susceptible to disruptions. The inability to handle diversity and adapt to unforeseen changes in a timely manner can result in serious operational and economic failure.

In contrast, antifragile organizations recognize the hazards of depending too heavily on a single maturity business, particularly in unstable markets, and flourish by embracing operational diversity. At the heart of their success is the ability to simultaneously manage multiple, quite diverse business activities at different levels of maturity along the Innovation Cycle outlined in Section 3.3.

Their multi-opportunity approach spreads risk and provides multiple avenues for growth. One autonomous business unit may refine an established product, while another pioneers into an uncharted market segment. This layered strategy acts as a bulwark against market fluctuations, turning potential obstacles into opportunities for growth and innovation. This concept of simultaneous exploitation and exploration — evolving and adapting in synchronicity with changing market dynamics — builds upon the Innovation Cycle, particularly the challenges that traditional organizations face in moving from Stage 4 to Stage 1. These challenges need to be overcome, and the more frequently a company is able to do this, the faster it can turn new opportunities into profit.

Otherwise, companies can easily get caught up in optimizing existing processes and structures, losing sight of the bigger innovation picture and neglecting to build the capabilities required for operational
flexibility. While striving for a streamlined operational model tailored
to idealized customers, traditional business process management systems inadvertently stifle creativity, innovation, adaptability and the
ability to serve a diverse customer base with a multitude of needs.

The following example from home appliance manufacturer Haier
shows the power of operational diversity. The company builds washing machines that cater to unique environments. It recognizes distinct
regional needs and produces specialized models suited to these markets,
such as those for rural regions where muddy work clothes are common,
and others for urban settings where limited living space is the norm.
With slight operational modifications, Haier produces a remarkably
inventive range of washing machines that satisfy a multitude of customer needs. This strategy reflects a deep understanding of the diverse
requirements of their customer base and a dramatic departure from
the one-size-fits-all approach.[15]

By focusing on specialized products tailored to specific customer
needs, Haier demonstrates how managed variety can lead to a competitive advantage. This allows them to thrive amid market volatility
and technological disruptions. It represents a significant shift from
uniformity to a more nuanced, flexible approach that values diversity
as a core strength.

While the adoption of diversity in operations enhances organizational agility, its effectiveness hinges on well-defined ownership
and rigorous accountability. This need is especially critical in multi-
opportunity business environments, where teams are operating autonomously across various business activities and maturity levels.

Empowered Ownership of Operations and Processes

In antifragile organizations like Amazon and Netflix, the principle of *Accountability* plays a pivotal role in fostering operational diversity and agility, as discussed in Section 2.2. These companies demonstrate how empowering teams with ownership and instilling strict accountability can lead to remarkable success in rapidly evolving markets.

Amazon Web Services, for example, famously operates on the principle of *two-pizza teams*. This concept involves forming small, autonomous teams nimble enough to innovate and swiftly respond to changing market conditions. Each functions almost like a mini startup within the larger organization, taking ownership of their projects from inception to delivery.[12] This level of *empowered ownership* encourages deep investment in their work, driving innovation and proactive problem-solving. Additionally, the accountability inherent in this model motivates teams to focus on customer satisfaction and business impact, aligning their efforts with the organization's overall objectives. The *two-pizza teams* concept is used across both Amazon and Amazon Web Services. This enforces ownership, efficiency and scalability, and allows business teams to focus on a single product or service, nurturing innovation and speed.

Netflix's culture, rooted in the values of *Freedom and Responsibility*, complements this approach. The company gives its employees significant autonomy, trusting them to make decisions that align with broader organizational goals. This empowerment encourages a sense of ownership. Netflix's approach to accountability is equally important. The company upholds high performance standards, with a clear expectation that every team member is responsible for the quality and impact of their work. Despite decentralized decision-making, accountability helps instill a sense of coherent direction and purpose in all actions across the organization.[80]

The implementation of these principles is further supported by advanced digital tools and a dynamic system of business process management. AWS and Netflix utilize sophisticated data analytics and cloud-based tools to provide essential, real-time market and operational data. This technology empowers teams to make informed, responsive decisions. Moreover, the synergy between clear role definitions and dynamic business processes allows stakeholders at all levels to remain informed and act effectively, so that individual efforts are in line with the organization's overarching goals.

In fact, technology is an absolute necessity for these very small teams to be able to run their operations. Their sheer numbers of customers can only be served through massive digital automation of business operations. AWS's *two-pizza teams* are essentially in charge of establishing, maintaining and adapting a suite of fully automated digital business processes for each service they offer.

In both Amazon and Netflix, assigning clear ownership to each product or service nurtures continuous learning and improvement. Owners, having full responsibility and authority over their products or services, can swiftly make and implement decisions. They can also learn from failures and take the risks associated with decisions, a critical aspect of ownership. This is vital for antifragile organizations in dynamic markets, where learning from and leveraging change provides a key competitive edge.

To a significant degree, the success of antifragile organizations can be attributed to their emphasis on empowered ownership. Without distinct ownership and accountability, there is a heightened risk of inefficiencies, oversights, unnecessary delays in decision-making and misunderstandings. Empowered ownership enables operational diversity and rapid innovation in a multi-opportunity business.

Having said that, any empowerment reaches the limits of its autonomy and authority when it comes into conflict with the interests of other stakeholders, or when it endangers the overall alignment of the organization's overarching purpose, strategies or goals. The variety of operations, products and services therefore needs to be managed to some extent, as we will see in the next section.

The Managed Variety Engine

The lack of variety in achieving specific outcomes is a significant challenge, closely related to the issue of insufficient diversity we discussed earlier. Traditional organizations, often trapped within rigid frameworks, tend to outline singular, pre-defined pathways, advocating a specific, predetermined way to achieve results. This strict adherence to established patterns can inhibit innovation and limit adaptability in the face of evolving business. Fostering and managing variety in business processes and operations is emerging as a critical tool for innovation, adaptability and flexibility. In short, variety provides decision-makers with more options to achieve desired outcomes.

Consider a common scenario: An organization requires the purchase and delivery of goods for its operations. A conventional approach may entail a uniform, generic procurement process. This usually involves optimizing purchase prices for large quantities of items, deprioritizing other aspects, like the total speed of procurement from request to delivery. This can create time issues for innovation teams, who often need to acquire small quantities of special equipment, like 3D-printers for fast prototype builds. Procurement agents routinely shuffle such requests into waiting queues, because they consume much of their time without offering significant cost-cutting opportunities. Such requests therefore immediately become low-priority, meaning that innovation teams wait a long time for delivery, despite the fact that they need them quickly, not necessarily at the lowest possible price point. However, by implementing managed variety, the organization can enhance its procurement system's dynamism and responsiveness. A diversified system can offer various procurement methods, including a fast and effortless option.

The concepts and steps associated with a more dynamic process system work as we will describe below, as introduced by the authors into the process organization of a large automotive supplier.

Modularization of Process Landscape
Structuring a system of processes into modular components is the first step. This makes it much easier to adapt, modify or configure individual process variants as needed. Modular process libraries provide

a set of individual modules, allowing teams to select and customize the components of business processes based on their specific operational needs and business maturity. Modularity supports process evolution in line with market dynamics and organizational learning, leading to increased operational efficiency and facilitating innovation.

Differentiation and Customization

Depending on business requirements, various process modules can be chosen and combined, making it possible to prioritize either speed, cost-effectiveness or local sourcing in each procurement activity (Figure 3.4).

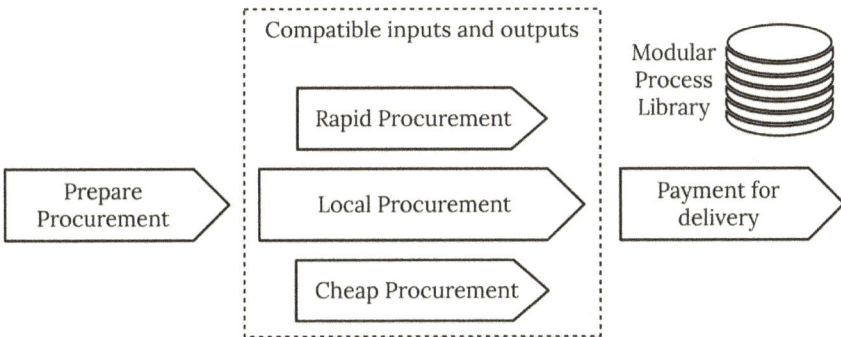

Figure 3.4:
Process Modularization and Differentiation

For instance, urgent purchasing needs can trigger a streamlined process that prioritizes speed, skipping non-critical checks or approvals for the sake of expediency. A straightforward method is to provide innovation teams with a corporate credit card for their purchases, while expecting them to abide by legal compliance xaall purchases. Innovation teams can either follow the standard organizational procurement process or tap their assigned card, depending on the situation. This enhances the team's flexibility, and once it has been successfully piloted it could be offered to all innovation teams, creating a new process variant for the organization. Each new process variant contributes to its library of business processes, which serves as the basis for the value-creating business operations. This library helps the organization efficiently perform a growing range of tasks, extending the scope of the business and speeding up new operations through rapid customization of their underlying processes.

Rapid Evolution and Addition of Process Variants

Thanks to the modularization of each process variant, process module changes can be made independently, facilitating their modernization. This facilitates quick adaptation to changing contexts without disrupting processes in other contexts. Established business operations are not affected by new variants and can continue to use their current processes. This allows for a safe acceleration of change within an organization's process framework. Otherwise, changing existing processes poses a risk to established business operations, potentially slowing down process improvement and innovation. For example, if the company relies on only one procurement process, any alteration can impact its efficiency and functionality, leading most process managers to shy away from modernizing it.

Modularity greatly reduces the risk of breaking a running system. It allows for the quick and safe implementation of any desired change into a new process variant. For instance, a business operation pursuing sustainability goals can develop a procurement variant that guarantees purchasing from certified eco-friendly sources. Its integration into the process landscape can expand applicability beyond the original intent, allowing its use in other business operations. As a result, the number of available procurement options within the organization grows. This promotes flexibility, facilitates cooperation and enables sharing of lessons learnt across all operations. The ease of implementing process changes not only enables the rapid addition of process variants but also significantly speeds up the evolution cycle of processes in general.

Highly adaptive processes are characterized by their agility, helping companies respond to evolving market conditions and internal demands without much delay. The perceived agility of processes is the result of being able to frequently run through a learning and improvement cycle. Fast iterations then make processes highly adaptive and responsive to changing conditions or requirements.

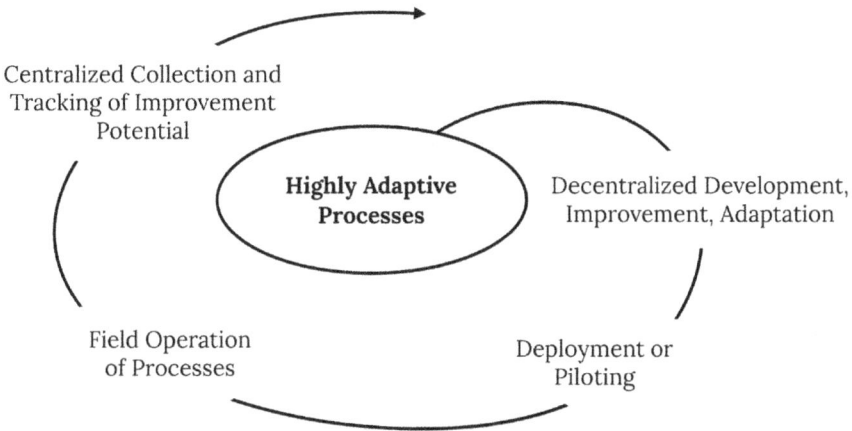

Figure 3.5
Highly Adaptive Process Cycle

This lifecycle of process evolution, depicted in Figure 3.5, starts with a rapid design phase in which process variants are created or adapted based on real-time feedback or emerging requirements. After deployment, each variant is continuously monitored to assess its performance and alignment with strategic objectives. This real-time evaluation then feeds a dynamic refinement phase in which processes are iteratively improved or retired, based on their effectiveness and relevance.

Furthermore, highly adaptive processes are implemented and piloted with a *learn-fast* mentality, where improved variants can be tested in controlled environments and lessons learnt are quickly incorporated into the next iteration. This approach reduces risk and speeds up learning from each process variant, cultivating an environment that encourages innovation and ingrains adaptability in the organization's DNA. The following sections will explore in detail how to achieve this rapid learning cycle.

Standardization of Interfaces and Dynamic Process Architecture

While it is important to allow for diversity in process modules, standardizing certain interfaces and interactions remains important. Standardization facilitates smooth coordination and increases cohesion among different work streams. This can help deliver seamless functioning of the overall process architecture, at various levels. Standardization also enables learning opportunities and knowledge transfer to and from other operations. As standardization necessitates oversight and coordination, it should be performed in a well-synchronized manner among all affected process stakeholders. This typically leads to the creation of a distributed process organization that governs standardization and differentiation decisions based on the principle of subsidiarity. It mandates that decisions be made at the lowest appropriate level capable of achieving an effective solution, but not lower than that. For instance, each variant of the procurement process must comply with identical standards at the interfaces, particularly concerning input and output data for preceding and subsequent processes. Otherwise, downstream processes would not know what data to expect, which would severely impact their efficiency and functionality.

The standardization of process interfaces creates a framework that promotes compatibility among process variants across all of the company's value creation chains. It essentially establishes the organization's process architecture. This architecture requires a governing body that looks beyond individual business operations, scrutinizing the big picture of interoperability, flexibility and cooperation.

The framework for processes resulting from modularization, managed standardization and fast differentiation should be highly flexible, capable of dynamically balancing innovation and efficiency needs. As such, it also needs to be subject to the highly adaptive process lifecycle discussed earlier. The balancing act needs to be performed all the time, with high frequency. Otherwise, it would impose outdated standards that are a hindrance rather than an asset.

Iterative Development and Continuous Improvement

Adopting an iterative approach to process improvement is a well-established practice within traditional process management. However, it often proves insufficient in dynamic business environments where process architectures must keep up with the pace of change in the outside business environment. Process users are typically the first to notice such change, when certain prescribed process details do not make sense, are incorrect, or turn out inefficient in a changed context. Any such change should trigger immediate improvement or adaptation actions. Having feedback loops at various levels integrated into each business process is the fastest way to discover the need for action. They are the most effective way to solicit guidance, frequently and methodically, identify areas for improvement and address user-perceived issues. This enables rapid refinement of operations, and promotes agility and adaptability in dynamic environments. The success of feedback loops depends on users being able to easily report issues, and process owners being able to quickly improve their processes. Therefore, process owners need to be promptly informed of any necessary adaptations, corrections or improvements, and empowered to quickly implement required process modifications and upgrades. Employees in business operations can offer suggestions for improvement, and provide early feedback on pilot efforts. When the improvements are incorporated into the process library, all of the organization's business operations can benefit.

Technology can reduce this process improvement cycle time to a few days or minutes, even in large and distributed organizations, significantly enhancing the value of business processes and the process improvement system's reputation among employees. Speed of action and communication, especially with process users, is key. Otherwise, process users may lose trust in the ability and willingness of process owners to support the business processes and adapt them to new needs. This can lead to a slow degradation of the process framework's effectiveness, followed by a breakdown of the organization's ability to collaborate efficiently.

Decentralized Decision-Making and Empowerment

The large volume of process improvement or differentiation requests in a fast-paced business environment can quickly exceed the process owners' ability and capacity to promptly implement them. When process improvement cycles need to be performed faster and more frequently across the whole operational system, as discussed previously, there is only one viable solution. Namely, process ownership should be delegated and distributed to a larger number of individuals within the organization, allowing process users at the operational level to customize business processes and align them with their specific working conditions. This change can only be effective if those who are given such customization authority also accept ownership and responsibility for process improvement. Rather than having a handful of process owners, with very limited improvement capacity, the organization can then engage dozens, hundreds, or even thousands of individuals for its process adaptation and improvement efforts. This approach makes perfect sense: Since the need for process landscape differentiation or adaptation is often detected at the operational level, where value is directly created, it is essential to equip individuals in these operations with the tools and knowledge needed to formulate and implement enhanced solutions. The quicker and smoother the customization, differentiation or adaptation can be performed, the more flexibility can be achieved in the overall process landscape. Therefore, enabling the operational level to perform changes in business processes, differentiating and adapting them, is a key concept that speeds up improvement cycles, greatly enhancing ownership and responsibility for process improvement among employees.

Balancing Differentiation Requirements

The multitude and diversity of business processes that arise from the previously discussed steps raises the risk of complete fragmentation of the process landscape, to the point where commonalities between operations disappear, making it impossible to maintain the standards required for effective collaboration across operations. This must be avoided at all costs, as it significantly undermines the ability to cooperate, learn and innovate across business operations. The long-term challenge of achieving variety and differentiation comes in striking a balance between fulfilling the diversity of operational needs and ensuring efficiency and control across the organization through standardization. This balance can be achieved through a clear understanding of where differentiation is necessary and where standardization is beneficial. Effective governance of the process landscape necessitates prompt and well-coordinated communication and consultation among its stakeholders. Digital technology can significantly aid this communication, particularly in large and distributed organizations that have many process stakeholders.

In the procurement example, the organization benefits from the implementation of standardized interfaces between the different procurement process variants because it maintains the integrity and efficiency of its operations. This standard, even if only a visual representation of complex operations, promotes a common understanding across the company of what procurement is, how it can be initiated and what it entails. As a result, communication and collaboration between different parts of the organization are enhanced by this standard. Otherwise, achieving consensus and understanding of the nature, objectives and scope of procurement procedures would be challenging and time-consuming. If each business operation had a completely different methodological approach, this would impede joint procurement efforts, such as aiming for larger economies of scale across business operations.

The implications of this procurement example extend far beyond a single business function. The approach can in fact be applied to the management of all business processes. Identifying common ground for standardization, and implementing it, is a continuous, dynamic effort that must be balanced with evolving differentiation needs. The key to successfully doing it is efficiently organizing transparent communication among process owners, and establishing clear procedures for process improvement and further development of the process architecture. Digital technologies can greatly facilitate this management challenge, with off-the shelf *teamware* solutions for issue tracking, communication and resolution.

Process Synchronization and Integration

To facilitate coherent operations across a distributed process framework, process synchronization and integration are key requirements. They guarantee a consistent flow of data and resources across various functional areas, enabling informed decision-making and collaborative endeavours. This synchronization is improved by establishing clear communication channels for process changes across the different standardization levels and a transparent, coherent change implementation framework. Figure 3.6 illustrates how a distributed process organization achieves the synchronization of individual process changes with overall standards. Far from being a theoretical concept, it is actively implemented by world-leading automotive suppliers such as Bosch Engineering GmbH, which provides systems engineering and product customization services.

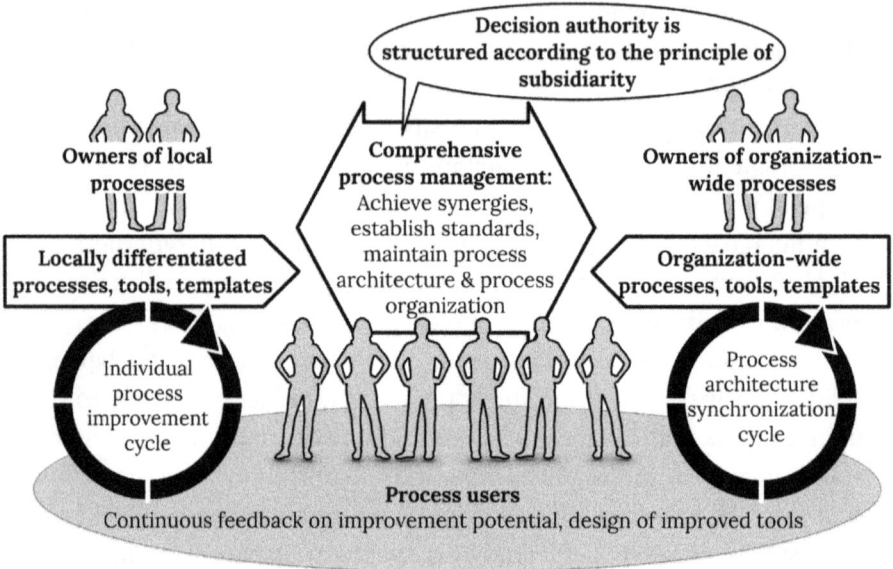

Figure 3.6
Distributed Process Organization

- **Owners of local processes** are responsible for those that are tailored to meet specific localized needs. They use locally differentiated tools and templates that are unique to their specific area of the organization. In a distributed process organization, there can be hundreds of local process owners, greatly increasing the organization's capacity for process improvement. Ideally, local process owners perform this role in addition to their daily operational tasks. At Bosch Engineering, local process owners are required to be regular users of their own processes. This principle helps ensure that their business processes provide practical and valuable solutions for daily challenges employees face, rather than hypothetical descriptions that are largely ignored, as in so many other companies.

- **Process users** are the individuals who rely on business processes to carry out their work. They provide continuous feedback on business processes, their representation in the process library and the tools aiding in their implementation. When their feedback leads to rapid improvements that facilitate their daily work, process users become avid drivers of process improvement, differentiation and change. At Bosch Engineering, the majority of process improvement requests stem from process users: Up to a thousand formally tracked requests are logged per year, in addition to thousands more that are implemented so quickly that they are not even tracked.

- Each local process owner continuously performs the **individual process improvement cycle** based on feedback and performance metrics. This cycle keeps local processes efficient, effective, and easy to understand and use. The duration of local process improvements can vary greatly, from mere minutes to months. Changes in one process often trigger the need for synchronization with adjacent processes and interfaces, setting in motion change management procedures that drive consistent implementation of changes across all business processes and their variants.

- The **process architecture synchronization cycle** addresses this challenge by relieving local process owners of many change-related communication and coordination tasks, which facilitates and greatly speeds up the management of changes in the overall process architecture. The cycle has a fixed duration, making it easy to synchronize individual changes. Process owners register planned changes for integration in the next architecture release cycle, and follow the process release procedures coordinated by the organizational body of *comprehensive process management*. Registration is particularly valuable for changes that involve adapting process interfaces or other organization-wide standards. Without a clearly defined synchronization cycle, implementing these changes consistently across the entire process architecture would take a significant amount of time. Worse, the slowest process to change in the chain of architectural dependencies would delay the timely deployment of an improved process architecture. Bosch Engineering avoids this. It performs the process architecture cycle every four months, delivering a reliable, consistent and aligned process landscape that integrates new business needs and facilitates collaboration across the company's diversified business operations.

- The organizational body of **comprehensive process management** is responsible for achieving synergies between different local processes, establishing standards, and maintaining the overall process architecture and organization. This virtual process organization helps ensure that all processes align with the business's top-line goals and objectives. It consists of local process owners, who can be organized in different chapters, and those responsible for coordinating changes, particularly process interfaces within their chapters. Additionally, these individuals influence the development and adaptation of organization-wide standards and can assume the role of *owners of organization-wide processes*. At Bosch Engineering, they collaborate with organization-wide process owners to make decisions regarding standardization and differentiation at both local and global levels of the process architecture. To identify decision needs and drive decisions forward, this organizational body self-manages several dozen meetings of process stakeholders per month.

- **Decision authority is structured according to the principle of subsidiarity**: Decisions are made as locally as possible. When necessary, they are coordinated and supported by higher levels of the organization. This supports fast decision-making and implementation, greatly increasing the capacity for change in the organization. At Bosch Engineering, the number of implemented improvement requests approximates the number of submitted improvement requests. That can end up being up to a thousand requests per year. For each request, this implies that numerous decisions may be required, often involving intricate negotiations among process stakeholders. Bosch Engineering is able to handle this volume of decisions thanks to the principle of subsidiarity, which enables effective governance in a large and distributed process organization.

- Formal authority and responsibility is placed upon the **owners of organization-wide processes**, who are tasked with facilitating the consistency and synergy of processes that are used across the company. They help ensure that organization-wide processes, tools and templates are standardized, and support the overall mission of the enterprise. At Bosch Engineering, formal decision-making authority regarding processes and standards is handed to a few dozen individuals, all of whom are highly skilled in aligning potentially conflicting interests and coordinating cross-department activities. They frequently report to high-ranking business managers.

- **Organization-wide processes, tools and templates** are standardized for consistency and alignment with the company's objectives. The owners of organization-wide processes maintain these standards based on continuous feedback from process users, local process owners and business managers. For example, Bosch Engineering applies the same tools and procedures for both local and organization-wide process improvements. This allows for efficient promotion of local process requests to the organization-wide level and vice versa.

As a result of all these unconventional methods of organization, the synchronization of the cycles of **individual process improvement** and the **process architecture** happens transparently and quickly, allowing for a dynamic balance of standardization and differentiation. It enables local innovations to be integrated into the wider organization's standards and practices, while seeing to it that organization-wide processes support and enhance local operations. This setup creates a rapid feedback loop where processes at all levels are continuously improved and aligned with each other. It also steers all processes to support the organization's broader set of collaboration standards, promoting a cooperative environment that takes advantage of its large variety of business capabilities to enable and sustain a multitude of more complex value chains.

While the practices of process synchronization and integration, as exemplified by Bosch Engineering, are at the forefront of managing complex, distributed business operations, they still only represent a tiny step toward the expected ultra-dynamic business process management of the future, potentially fuelled by advances in AI and process management software suites. The future will bring new challenges and opportunities that will further drive the evolution of practices in business process management, involving an even stronger focus on flexibility, variety, and delay-free organizational learning and adaptation.

In conclusion, managed variety is a strategic approach to process management that addresses the challenges posed by rigid and one-size-fits-all operating models. It leads organizations toward a highly flexible, responsive and innovative process culture that fully embraces diversity in methodologies and techniques.

Collaboration Standards and the Enterprise Process Stack

In a multi-opportunity business like Haier's, with its more than 4,000 micro-enterprises, the potential for operational chaos is significant. Diverse stages of business maturity and contradictory objectives can lead to misalignment and inefficiency, posing a substantial challenge to maintaining consistent operations, cooperation, compliance and strategic alignment. Without a clear framework for interaction, the complexity of autonomous operations could undermine the very agility and inventiveness that the decentralized setup aims to achieve.

The Enterprise Process Stack, as shown in Figure 3.7, effectively addresses these issues by providing a comprehensive framework that balances standardized operations with the flexibility and customization necessary for a multi-opportunity business.

The stack is organized into three interdependent layers, each of which addresses different operational needs and serves a different purpose. While the top of the stack deals with immediate value creation, and must therefore cover a wide range of diversity, the bottom end needs to deliver high efficiency and reliability from the multitude of basic, recurring interactions required for cooperation, such as standard mechanisms for internal messaging or contracting. This promotes uniformity at the foundations of the operational system.

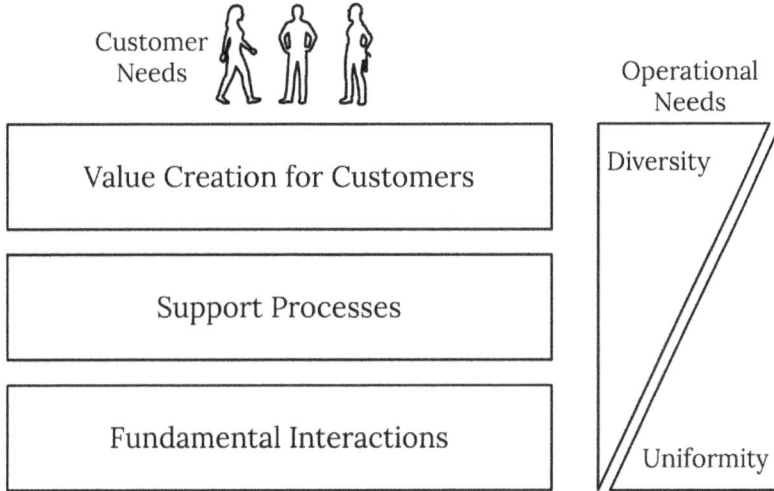

Figure 3.7
Enterprise Process Stack

Value Creation Layer

This layer represents the pinnacle of operations, where business processes are completely tailored to specific products, services or customer segments. In this context, micro-enterprises, driven by their unique market maturity, develop distinctive strategies and services for diverse customer groups. This operational nuance cultivates a deep understanding of customer needs, as showcased by Haier's micro-enterprise approach. This strategy enables the creation of tailored solutions, adeptly capturing short-term opportunities and tapping into niche markets.[67]

Support Layer

This layer encompasses business processes that enhance and support value creation, such as IT services, logistics, procurement and recruiting. For example, one business team may require customized advanced data analytics services to understand consumer behaviour, while another may need services for rapid prototyping. It would be inefficient for the *Value Creation Layer* to create all of these supporting functions from scratch, and to allocate their own resources for this task. Therefore, antifragile organizations try to build such supporting capabilities once, and share them as specialized services across all organizational units. As internal service providers, these functions can perform specialist work for any business operation, ensuring efficiency, high quality standards and compliance with technical or regulatory requirements through the processes that their specialists follow. For example, procurement functions must abide by specific procurement regulations and defined procedures.

As previously discussed in *Balancing Differentiation Requirements*, providing different options makes it easier to customize the service to various business needs, such as buying items quickly, cost-effectively, locally or sustainably. Supporting processes therefore need to balance the need for operational standards while also addressing the differentiation needs of the Value Creation Layer. In traditional business management, support processes are often standardized for the sake of organizational efficiency and cost reduction, rather than being developed and differentiated according to the needs of the Value Creation Layer. In contrast, antifragile organizations treat supporting processes and functions as enablers of value creation. Therefore, these supporting functions and processes can be developed and differentiated based on the business value they provide, rather than solely on their costs.

Haier takes this to the extreme, treating supporting functions as profit and loss responsible service providers, paid by their internal customers. This way, internal services keep delivering value, rather than solely promoting uniform solutions. The Support Layer needs to strike a good balance between diversity and uniformity, making work in this layer similarly dynamic and entrepreneurial on the customer-facing end. It needs to continuously and effectively mediate the different stakeholder needs coming from the front-end and back-end of operations, and come up with solutions that serve both.

Fundamental Interaction Layer

Fundamental interactions provide a coherent platform upon which the other layers can effectively function. They establish standards for communication, engagement of resources and interaction within the organization. This includes the very basic interactions involved in delegating and accepting responsibility for specific outcomes, contracting work within and across teams, accounting for work efforts, internal invoicing of services, and providing accountability, safety and security. Its purpose is to establish a consistent and efficient *modus operandi* throughout the organization, while also providing fair, safe and secure conditions for all participants. This lays the foundation for trust among employees, greatly improving the efficiency of myriad individual cooperation tasks in the value creation and Support Layers. Uniformity of foundational interactions facilitates their automation, further reducing the effort associated with coordination. Technology serves as a big enabler of progress in this layer. Ahead, Section 3.5 contains in-depth studies of several outstanding organizational practices.

The *Enterprise Process Stack* provides a structured approach that effectively mitigates risks associated with decentralization. This framework guides the development of practical and differentiated solutions in the area of business process management. It ensures that each team can operate with the necessary autonomy for rapid innovation and market responsiveness, while providing cohesive and streamlined operational standards for efficient cooperation across the entire organization. In short, it achieves the required balance between autonomy and unity, innovation and reliability.

Conclusion

The discussion thus far has systematically analysed the essential organizational attributes of dynamic business processes and operations. The main points are that the operational agility of antifragile organizations stems from their structured yet flexible business process frameworks. These frameworks facilitate rapid adaptation to market changes. Modular operations, empowerment of operational levels and effective cooperation standards promote trust, rapid learning and innovation across the entire company.

These operational strategies achieve their full potential when integrated with advanced digital infrastructures. The following section will focus on the digital backbone, which is the technological enabler for efficient implementation of many of these strategies.

3.5

Digital Backbone

The boundaries of an organization's potential are defined by the breadth of its communication and collaboration capabilities. As these capabilities expand through digital technology, so too does the organization's ability to innovate, adapt and thrive in a complex, interconnected world.

The digital backbone plays a central role in empowering autonomous operations and ensuring effective collaboration, learning and innovation across organizations. It resembles a central nervous system, providing the necessary infrastructure for the seamless flow of information, decision-making and coordination of efforts. The digital backbone's role is thus twofold: it underpins the dynamic characteristics of business operations and catalyses the continuous evolution of organizational capabilities. The development of such a backbone is a progressive journey through various stages of digital maturity. As organizations evolve through these stages, they enhance the power and versatility of their business capabilities.

Stages of Digital Maturity

The evolution of digital capabilities has become a critical determinant for the progression of an organization. This evolution typically takes place in several stages, each building on the previous one to create the digital backbone that is essential for an antifragile organization.

Digitization

In the first stage, a company converts its analogue data into digital formats. This foundational step is important for making information more accessible and manageable, setting the stage for further digital advancements. It involves transitioning from paper to pixels, allowing for the initial collection and storage of digital data. The characteristics of the digital formats greatly influence the possible usage scenarios, for example, how efficiently data can be shared, and how much value digitization offers for practical applications. Ideally, the chosen digital formats are standardized to provide compatibility across different systems and support the easy, fast and reliable exchange of data across the organization. This requires building and learning to use a basic digital infrastructure for storing and accessing data. Companies at this stage are still constrained in their ability to implement digital business models due to their limited digital capabilities. The organization is just beginning to learn how to efficiently manage digital data and the associated tools.

Digitalization

Organizations progress from digitization to digitalization by using and managing digital data as key elements of their business processes, which requires digitalizing big parts of the process landscape. A more cohesive data structure emerges, enabling improved process efficiency and data accessibility. It allows for sharing and using information across different functions and in multiple processes at the same time. In this stage, the digital backbone emerges as the connecting element between processes and business operations that need to access and share the same data. As such, it needs to provide the single source of 'truth' for shared data, ensuring data integrity and promoting a unified approach to data management. This requires the implementation of an efficient data administration system that identifies relevant data and then enables appropriate handling, security and traceability. These measures collectively contribute to the confidence stakeholders have in digital data and digital processes.

At this stage, companies are beginning to recognize the strategic value of data and digital processes, which allows them to enhance operational efficiency, increase productivity and innovate service delivery. The digital backbone becomes increasingly important as it connects disparate business processes, offering a unified platform for seamless data flow and efficient collaboration through digital channels within the organization.

Yet, if not properly implemented, this can lead to data being managed in silos, isolated from other business operations. While this approach can improve operational efficiency within individual business units, it largely inhibits data sharing and collaboration across business operations, reducing the strategic potential of digitalization. If implemented correctly, this stage lays the foundation for shared data management across business operations and enables organizations to use data for strategic decision-making, which serves as a cornerstone for antifragile organizations.

Automation

Automation represents another significant milestone in an organization's digital evolution. It frees up human resources from repetitive administrative tasks, so they can focus on discovering and enhancing customer value and achieving strategic improvements. At this stage, it is necessary to enhance the capabilities of the digital backbone and the skills required to manage automation. Organizations need to learn how to govern the automated data flow and manage the connectivity of automation interfaces across operations. They utilize predictive analytics and real-time decision-making based on accurate and timely data. Advanced automation technologies, such as AI and machine learning, enable the execution of autonomous tasks and help in further streamlining operations. For certain business functions, such as cybersecurity, the automation of many busy operations becomes a necessity. For an organization that aspires to be antifragile, achieving this level of digital maturity is a minimum requirement. Otherwise, it would simply not be fast enough for hyper-dynamic markets. Automation helps ensure that companies are not engulfed in the manual management of recurring transactions, but can concentrate their cognitive efforts on new opportunities, swiftly pivoting their business operations, innovating and growing.

Transformation

The transformation stage is where organizations can expand their organizational capabilities by harnessing the full potential of digital technology. Here, the digital backbone incorporates advanced analytics tools and AI capabilities that help predict trends, identify opportunities and make data-driven decisions. Additionally, it integrates cloud computing platforms into business operations that improve scalability, flexibility and the ability to quickly deploy new applications and services. These digital capabilities now allow for a comprehensive reimagining of business models and the organizational setup, building on the advancements made in the previous stages. Companies that have mastered this stage demonstrate an exceptional ability to continuously innovate and adapt. Teams in these organizations can act with a high degree of autonomy. They utilize open platforms that foster collaboration and co-creation of value. This encompasses collaborative tools and digital marketplaces that allow interaction and co-creation with adjacent teams, customers, partners and other stakeholders. They can significantly increase flexibility and adaptability, enhancing the value of organizational capabilities and business relationships. In this maturity stage, the digital backbone helps companies take advantage of the collective intelligence and creativity of business teams, leading to the development of new products, services and business models that were previously unimaginable. Achieving this state of maturity is essential in an organization's journey toward becoming antifragile.

As companies progress through these stages, they reach a point where they can fundamentally reconsider how they interact with markets and customers. Haier's realignment has led to the creation of innovative organizational setups, such as its ecosystem of micro-enterprises. This ecosystem is built on deep digital integration and advanced data analytics capabilities.

Similarly, Amazon's journey through these stages, particularly its mastery of automation, has allowed it to redefine retail and cloud services.[12] Companies that are able to continuously innovate and adapt during the transformation stage demonstrate a flexible and adaptable business model, supported by a strong digital backbone.

These companies demonstrate that achieving antifragility requires a high level of digital maturity. It enables them to be nimble and innovative, while at the same time being able to quickly scale successful ventures and operations.

Case Study: Amazon Web Services (AWS)

Digitization Stage

AWS started as a digitization effort of Amazon's internal infrastructure, converting physical servers and data centres to a digital, cloud-based format. This allowed Amazon to manage its vast amounts of data more effectively and set the stage for the cloud revolution.

Digitalization Stage

AWS progressed by integrating various digital services, like computing power (EC2), database management (RDS) and more. This stage marked a significant shift from being an organizational function of an e-commerce company to becoming a digital service-driven company.

Automation Stage

AWS incorporated advanced technologies such as AI, machine learning (with services like SageMaker), and automated deployment and management tools (like CodeDeploy and CloudFormation). On an organizational level, this required that all organizational functions be made available, connected and managed exclusively through digital processes and automated interfaces.

Transformation Stage

AWS transformed its business model, shifting from basic cloud services to innovative, wide-ranging solutions like AI and machine learning. This involved a complete reevaluation of operations, focusing on flexible, customer-centric service offerings. AWS's organizational structure evolved, prioritizing innovation and agility. This transformation redefined AWS's role, positioning it as a strategic partner in digital transformation, constantly innovating and adapting to market trends and enhancing customer value through advanced technology-driven solutions.

The Role of the Digital Backbone in the Enterprise Process Stack

To facilitate rapid adaptation and growth, the Enterprise Process Stack is highly relevant, as described in Section 3.4. Its layered approach, consisting of the *Value Creation Layer*, *Support Layer* and *Fundamental Interaction Layer*, aligns perfectly with the capabilities of the digital backbone.

Supporting the Value Creation Layer

The digital backbone can enhance the ability of the Value Creation Layer to customize processes for specific products or services. By providing advanced analytics and real-time data on products, services and customer needs, it empowers autonomous teams to develop unique strategies and innovative solutions. This cultivates continuous improvement and customization. Haier's digital backbone, for example, enables real-time tracking of home appliance performance data, allowing the company to quickly innovate and customize products based on customer usage patterns. Similarly, consumer electronics maker Xiaomi has integrated direct chat channels into their mobile phones, allowing users to request new features or individual support.

Optimizing the Support Layer

The digital backbone provides the Support Layer with access to a variety of flexible and customizable digital tools, so that support services are effective and efficient, tailored to the specific needs of different operational streams. The ability to rapidly customize digitalized business processes facilitates dynamic rebalancing of standardization and differentiation needs. Moreover, the support services themselves can be deeply integrated into the digital backbone, making their support capabilities available throughout the organization as digitally managed services, further facilitating their integration into automated value chains. For example, development teams at AWS can leverage the support services of SageMaker, a fully managed machine learning service, to boost their own analytics with powerful machine learning capabilities in the digital backbone, allowing teams to innovate faster.

Automating Fundamental Interactions

The Fundamental Interaction Layer can greatly benefit from automation capabilities of the digital backbone. To maintain operational coherence in a decentralized organizational set-up, and to set the basis for automation in higher levels of the process stack, it is critical that recurring foundational transactions are conducted uniformly and efficiently, and that automation provides this reliability. Automating standardized processes, such as internal invoicing, contracting and compliance, significantly improves efficiency and reduces the burden on human resources. Haier automates many standard processes, such as reporting, internal invoicing and compliance checks, through its digital backbone, which significantly increases operational efficiency, internal service reliability and trust among its micro-enterprises.

The digital backbone and Enterprise Process Stack can perfectly complement each other. Ideally, they seamlessly work together to manage and share business processes, data and services across organizational domains. This sharing of resources and capabilities requires multiple organizational stakeholders to constantly collaborate, quickly and efficiently, on many cross-domain governance issues. Especially important are those related to ownership, safety of data, design of process interfaces, and training and support of users. The sophisticated digital infrastructures in companies like Haier and Amazon demonstrate that such collaborative governance requires a foundation of transparency, traceability and accountability in all organizational activities. A digital backbone is perfect for building this.

Transparency and Accountability in the Digital Backbone

The digital backbone acts as a reliable custodian for organizational transactions. Each transaction processed through this infrastructure creates a traceable trail, ensuring that every activity is logged with clarity and authenticity. The resulting precise records about each internal and external transaction provide an unparalleled level of transparency. Stakeholders, whether internal or external, can easily trace each transaction back to its origins, leaving no room for doubt or uncertainty about the state of transactions, and providing useful, real-time indicators of the progress made toward desired outcomes.

The digital backbone can also establish unprecedented levels of transparency regarding the responsibilities and ownership involved in the management of data, value chains, processes, services, goods or governance rights. In a digital environment with a wide variety of stakeholders and frequent changes, paper records might not keep up with the developments. The digital backbone provides an accurate, reliable single point of truth at all times, enabling rapid identification of owners and decision-makers, facilitating quick resolution of otherwise lengthy disputes among stakeholders.

The integration of advanced digital solutions into the digital backbone, such as blockchain technology, can create a transparent and immutable record-keeping system. This is particularly important in complex supply chains, where multiple parties are involved and the safeguarding of sensitive data is critical.[81] By providing a transparent and unalterable record-keeping system, blockchain technology instills a higher degree of trust among stakeholders. Any attempt to unilaterally modify a transaction recorded in a blockchain would require significant effort. Securing critical records, such as internal or external contracts, with blockchain technology therefore instills confidence in the authenticity of records, which enhances trust among the cooperating entities and their stakeholders. In addition, transactional logs establish a clear path of accountability, promptly flagging any discrepancies, tracing their origins and quickly identifying the involved parties. This function promotes accountability and helps deter unethical or irresponsible conduct.

Thus, digitally recorded transactions help establish compliance with standards and regulations. Many checks can even be automated, reducing the risk of unauthorized human intervention or error. Depending on the regulatory environment of specific industries, the digital infrastructure can assist compliance custodians, making their work much more effective and enabling them to spend more time on difficult cases involving ambiguous behaviour or unclear ethics.

The emphasis on transparency and accountability in the digital backbone enhances trust among all parties involved. This includes employees seeking validation, customers in need of reliable transactions and partners striving for fair dealings. The focus on clarity in every transaction goes beyond mere data exchange; it embodies the organization's commitment to honesty and responsibility. To achieve antifragility, organizations must be dedicated to transparency and accountability. It allows them to build and maintain trust even during turbulent times, promoting effective teamwork and establishing long-lasting relationships.

The European Federation of Pharmaceutical Industries and Associations' EFPIA Code of Practice[82] is an example of the desired transparency and accountability. The code reflects the industry's commitment to operating in a professional, ethical and transparent manner. Among other practices, EFPIA members voluntarily disclose all payments and transfers of money to healthcare professionals, healthcare organizations and patient organizations, bringing transparency and clarity to these partnerships. A digital backbone could help implement such a practice more efficiently and effectively.

As we explore the multifaceted role of the digital backbone in enhancing organizational agility, data integration and technological sophistication, it becomes clear how valuable these elements are in real-world applications. The following case studies exemplify the practical implications of these concepts. They demonstrate how the strategic deployment of a digital backbone enables organizations to rapidly adapt and thrive when confronted with dynamic market challenges.

The Digital Backbone in Action

Henkel: Harnessing the Power of Digital Transformation and Real-Time Data Management

Henkel, a global leader in brands and technology, has been recognized by the World Economic Forum as an Industry 4.0 pioneer — one that leverages rapidly evolving technology to transform how people live, work and relate to each other — for its strategic and comprehensive digital transformation.[83] The company's success is deeply rooted in its digital backbone, a cloud-based data platform that connects more than 30 production sites in real time. This digital infrastructure enables

Henkel to keep pace with ever-increasing customer expectations and to develop sustainable production processes.[84]

A key focus of Henkel's digital strategy is interoperability — the integration of its systems and services. This seamless integration facilitates communication and collaboration across different departments and operations. It enables them to respond quickly to market changes and customer needs, driving business growth and customer satisfaction. By leveraging advanced analytics, machine learning and AI algorithms, Henkel can process and analyse vast amounts of production and order data in real time and share it across its operations. This allows it to maximize the effectiveness of procurement, minimize the risk of shortages, and keep production lines running smoothly. In addition, by implementing its *Connected Worker* program, Henkel is able to share real-time data with machine operators, enabling continuous connectivity throughout the production process.

Henkel's strategic use of digital technologies, and its focus on enhancing customer experience and promoting co-created value, suggest that the company is on the brink of fully harnessing the opportunities of a mature digital backbone, which would pave the way for the transformation stage.

Tata Steel: Data-Driven Digital Backbone and Advanced Analytics

Tata Steel, a leading Indian multinational steel manufacturer, strategically positions its Data Office at the heart of its operations, harnessing the power of data analytics and digital transformation to enhance business efficiency and drive value creation. At the core of Tata Steel's digital strategy is its Data Office's commitment to meticulous data collection and management. The office diligently gathers data from diverse company sources, including manufacturing processes, the supply chain, sales and customer interactions. The comprehensive data collection is supported by sophisticated data storage solutions and databases, ensuring organized, accessible, high-quality data. This foundational work is critical in driving data-centric operations and decision-making processes across the organization. Tata Steel's Data Office excels in data analytics and reporting, using these insights to inform and guide business decisions. The office analyses patterns and trends to create detailed reports and dashboards customized for various departments. This practice informs strategic decisions and empowers different sectors of the company with the data they need to optimize their operations.[85]

Collaboration is key in Tata Steel's approach. The Data Office works closely with various departments to understand their data needs and support data-related projects. This collaborative effort extends to providing advanced IT services and training to employees, promoting a data-driven innovation culture within the organization. At the Kalinganagar plant, the company's commitment to digital innovation is evident. By analysing two years of operational data, they have developed predictive models for the superheating process in steel production, achieving an impressive 75% accuracy.[86] This initiative is part of a broader strategy to optimize key performance indicators such as energy consumption, throughput, quality and yield, exemplifying the company's drive for operational excellence. Furthermore, their work on creating digital twins of their Jamshedpur factories highlights a forward-thinking approach to Industry 4.0, focusing on essential operational aspects like yield, energy, throughput, quality and productivity, and enabling remote operations.[87]

Emphasizing collaboration across teams, the Data Office has introduced advanced analytics in various domains, including sales, operations planning, demand forecasting, stock management and maintenance planning. The initiative, dubbed *Future Value Chain*, has resulted in significant improvements, such as reduced order backlogs and enhanced delivery performance.[88] Tata's integrative systems and tools, supported by the centralized Data Office, exemplify their commitment to interoperability. It is this harmonized digital backbone that drives improved efficiencies, minimizes operational friction and delivers on the steelmaker's forward-looking digital strategy.[85]

Alibaba: Powering Innovation

Alibaba, a Chinese global leader in e-commerce and technology, has also built a digital backbone that supports its vast operations and innovative ventures. This digital infrastructure is the foundation of Alibaba's e-commerce empire and the driving force behind its expansion into various sectors, including cloud computing, digital media and retail.[89]

Internally, Alibaba's digital backbone promotes collaboration within teams and beyond. This is achieved by using an advanced technology infrastructure and digital tools that enhance communication, stream-line workflows and connect otherwise disparate groups within the company's ecosystem. Alibaba Cloud serves as its primary cloud-based platform, enabling teams to collaborate effectively by sharing docu-ments, conducting data analysis and deploying applications in a seam-less manner. It facilitates a collaborative work culture in which infor-mation is easily accessible, helping drive collective decision-making. The company's internal AI-powered tools analyse project data in order to predict timelines, allocate resources efficiently and identify potential bottlenecks. This lets teams collaborate more effectively by focusing on high-priority, high-value tasks and workflow optimization.[89]

In addition to facilitating internal collaboration, Alibaba's digital backbone serves as the foundation for all of the company's business operations. This comprehensive digital infrastructure supports and enables its digital and operational capabilities, driving innovation and efficiency across Alibaba's e-commerce platforms, including Taobao and Tmall, digital finance through Ant Financial, logistics with Cainiao Net-work, and beyond.[90] These platforms facilitate an enormous number of online transactions, with some 2.32 billion transactions recorded in 2020 alone.[91] This is made possible by the digital backbone that sup-ports high-volume online traffic, payment processing and data analyt-ics. An outstanding example is Alibaba's *Taobao Villages* initiative, which developed more than 4,000 digital communities into e-commerce hubs. This initiative demonstrates how Alibaba's digital backbone drives eco-nomic development and empowerment at the grassroots level.[92] In dig-ital finance, Ant Financial has transformed access to credit with micro-lending services, which provide loans to small and micro businesses. By automatically leveraging digital transaction history and behavioural analytics, Alibaba can provide credit solutions within minutes.[93]

Finally, the digital backbone is essential to collaboration and synergy among its many merchants, consumers and service providers. The com-pany shares data and consumer insights, enabling its partners to tailor their offerings, rapidly and effectively aligning their strategies. Open innovation platforms like Alibaba Cloud and the DAMO Academy, its research arm, offer tools for developers, startups and researchers to col-laborate on technology projects, further encouraging collaboration across the tech community and driving the development of new solutions.[89]

All told, Alibaba's digital backbone is a key enabler for creating a collaborative, efficient and innovative business ecosystem.

Amazon: Interoperability and Real-Time Data Management

Amazon has built an exceptional position in the digital world by strategically leveraging a comprehensive digital infrastructure that is unparalleled in scale and reach. The cornerstone of Amazon's success is its interoperability, or the ability of its systems and services to work together seamlessly. This is evident in its vast technology ecosystem, which spans the company's widely recognized e-commerce platform, its AWS cloud computing division and myriad other digital ventures.[94]

The company is built on a seamless digital communication and interaction backbone spanning its wide range of business segments. Amazon's exceptional ability to manage data in real time, a critical element in the digital age, drives efficiency and cultivates a culture of innovation within the organization.

By leveraging its robust digital infrastructure, Amazon has been able to deliver personalized customer experiences that are essential for today's customer-centric business environment. Based on the continuous flow of customer data, the company makes real-time adjustments and improvements to its operations. This ability to adapt and respond in real time has set a new benchmark in the industry and provides a model for others to follow.

Amazon's strategic focus on interoperability and real-time data management has been central to its success. This combination has established a groundbreaking standard in delivering digital services and personalized customer experiences, demonstrating the power of a dynamic and responsive digital infrastructure.

Haier: Micro-Enterprises and Real-Time Adaptability

Haier's transition to nimble, networked micro-enterprises is at the forefront of its operating model. These micro-enterprises, supported by a powerful digital backbone, foster a collaborative and customer-centric ecosystem. To further enhance this model, Haier integrated AI, big data and Internet of Things (IoT) services, leveraging its digital backbone to gain real-time insights and help ensure rapid response to evolving market demands.

One component of Haier's digital infrastructure is the *Workbench*, which was developed as the cornerstone of an organization that adopts algorithms and a smart contract framework to manage dynamic cooperation among its entities.[35] Through the *Workbench*, Haier orchestrates its ecosystem of micro-communities and micro-enterprises, significantly reducing internal transaction costs while promoting flexible collaboration and dynamic alignment of different organizational units. The integration of blockchain technology within this framework has further streamlined the coordination processes, particularly in managing transactions, contractual agreements and performance metrics, delivering absolute clarity and accountability.

The organizational transition to ecosystem micro-communities in 2019 has replaced many individual contracts between micro-enterprises with a simplified system that requires only one collective contract per ecosystem micro-community, solidifying trust and transparency among its cooperation micro-enterprises. Automated and immutable processes align the goals of smaller teams with broader organizational goals of the ecosystem micro-community, ensuring fairness and clarity.[35]

Haier's *Workbench* ensures that both micro-enterprises and ecosystem micro-communities comply with the protocols of the Fundamental Interaction Layer, which are essential for compliance with financial, human resources and legal aspects of collaboration. Together, these elements represent the indispensable role of the digital backbone in supporting Haier's innovative organizational model, which prioritizes frequent, dynamic adaptation and improvement of all its operations.

These case studies demonstrate the transformative power of digital infrastructures in business. However, it is important to recognize that the success of these digital backbones is not solely a result of strategic vision, but attributable to the extensive hard work in data engineering, process engineering and the governance of processes and data.

The integration of AI, the Internet of Things, advanced analytics and cloud-based platforms requires meticulous data engineering to ensure data quality, relevance and security. These include the collection, storage, processing and analysis of vast amounts of data. Equally critical is process engineering, which requires constant refinement and optimization of business processes to align with digital tools and platforms.

Furthermore, the governance of these digital systems is a complex yet essential aspect. It involves developing robust policies and protocols to manage data integrity, interoperability of systems, privacy, compliance with regulations and ethical considerations. Effective governance makes sure that the digital transformation journey is not only feasible, but also sustainable, responsible and aligned with broader organizational goals. The success of organizations in utilizing their digital infrastructure demonstrates the importance of rigorous data and process engineering, and their strict governance. The primary takeaway is that digital transformation offers substantial promise, but it requires a fundamental commitment to hard work and management attention to these critical areas before its full potential can be realized.

Conclusion

In conclusion, the digital backbone is central to organizations, serving as a key element in improving operational agility, seamless communications and effective use of data. Its sophisticated combination of technologies, strategies and processes forms the central nervous system of organizations, enabling them to be dynamic, adaptive and, ultimately, antifragile. The transformational impact of the digital backbone can be clearly seen in the progression through different stages of digital maturity. It supports decentralized decision-making, breaks down departmental silos and promotes transparency and continuous innovation. This journey to digital maturity equips organizations with the agility needed to thrive in a rapidly evolving business environment.

The following section builds on the foundation laid by the digital backbone. Data-driven decision-making is emerging as a key strategic priority, enabling organizations to apply real-time analytics to drive insightful, innovative and customer-centric strategies.

3.6

Data-Driven Decision-Making

Data-driven decision-making, grounded in robust digital infrastructures, has become essential for organizations to better navigate the complexities of today's business environment. A well-developed digital backbone facilitates systematic data collection and management, enabling businesses to convert raw data into valuable insights. These insights drive strategic and customer-centric initiatives.

Data analytics allows organizations to identify patterns, providing them with the ability to anticipate and adapt to upcoming market changes. Companies such as Haier and Amazon utilize data analytics to predict user behaviour and optimize their product features, helping them build and maintain a competitive edge. For example, Haier employs data from IoT-enabled products to enhance customer satisfaction, aligning their decisions with consumer needs and preferences.

Real-time analytics significantly enhance strategic decision-making, enabling businesses to interpret and react to data as new trends, events and opportunities manifest. This capability is critical in fast-paced market environments where timely responses can provide a competitive edge. For example, in inventory management, real-time data analysis allows companies to adjust their stock levels preemptively and dynamically, ensuring optimal availability of products and swift adaptation to volatile changes in consumer demands.

Making decisions based on actual, real-time customer data, rather than hypothetical or assumed needs, helps ensure that the solutions delivered are truly relevant and effective. Amazon, for example, uses advanced recommendation algorithms to refine user experiences and guide decision-making. Early identification of emerging trends enables proactive experiments on a small scale, with minimal risks, before quickly scaling up operations. As a result, organizations can rapidly shape their tactics in response to insights they gain, ensuring that strategies are aligned with the heartbeat of the market. (Also see Sections 3.1 and 3.2.)

By diving deep into customer data, companies gain unparalleled insights into preferences, behaviours and emerging needs. For instance, Haier's *Internet of Food* initiative analyses kitchen appliance usage in real time and customizes providing recommendations based on usage patterns. This includes suggesting personalized dietary tips and recipes, tracking refrigerated items' expiration dates, suggesting popular regional meals for New Year dinner parties, and promoting local food chain offerings. This demonstrates a responsive strategy to market preferences, allowing the company to provide tailored product offerings and usage tips that enhance customer satisfaction and loyalty. In addition, these insights can uncover operational inefficiencies, presenting opportunities for optimization and growth.

Companies that extensively utilize data analytics, such as Netflix, can easily identify emerging trends in viewer preferences, uncover latent market opportunities and design innovative solutions that address unmet needs.[95] This allows Netflix to create appealing content and strengthen customer loyalty. Additionally, monitoring of real-time data and automated matching with key performance projections serves as a watchtower for strategic risk management, identifying potential risks early on and ensuring that preemptive strategies are in place.

Effective data analytics depend on sound governance of data and, if possible, governance of the processes generating the data, thus ensuring integrity and quality of the data used for decision-making, as well as compliance with regulatory standards. Data governance is essential for generating reliable, actionable insights from data streams. The value of the generated insights is maximized when employees possess the necessary skills to interpret and apply the results effectively, highlighting the need for ongoing training and development in data literacy.

Case Studies

Data-driven decision-making is becoming a key element of business strategy across various industries. Section 3.5 showed how companies such as Henkel, Tata Steel, Alibaba, Amazon and Haier use data to inform their business operations and strategies. These companies have integrated data analysis into their decision-making processes, so that resulting actions are both informed and effective. The ability to swiftly adapt business strategies in response to dynamic market conditions demonstrates the value of comprehensive data analytics frameworks. To further illustrate the practical application of data-driven decision-making, we return to the case studies discussed in Section 3.5.

Henkel

Henkel's approach involves a thorough analysis of customer data to inform product development and see to it that products meet and exceed performance standards. By gathering and analysing feedback, Henkel tailors its offerings to customer needs. The company also uses data-driven insights to improve its supply chain efficiency and drive sustainability initiatives. Data-driven insights underpin Henkel's decisions, and help ensure that their choices meet market demands and support environmental goals. Combined with high levels of automated production, this allows Henkel to participate in new business models and cooperations, where profitability depends on excellence of data management throughout the value chain. It is therefore no surprise that Henkel is one of the few companies able to seamlessly participate in Haier's SmartHome business ecosystem, providing individualized detergents for Haier's washing machines.[96, 97]

Tata Steel

Tata Steel applies real-time machinery data to improve operational efficiency, particularly in predictive maintenance. The organization also uses data analytics for market analysis, enabling timely responses to market trends and refining production strategies. This focus on data-driven insights allows Tata Steel to make informed decisions about production strategies and adapt to market demands.[85, 88]

Alibaba

Alibaba harnesses the power of big data analytics to inform strategic decision-making across its vast e-commerce platforms. By analysing user data, the company effectively tailors marketing strategies and optimizes logistics, so product availability aligns with consumer demand trends. This approach enables Alibaba to maintain a competitive edge by rapidly adapting to market changes and enhancing customer satisfaction through personalized experiences.[89, 93]

Amazon

Amazon utilizes advanced recommendation algorithms to refine user experiences and guide decision-making. The company's strategy includes using predictive analytics for inventory management and selecting prime video content. By leveraging these data-driven insights, Amazon can make informed decisions about product offerings and content availability, ultimately enhancing operational efficiency and the user experience.[94]

Haier

All of Haier's decisions rely heavily on user feedback and data from actual product usage, which are collected in real time. By enhancing their user-centric innovation approach with data from IoT-enabled products, the company is able to discover unmet consumer needs and improve customer satisfaction. Haier's data-informed, direct-to-consumer business model is a key enabler of this strategy.[72]

Challenges of Data-Driven Decision-making

Data-driven decision-making holds the promise of revolutionizing organizations, yet its successful implementation comes with significant challenges. This necessitates not only new capabilities but also a profound cultural transformation within the organization, challenging traditional decision-making norms. This is evident in surveys of executives at Fortune 1000 companies, which reveal a stark disparity between the aspirations for and the actual implementation of data-driven decision-making.[98] This gap reflects the complexities associated with incorporating data analytics into core decision-making processes. Therefore, several key challenges must be addressed to help ensure effective outcomes.

- **Data quality and integrity**: Ensuring data quality and accuracy is a fundamental requirement. Decisions based on incomplete, obsolete or unrepresentative data can be misleading and result in erroneous strategies and actions.

- **Real-time data processing**: In rapidly changing industries, real-time data processing and analysis are essential. Developing the infrastructure to support real-time analytics is complex and resource-intensive, but necessary for maintaining agility and responsiveness in fast-paced business environments.

- **Data overload**: The overwhelming amount of data available can lead to data overload, where organizations struggle to filter and extract relevant information from large data sets. This can result in analysis paralysis, where decision-making is hindered by an overwhelming amount of data.

- **Integration and sense-making of different data sources**: Integrating disparate data sources is a significant challenge for organizations, due to the diversity of data formats and storage locations. This often leads to a disjointed understanding of situations and impedes effective decision-making.

- **Lack of skilled personnel**: Proficient data analysis requires specialized skills in both data interpretation and business acumen. A shortage of skilled personnel can hinder the translation of data into actionable insights, limiting the effectiveness of data-driven strategies.

- **Data privacy and security**: The increasing importance of data in decision-making raises the risk of data breaches and privacy violations. Providing data security and complying with privacy regulations is vital, but this can be challenging due to the constantly evolving nature of cyber threats and legal frameworks.

- **Interpreting data correctly**: Data interpretation can be complex and prone to errors, which can lead organizations astray. Therefore, it is critical to approach data analysis with rigour and skepticism to avoid making misguided decisions.

- **Balancing data with intuition**: Maintaining a balance between data models and human intuition and experience is essential in decision-making. It is important to continuously reevaluate data models and insights, to verify their ongoing relevance and value, and to prevent unintended consequences.

- **Human oversight**: Like any automated system, data models and algorithms are inherently flawed, because they represent only an approximation of the real world. Data and models are therefore incomplete and possibly outdated, especially in a highly dynamic environment. Unmitigated high-speed interactions of automated systems can cause sudden unexpected and unwanted effects, such as the flash crash of the Dow Jones in May 2010. Intuition and human oversight needs to be employed to continuously review and monitor automation models, and to look out for security threats and other unwanted effects of largely automated systems.[99]

Addressing these challenges requires a strategic, multi-dimensional approach encompassing technological solutions, skilled human resources, and a balanced perspective on the role of data and automation in decision-making.

One of the most significant challenges is the risk of misinterpreting data, especially in the absence of domain expertise. A notable example of this risk is the initial misinterpretation of *Google Flu Trends* data. Google's algorithm, designed to predict flu outbreaks based on search queries, initially showed promise, but eventually led to significant miscalculations. It substantially underestimated the impact of the 2010-2011 flu season, inaccurately predicted the 2011-2012 outbreak, and then missed the peak 2013 flu period by 140%. This demonstrated how important domain expertise is in accurately interpreting data analytics. Misinterpreting data can lead to flawed conclusions, further compounded by dismissing human intuition and experience. In today's data-rich era, the introduction of bias through data and analytics poses additional challenges that can potentially undermine the integrity of decisions.[100]

In response to these challenges, organizations must develop extensive data management and data governance capabilities. As demonstrated in the above case studies, these capabilities are best honed through continuous, decentralized, rapid and multi-disciplinary efforts involving many different perspectives and stakeholders, ideally also including independent expertise. And, the work of data teams does not end with building data-driven decision engines. That is only the start of an even more complex improvement and adaptation cycle. Establishing and continuously refining data governance capabilities in organizations is clearly a task of leadership, and we will look at this domain in Section 3.7.

Recommendations for Artificial Intelligence

The European Union's AI Act establishes a frame of reference for data governance and automated decisions. Although it is legally applicable only for the utilization of AI in business operations, it is also useful for any data-driven decision strategy. The regulation limits the use of AI in business operations. The technology can be used as a consultative tool to improve decision-making processes, but human authority and accountability has to be maintained at all times. Humans must ultimately always remain in control of decisions. With more companies relying on vast amounts of data for making strategic decisions, the EU legal framework's focus on responsible, transparent, human-controlled decision-making is becoming increasingly relevant.[101]

Human Oversight in AI Supported Decision-Making

The EU emphasizes the use of AI as an assistant, rather than a decision-maker. In a rapidly changing world, organizations must quickly navigate a tangle of uncertainties. The ability to use this technology for comprehensive data analysis and rapid decision-making, while maintaining human oversight, is becoming increasingly important. By establishing AI in a supportive role, a harmonious fusion of empirical evidence, human intuition and ethics can be achieved. The AI Act emphasizes the importance of human oversight to help ensure that insights generated by AI supplement human judgment, especially in complex and nuanced decisions. This balance is critical in ensuring that decisions are grounded in data, yet are being enriched with the contextual understanding and ethical considerations that only human insight can provide.[101]

Ethical and Responsible Use of Artificial Intelligence

The EU's AI Act provides guidance on the ethical and responsible use of this technology in business strategy. This includes a strategic approach to the design and implementation of AI systems, with a focus on ensuring their short-term effectiveness, long-term sustainability and adaptability, while seeing that humans retain control over outcomes.

To achieve reliability and transparency, businesses need to design AI that is capable of handling evolving business needs and technological advances, ensuring their relevance and effectiveness over time. It is important to consider how these systems can continue to deliver value in the future, beyond short-term gains.

Self-regulation is a key aspect of this approach. AI needs to be equipped with mechanisms that allow it to continuously monitor its own performance. This involves not just tracking efficiency and accuracy but also identifying and highlighting potential errors to human supervision. This is necessary to align AI with the ethical guidelines and compliance standards set forth by the AI Act.

Furthermore, the EU's regulation requires a dynamic feedback loop in which human supervisors can comprehend the impact and results of AI-supported interactions within their own business operations and the wider business environment. This allows them to improve the algorithms and decision-making processes to more sustainable outcomes.

As companies increasingly rely on data analytics and AI for strategic decisions, adhering to frameworks like the EU's helps ensure that these technologies are used in a manner that enhances human decision-making capabilities while upholding ethical and social responsibilities.

Automation of Management Tasks

AI's role in automating management tasks highlights a significant paradigm shift in methodologies, where automation is progressively reshaping and, in some cases, fundamentally altering traditional management practices.

A noteworthy example is the application of AI in workforce management, where it can address a multitude of administrative tasks, ranging from forecasting staffing needs, accurately scheduling jobs, real-time monitoring of job completion and the management of work shifts. This last example, the detailed management of employee work schedules, is a good example how automation can beat humans in many administrative and managerial tasks. Assigning employees to specific duties and hours, meticulously matching work and qualifications, is quite time-consuming for humans. Managers can realistically perform this chore only once or twice a day, and they do it with a significant margin of error, without even knowing it. This regularly results in mobilizing more resources than necessary for certain work shifts, as well as resource shortages during peak demand periods.

Workforce automation software is much better suited for this management task than humans. Automated solutions can make predictions and prepare decisions that previously required human judgment, using rich data sets based on both historical patterns and real-time information. They can also perform scheduling and match-making much faster, without getting distracted and tired. This significantly improves scheduling: Work shift planning can be done in much smaller increments and much more frequently. These systems can reschedule jobs every 15 minutes, greatly increasing the flexibility of assignments, reducing slack times and giving the workforce much more control and options regarding their time off. Jorge Amar and his colleagues, experts at McKinsey & Company in operations and workforce management, have analysed[102] that the impact of these advancements is substantial. For instance, the implementation of AI in workforce management can boost the productivity of field workers by 20%-30% and the productivity of schedulers by 10%-20%. The outcome is a more stream-lined, agile and intelligent approach to handling a vital organizational resource — the human workforce.[102]

In the manufacturing sector, software-driven production planning and scheduling can improve efficiency, reduce lead times and optimize resource allocation. AI-powered systems automate complex production plans, maintain optimal production levels and react automatically to deviations. This can significantly reduce lead times and optimize resource allocation.[103]

In general, automation and assistant systems can significantly reduce the managerial workload. Where does that leave managers? To what extent do organizations need them as a full-time resource? Should automated systems replace human managers? The answer depends on the managerial tasks at hand.

- **Planning**: Automation tools can assist in data gathering and analysis, making it easier to forecast trends and make informed decisions. Software for project management can automate scheduling, resource allocation and timeline tracking.

- **Organizing**: Automation in document management, employee scheduling and resource allocation can streamline organizational tasks. Systems like Enterprise Resource Planning can integrate various functions, simplifying the management of resources and information.

- **Staffing**: Parts of the recruitment process can be automated by sorting through resumes, scheduling interviews and conducting initial screening. Training programs can also be automated and allow for individual qualification plans.

- **Directing**: Task management and workflow automation tools can help in assigning tasks, setting deadlines and tracking progress, reducing the need for constant direct supervision.

- **Controlling**: Performance monitoring can be automated with tools that track key performance indicators. Automated reporting systems provide regular updates on various metrics, allowing for transparency and quicker response to issues.

- **Budgeting and financial management**: Financial processes, including budgeting, invoicing, payroll and expense reporting, can be largely automated with the right software, leading to increased accuracy and time savings.

- **Problem solving and decision-making**: Data analysis tools can automate the collection and processing of large data sets, providing insights that aid in decision-making. Predictive analytics can help in anticipating problems before they occur.

- **Quality control and process improvement**: Automation tools can monitor production processes, identify variances from quality standards and initiate corrective measures. Process mining software can analyse workflow data to identify bottlenecks and suggest improvements.

- **Communication and reporting**: Automated reporting tools can generate regular operational reports, financial statements and other necessary documentation, saving time and reducing errors. Communication tools can automate reminders, notifications and updates to team members and stakeholders.

- **Compliance and legal responsibilities**: Compliance management software can track changes in regulations, ensure that the organization is compliant and automate reporting to the appropriate authorities.

Automation can greatly enhance efficiency, accuracy and consistency in these areas. However, it is important to balance this with human oversight so complex, non-routine and strategic tasks are handled with the necessary expertise and judgment.

Therefore, managers remain accountable for the results of their software assistants and must oversee their work, initiating any necessary corrective or optimization actions. They must acquire new skills to effectively supervise their machine assistants and continuously guide their evolution in a dynamic environment. Thus, for managers, the development of leadership skills becomes more important, focusing on areas where human judgment, creativity and emotional intelligence are essential.

Conclusion

Antifragile organizations successfully integrate vast amounts of data and analytics into their decision-making processes, demonstrating the benefits of a data-centric approach in driving continuous innovation and adaptation. Yet, transitioning to such a system requires not only technological integration but also successfully addressing many managerial and governance challenges to maintain control of outcomes. This is especially important in highly dynamic business environments. The tasks involved are complex and require the development of new skills, with significant implications for leadership, organizational culture and, ultimately, organizational structures.

3.7

Leadership and Organizational Culture for Complexity

Leadership and organizational culture are deeply rooted in the natural evolution of an organization as it grows. In the early stages of a business, the primary focus is on developing a product and business model that meets market demands and generates revenue, followed by strategies that direct growth and repeated value creation through business processes, technological competence and people skills. Organizational culture develops from key lessons learnt during these early growth periods, the attitudes of leaders and the resulting stories that are widely shared among employees.

All of these shape the shared values, norms and attitudes that influence how employees within the organization act, behave and make decisions. Culture is the sum of what an organization has collectively experienced and learnt over time. Culture plays a very important role for organizations: it provides members with a common, but largely intangible, set of beliefs and social interaction norms that greatly simplify the complex tasks of communication, coordination and alignment of collective activities. Culture can therefore either enable or hinder certain collaboration efforts, depending on how they feed into an organization's cultural norms.[54]

In a complex environment that continuously creates new challenges, organizations benefit from a culture that rewards innovation. Leadership plays a crucial role in shaping such a culture. The accelerating pace of change compels organizations to make more strategic decisions in less time. This necessitates leaders and teams being closer to their customers and quickly developing a deep understanding of the problems they face. This close proximity enables them to directly observe the impact of events and outcome of decisions, providing immediate feedback on their effectiveness, and initiating swift adaptation of strategies to meet real-world demands.

The Bottleneck of Decision Hierarchies

In traditional organizational structures, strategic decision-making processes still follow a centralized pattern, a legacy of the Tayloristic division of labour we talked about earlier. This management approach prioritizes a top-down, rigidly divided labour structure, which was effective in an era marked by less complexity and more predictable market dynamics. It reflects a belief in the superiority of high-level decision-makers, with supposed access to all relevant information, over grassroots insights from the shop floor.

In addition, communication within Tayloristic structures often reflects this centralized approach, being predominantly one-way and top-down. This pattern stifles open feedback and dissent, effectively silencing the valuable perspectives and insights from the workforce. Rooted in decades of tradition, there is an implicit assumption within the organizational culture that employees at lower levels are merely operators, not strategists. This belief curtails collective intelligence, because it excludes large parts of the workforce from contributing valuable insights to strategic decision-making, limiting the organization's overall adaptability and true potential.

Any decision-making process that is predominantly unidirectional — and that concentrates decision-making authority, accountability and power over the decision-making process in the hands of the same small set of individuals — is in direct conflict with the antifragile principles discussed in Chapter 2. One way or the other, these practices always lead to decision-making hierarchies that concentrate strategic authority in the hands of a few individuals at the top of organizations.

It is a common pattern, even found in alternative management systems like Holacracy — which aims to put decision-making in the hands of self-organizing employee teams — because it provides a clear and reliable chain of command, authorization and control. The simplicity and efficiency of this system is hard to beat, especially when it delegates authority for certain recurring decisions to lower levels, conveying the impression of decentralized control. And while this increases the organization's decision-making capacity and reduces decision time for many well-understood problems, it still concentrates strategic decision-making. For unprecedented needs or opportunities, this system works poorly, as it increasingly delays decisions as the organization grows.

The greater the complexity and the higher the risk a decision entails, the closer to the top it must be placed. This naturally limits an organization's decision-making capacity, because there are only a few decision-makers at the top. These individuals are well-known, easy to find, and it is clear how to approach them. Whenever someone in a lower echelon of the hierarchy feels uncomfortable making a decision, or reaches the limit of their own decision-making authority, they can simply push it up the hierarchy. This behaviour is culturally expected and accepted, sometimes even rewarded. However, the limitations of this approach have become increasingly apparent as the business world has evolved to become more dynamic and complex.

Although they provide a sense of control and order, decision hierarchies create bottlenecks that often result in delayed response times and insufficient oversight of the subtle complexities of real situations. Especially when an event or situation requires a decision that does not clearly match responsibilities within the delegated authority structure, it needs to be elevated to the top. Only the top has the authority to reassign responsibility for the new situation. Unexpected events, such as the COVID-19 crisis, immediately overburden the top of decision hierarchies, flooding it with requests. Decisions made in such a top-down manner cannot effectively address the nuanced needs for action on the ground, and they simply take too long in a dynamic business environment that requires immediate responses and actions.

Closely connected with decision-making hierarchies is the assumption of traditional leadership models that leaders control the future and need to have all the answers.[104] These beliefs underlie and reinforce static, inflexible systems of leadership and management. They seriously undercut more decentralized models that promote self-management, self-control and self-directing capabilities, all of which are increasingly required in today's complex and fast-paced world of business.

Today, the standard method of breaking down goals into smaller, tractable segments, commonly known as *decomposition*, is no longer effective. This is mainly due to the fact that the elements of complex and dynamic systems interact in unpredictable ways, resulting in many outcomes that cannot be understood or influenced by examining the components of the systems in isolation. The overall outcome of complex systems exceeds the sum of their individual parts. In such settings, static efforts to break down goals disregard the interconnectedness of system components, resulting in strategies that are too simplistic, inappropriate and inflexible. Complex environments require a new, more inclusive paradigm of leadership and decision-making.

Leadership in Complexity

Navigating complex environments calls for a holistic, systems-oriented approach. This means understanding the organization and its business environment as an interconnected whole, acknowledging the relationships and interactions among various components, and how changes in one part can influence the entire system. In this context, the focus of goal-setting shifts from individual performance to aligning individual contributions, considering the impact they might have on the system, and the bigger purpose and goals of the organization. This alignment effort is what we refer to as leadership in a complex system. It boils down to this simple definition:

The one who aligns contributions toward a goal, leads.

Instead of trying to control and break down potential contributions beforehand, leaders need to create clarity about the goal, find people who want to contribute to that objective, and then align their achievements and contributions as they continue to emerge. This dynamic alignment helps ensure that all contributors are working toward the same overarching goals. Implementation of this approach requires clarity about achievements, and also continuous reassessment and rea-lignment of goals and contributions in light of additional insights and changed circumstances. Implementing such a broad, continuous and dynamic alignment requires all contributors to take responsibility for aligning their own contributions with those of others.

In antifragile organizations, everyone can make contributions to leadership, and will be recognized as a leader in their own right when they do. Leadership therefore emerges as a shared organiza-tional capability, not a fixed role assigned to individuals. This different understanding of leadership reflects the principle of *Enabling Others to Act*,[105] as posited by executive consultant Jim Kouzes and the academic Barry Posner in their influential work, *The Leadership Challenge*. It cul-tivates a culture where leadership is shared and collaborative, a trait that is essential for navigating today's dynamic business landscapes. This reinforces the need for leaders to inspire and empower at every level. Indigenous tribes, such as the nomadic Maasai of Kenya and Tanzania, have been practising this form of leadership for centuries, emphasizing collective responsibility and service to the community as core values. Their leadership model values service over authority, highlighting the effectiveness of stewardship in complex systems, where success is rooted in purpose-driven alignment and collective decision-making.[106] The Maasai use the collective capacity of the tribe and the subject matter expertise of members to select their leaders based on the challenge or opportunity at hand. Individuals who are trusted by others to have the most expertise in a given situation align the tribe's collective efforts, assuming a temporary leadership role. This dynamic leadership model not only nurtures a sense of ownership and accountability within the collective, but also helps ensure that the most qualified people, who have earned trust in their abilities, guide the team in specific scenarios. This leads to more innovative solutions, a stronger sense of collective purpose, and greater ability to respond quickly to new challenges and opportunities.

The concept of leadership as a dynamic process was advocated by thinkers like Mary Parker Follett long ago. Today, this idea is particularly relevant. Follett[61] championed a *power-with*, rather than a *power-over*, approach, viewing power as a dynamic, co-created process. Leadership in this context is not about exerting authority, but about jointly creating solutions and empowering individuals at all levels to lead in areas where they have the most knowledge or expertise. This approach fosters empowerment, where decision-making and direct action are closely linked, enhancing the organization's responsiveness and effectiveness. Effective problem-solving and conflict resolution arise from an integrative process that synthesizes varied perspectives rather than compromising them, leading to innovative and comprehensive solutions.[107]

By shifting from a directive to an enabling and aligning approach, leaders can empower their teams to perform better in complex environments. In such environments, outcomes cannot be predicted, but emerge from a multitude of interactions and contributions that move the group closer to its goals. True leaders then emerge as facilitators who enhance the organization's adaptability and innovation capabilities.[104]

Everyone a Leader

An organization that has successfully employed this leadership approach for decades is Morning Star. As described earlier, the California-based tomato-processing company operates on a self-management model, where *the mission is the boss*. As detailed by Gary Hamel, a renowned management thinker and strategist, in his article 'First, Let's Fire All the Managers,'[108] this company has no traditional managers or job titles. Instead, each employee is independently responsible for making and keeping clear commitments, coordinating their activities with others and meeting designated goals. A cornerstone is the shared belief that decisions should be made by those with the most insight and knowledge, underscoring the importance of trusted expertise and a profound understanding of the task at hand in complex settings. Morning Star cultivates an environment that empowers employees to assume ownership of their roles and responsibilities, aligning commitments to co-workers in a transparent way.[109, 110]

To that end, Morning Star has established *Colleague Letters of Understanding* (CLOUs). Each CLOU defines an individual's responsibilities and commitments, and helps ensure that his or her work is aligned with that of colleagues and the company's mission. Perhaps more important than the CLOU itself is the processes of negotiation, collaboration, mentoring, peer coaching and feedback through which each individual develops and adapts their commitments.[108]

The process of creating these letters of intent starts with colleagues negotiating their responsibilities, goals and contributions to the organization's objectives. These agreements are then carefully documented in the CLOUs, which outline the commitments and expectations of each party. Finally, the documents undergo a review process, often involving peers or relevant stakeholders, to establish alignment with broader goals and facilitate transparency and accountability within the company's self-managed structure.[111]

Such a leadership model creates an environment where the principle of accountability is deeply ingrained. In these settings, every team member is encouraged to take responsibility for their work, and encouraged to take care of their own personal growth and development before assuming such responsibilities for others. Morning Star strikes a careful balance between individual autonomy and alignment with the organization's overall purpose and operational goals, so contributions and decisions are in line with strategic directions. This alignment, from purpose down to operational practice, is not easy to attain. It requires a continuous process of self-reflection and genuine passion for an organization's values.

As described previously, Patagonia is a prime example of an organization firmly grounded in values and purpose. All aspects of the organizational culture demonstrate their resolute dedication to environmental and ethical principles. Patagonia's decision to discontinue steel spikes in favour of eco-friendly aluminium chocks, despite the risks of market acceptance, underscores the company's commitment to value-driven innovation. Such decisions are indicative of a culture that is grounded in a deepseated commitment to core values. At Patagonia, employees are not merely part of a company, but part of a movement — a community that treasures and embraces the great outdoors. This alignment fosters a sense of unity and purpose that goes beyond typical corporate objectives. Furthermore, Patagonia's leadership encourages decision-making that encompasses a larger perspective, beyond profit and loss, and considers the broader impact on society and the environment. The hiring process prioritizes a strong cultural fit, ensuring alignment with the core mission and values. In essence, Patagonia's culture is defined neither by profit margins nor corporate strategies, but characterized by a joint commitment to promoting environmental responsibility. There is a common sense of mission, and a firm conviction in ethical and sustainable conduct.[30]

Cultivating Trust and Accountability

The renowned animation studio Pixar has long been celebrated for both its creative output and its unique organizational culture. At the heart of Pixar's success is a deep commitment to psychological safety, a concept that enables team members to feel comfortable expressing their ideas, take risks and admit mistakes without fear of reprimand or ridicule. This culture was cultivated by Pixar co-founder Ed Catmull, who believed the key to innovation was creating an environment where creativity could thrive.[78]

Braintrust meetings, where directors and other key creatives meet to review the progress of a movie, are a cornerstone of this environment. In these sessions, everyone, regardless of rank or role, is encouraged to speak openly and honestly about the strengths and weaknesses of the project. The emphasis is on openness and constructive feedback, not hierarchy or authority. For Catmull, good ideas can come from anywhere, and it is important that all team members feel empowered to contribute. With no penalty for speaking up, employees feel free to take risks. They trust their managers and peers to value their contributions, however ridiculous they may first seem. This deep trust has enabled Pixar to tap into the collective intelligence of its diverse teams, resulting in more innovative end products. And this culture of trust extends beyond formal *Braintrust* meetings. It permeates daily interactions, where employees are encouraged to share their thoughts and collaborate across departments. Leaders who model vulnerability and humility, acknowledging that they do not have all the answers and that mistakes are a natural part of innovation, foster this culture. Pixar has created a learning environment where individuals feel safe to experiment, and where the resulting trust generates great contributions and outcomes.[78]

Beyond the business world, groups like emergency response teams and special forces units add another important aspect to cultivating trust. These teams perform well in unpredictable and dangerous situations, where stress levels are high, and thinking clearly can become a challenge for the untrained. Well trained teams are able to stay focused and on-task, coordinate and dynamically adjust their efforts in such circumstances. Beyond all their training, this is enhanced by a deep sense of accountability, commitment and trust in their own skills, and the capabilities of their teammates.[112, 113]

Mutual trust is the foundational element that drives these teams, enabling decisive actions. This trust has been earned by each team member through accomplishments for and with the group. Team members know what to expect from each other, they know their strengths and limitations. Trust in the team's collective strength provides the necessary mental security to confront adversity and uncertainty head-on. It enables them to come up with action plans that they can realistically expect to perform, even if it stretches their abilities. Trust is therefore grounded in intimate knowledge of one's colleagues' abilities. Trust and open communication enable swift, informed decisions, as well as actions that adjust seamlessly to changed circumstances.

Accountability is another cornerstone of the team's success. It is required that every team member takes responsibility for their actions, regardless of their position. This sense of responsibility improves reliability and encourages individuals to perform to the best of their ability. Accountability helps ensure that failures are not only recognized but also analysed and used as opportunities for improvement. Constructive after-action reviews focus on lessons learnt and improving future scenarios, eliminating the blame game.

A shared commitment to a worthy cause is what binds team members together. This commitment must extend to collective action plans, or coordination of actions will become unreliable. Consent plays an important role in fostering commitment to team decisions. Consent is based on the idea that decisions should move forward not only when every member is in complete agreement, but also when there are no significant objections. This approach differs from seeking unanimous agreement and is instead focusing on avoiding strong resistance. By prioritizing the absence of substantial objections, consent enables teams to benefit from the collective wisdom and insights of all members, encouraging a more inclusive and agile decision-making process. This method respects the diversity of perspectives within the team and decisions are made more swiftly, preventing the stagnation that can occur in the quest for full consensus. Moreover, the principle of consent aligns with the foundations of trust and accountability by empowering team members to voice concerns openly. This nurtures a culture where actions are closely aligned with the organization's shared purpose and values, and responsive to complex and evolving situations.

Antifragile organizations thrive on a culture that embraces trust and accountability. In such cultures, failure is reconceived as a valuable learning opportunity, essential for personal growth, team development and creativity. Employees feel empowered to experiment and express diverse opinions through open, two-way communication. This is especially important in settings where leadership is not a fixed role but a versatile and distributed set of capabilities. In such environments, leadership is not limited to a single individual but emerges organically, depending on the specific field or problem at hand. Teams recognize the value of diversity and adaptability. They feel psychologically safe in expressing their own limitations, including when they feel unable to lead in certain situations. This facilitates the transition of leadership roles, so the most competent and contextually suited individuals are tasked with addressing each challenge. Such a culture and understanding of leadership promotes organizational agility and innovation. It expands the overall leadership capacity of the organization, effectively removing the limitations of traditional leadership that usually cause delays and decision bottlenecks in complex environments.

Technology for Organizational Awareness and Alignment

In dynamic and complex environments, strategic decision-making and alignment capacity must be expanded and connected with the edges of organizational structures, where dynamic situations and the outcomes of the organization's responses can best be assessed as they unfold. Digital technology opens up very fast and effective pathways for addressing this challenge.

By leveraging *teamware* technology, decisions can be made faster and with closer connection to customer and operational needs. These software applications provide collective communication and collaboration tools that can quickly identify all the relevant people who need to contribute to a particular decision or goal. *Teamware* can help gather a group's insights, disseminate relevant information and elevate individual assessments to a shared picture. The technology can support all contributors and stakeholders in quickly forging a strategic decision and an aligned action plan. Not only can these plans be implemented faster, but the technology can also help dynamically integrate new insights during execution.

Without this technology, it can take much longer to create the necessary organizational awareness and alignment. The risk is that strategic decisions arrive too late for effective execution, or that action plans are too static to redirect and realign responses quickly enough. In complex situations, the sheer number of stakeholders involved could cause insurmountable delays in response time.

In general, organizations should establish an open and transparent *dialogue of decision* that enables sharing of strategic information, intent and insights without delay across departmental boundaries. In this context, a well-designed digital infrastructure can play a decisive role in facilitating and accelerating communication and collaboration. It can foster an outward-looking perspective to quickly anticipate and adapt to market trends and customer needs.

Technology to help large organizations close the gap between strategy and execution is still in its infancy. Cloud-based *teamware* and Customer Relationship Management solutions already provide a tiny glimpse of how this may play out in the future. Specialized technology for organizational awareness and alignment in dynamic environments will significantly impact and reshape leadership and entire organizations.

Conclusion

In the face of rapidly changing markets and the need for fast, adaptive decision-making, leadership and organizational culture are taking a leap forward. Antifragile organizations prioritize adaptability, decentralized authority and a culture of trust and accountability in their leadership model. This new paradigm empowers individuals at all levels to contribute to strategic decision-making and cultivates a more responsive, innovative and collaborative organizational system. Success proves antifragile organizations right when they align teams around a common purpose, foster trust and continuous learning, and adopt a fluid leadership model that distributes responsibility based on expertise and situational context.

This evolution points us toward organizational structures that can fluidly adapt to changing needs and market shifts. The following section will provide insights into how antifragile organizations create this structural flexibility.

3.8

Redefining Organizational Structures

The purpose of organizational structure is to reduce the complexity of interactions by defining roles, responsibilities and information flows between its entities. This helps ensure that tasks can be efficiently distributed, decision-making processes are clear and resources are optimally allocated to achieve the organization's goals. Organizational structures can therefore only be temporary constructs, relevant as long as they facilitate the efficient implementation of specific strategies toward specific goals. When rapidly changing and complex business environments force organizations to constantly adapt goals and strategies, structures must be able to respond to these changing needs in an adaptable and timely manner. This calls for structures that are inherently adaptable by design.

The organizational case studies in the preceding chapters, ranging from Haier's ecosystem of micro-enterprises to BBVA's agile methodologies, illustrate a wide range of approaches toward this organizational flexibility. They also show the critical role of technology in enabling organizations to enhance their dynamic capabilities.

Given the need to frequently adapt organizational structures, a significant challenge arises: fixed dependencies between organizational entities make it difficult to implement changes. In conventional, tightly integrated and coupled systems, changes or disruptions in one area inevitably cause inconsistencies, creating the need for change in other areas. Continued organizational efficiency and effectiveness depends on smooth organizational flow.

Any change hinders this flow. It causes ripple effects throughout the organization, similar to the ripples caused by a stone thrown into a pond. These ripples can interfere with each other, creating a back and forth between change activities, until a new equilibrium, a new stable flow, has been established. This phase of internal turbulence and instability can drag on for a long time, leading to significant operational delays and a loss of efficiency. Fixed dependencies between organizational entities are the reason why. Each of them needs to be adjusted in time consuming processes. Although fixed dependencies help maintain alignment and unity, they hinder the organization's ability to respond quickly to external pressures, technological advances or shifts in market dynamics. The time it takes to successfully implement organizational change limits the possible frequency of change initiatives. Exceeding the typical rate of change that an organization is capable of will seriously erode operational efficiency: People and business processes then become disconnected and misaligned, making it much harder to work together. In a highly dynamic environment that is calling for adaptation all the time, such a disconnect has severe consequences: it threatens the organization's viability and market position.

The dilemma can only be resolved by increasing the typical rate of change that an organization can sustain without losing its operational integrity and efficiency. This requires the decoupling of organizational units, allowing them to adapt without affecting others, while at the same time enhancing their ability to easily connect and cooperate, temporarily pooling their capabilities for joint operations.

Key Principles for
Antifragile Structures

Modular, loosely coupled and highly reactive structures then emerge as foundational concepts for organizations that can rapidly find a new efficiency equilibrium without the necessity to establish fixed ties and dependencies.

A modular system is clearly defined by its independent yet interconnected modules, such as teams, departments or product lines. Each module has its own well-defined functionality and responsibilities, allowing it to perform its function independently and efficiently. Modules are meticulously designed to perform specific tasks or sets of closely related tasks, ensuring optimal performance and productivity. This specialization develops expertise within each module, such as manufacturing a specific product or mastering a particular discipline or technology.

Although modules can operate independently, they are designed to be part of a larger system. Modular systems define a clear framework for cooperation among modules to communicate, share data or work together toward specific goals. Each module is designed with compatibility and smooth integration in mind, so it can connect seamlessly with other modules within the system.

This allows for parts to be added, duplicated, removed, enhanced or replaced without disrupting the system, or any part of it. This kind of inherent adaptability and redundancy is essential for evolving in parallel with changing needs.

A modular organizational structure is both cohesive and flexible, able to seamlessly integrate into broader organizational ecosystems and capable of simultaneous, rapid adjustments in all of its parts. The flexibility of these ties creates an environment where innovation, pivoting or even failure within single modules does not compromise the overall stability and performance of the organization. It empowers the organization to take risks and make changes without the fear of destabilizing the entire system. The benefits of such an approach are manifold, including:

- **Rapid response to changes**: By designing modules to adapt and improve without affecting the whole, organizations can react more quickly to market shifts, technological advancements and competitive pressures.

- **Increased innovation**: A modular approach allows for experimentation without the risk of widespread disruption.

- **Easier scalability**: Organizations can more easily scale up or down, adding or removing modules of similar type in response to growing or reduced demand.

- **Reduced risks**: Decoupling reduces systemic risk by isolating failures within single modules and preventing them from cascading throughout the organization.

Antifragile organizations use modularity to strengthen their ability to adapt quickly and frequently. This aligns well with the need for decentralized decision-making, giving each modular unit or team the autonomy to respond directly to market changes and challenges. The resulting structures represent a significant organizational development. Each unit and team can act independently while still working toward the organization's broader goals and evolving business opportunities, transforming the organization into a cohesive, highly efficient ecosystem that can perform equally well in both stable and dynamic environments. The competitive dynamics between eBay and Alibaba provide a compelling look at these concepts in action.

Case Study: Alibaba – the *Crocodile in the Yangtze*

Alibaba's rivalry with eBay during the mid-2000s illustrates the influence of adaptability on competitiveness, as thoroughly analysed by Ying Lowrey,[114] an expert in global e-commerce and Chinese market dynamics. As the global leader in online auctions and shopping, eBay attempted to enter the Chinese market by replicating its global platform, emphasizing uniformity and control from its headquarters. In 2003, only about a year after its entry, eBay had reached almost total dominance of the local consumer-to-consumer market in China. Despite this initial success, growth stalled. It became apparent that eBay was not as successful as expected due to the unique demands and rapidly changing dynamics of the Chinese market, which required a more flexible and responsive approach.[115] For example, eBay's business model was dependent on widespread availability and adoption of internet services and secure online banking. In China, both of these were missing or still in their infancy at the time. Unwilling to adapt their business model to the local situation, eBay then faced a fierce local competitor.

In 2004, Alibaba was a Chinese business-to-business platform that had just reached profitability. Despite eBay not intending to expand into the B2B sector, Alibaba immediately felt threatened, because they could not afford to lose even a small portion of their business to eBay.[116] Alibaba's founder, Jack Ma, adopted a strategy deeply rooted in understanding local market nuances and consumer behaviour. Realizing the need for secure online banking and internet services across China, and especially in rural areas, the company quickly decided to build these services and internet access points itself. Through its newly founded Taobao platform, Alibaba implemented a secure online payment system built around an escrow service that connected all Chinese banks with Alibaba's customers. This Alipay escrow service directly addressed users' concerns about the security of online transactions, reflecting the company's customer-centric strategy and ability to innovate and adapt. Being a local business, Alibaba had a deep understanding of local market nuances, including consumer behaviour, regulations and internet usage patterns. Their localized, flexible strategy, supported by a modular and adaptable organizational structure, was key in Alibaba's ability to outperform eBay in China.[116]

In 2006, eBay left the Chinese market because Taobao had successfully taken away their market position.

Alibaba's structure was inherently decentralized, empowering local teams and individuals with the autonomy to make market-driven decisions. This approach facilitated Alibaba's agility, allowing the company to tailor its services and user experience to the precise needs and preferences of Chinese consumers. In later years, in addition to facilitating e-commerce in China, Alibaba has continued to build platforms for a variety of digital services, including online payments and cloud computing, and expanding beyond China, demonstrating the effectiveness of a modular organization.[115, 116]

The contrast between Alibaba and eBay captures the essence of adaptability in achieving competitiveness. The limitations of eBay's one-size-fits-all strategy contrast sharply with Alibaba's decentralized, agile organizational model and strategy, which allowed for rapid adaptation to consumer preferences and emerging trends. Alibaba's structure facilitated quick and effective responses to market changes without compromising overall organizational coherence and stability, cementing its dominance over eBay in China. It also sets an example for leveraging deep market insights and innovative strategic approaches within an organizational framework.[93]

This example shows that a global platform may work in one market but require a tailored approach to succeed in another. This can be summed up by Jack Ma's declaration: "eBay is a shark in the ocean. We are a crocodile in the Yangtze River. If we fight in the ocean, we will lose. But if we fight in the river, we will win."[117]

Case Study: Haier's Ecosystem Micro-Communities (EMC)

Haier's micro-enterprise model demonstrates how decentralized operations can easily adapt and smoothly align their structures to emerging business opportunities, and simultaneously focus on more than one business opportunity. Haier's micro-enterprises operate autonomously, making swift decisions close to market demands and customer needs. These micro-enterprises can join forces and multiply their impact through ecosystem micro-communities. Each of these communities provides a platform for alignment, collaborative problem-solving, knowledge sharing and resource pooling. Their symbiotic relationship enables micro-enterprises to overcome limitations and access a wider range of expertise, technology and markets. By joining forces, they are able to undertake projects or pursue opportunities they would not be able to accomplish on their own. This setup ensures that the organization can pivot or scale operations efficiently, in close alignment and response to arising opportunities or challenges.[71]

By leveraging its ecosystem micro-communities, Haier is able to translate its internal adaptability into external value. While decentralized units cover specific market niches and needs, they can also easily align their efforts to jointly implement larger user scenarios. Haier's *Internet of Food* initiative provides a practical example of the role of ecosystem micro-communities in practice. Built on the cooperation of multiple micro-enterprises, this community addresses the evolving needs of consumers in the areas of food storage, management and consumption, as discussed in Section 3.6. By grasping the intricate nuances of user scenarios and integrating cross-industry value chains, Haier's initiative offers comprehensive solutions that exceed the limitations of mere appliance manufacturing.[72]

The relationship between micro-enterprises and ecosystem micro-communities is not without its challenges. Disputes over strategies or stakes may arise, but the overarching shared purpose of creating value for users prevents disputes from becoming entrenched. The interdependence and tension between micro-enterprises and ecosystem micro-communities thus become a strength, as they facilitate the creation of value for users. Haier's organizational structure is a master class in embracing adaptability while maintaining focus. By balancing decentralization with clear customer-centric goals, this approach emphasizes radical transparency, employee empowerment and customer-centric innovation.[32]

Case Study: Buurtzorg

Building upon the findings from the case studies of Alibaba and Haier, the case of Buurtzorg adds another facet to the analysis. The Dutch home healthcare organization adheres to a purpose-driven, patient-centric approach, which has proven to be highly successful. The company demonstrates that a high level of efficiency and satisfaction in healthcare can be achieved through the use of small, self-managed nursing teams. The decentralized approach minimizes bureaucratic overheads while maximizing direct care. This allows for personalized, patient-centred care and represents a significant shift away from the traditional, hierarchical structures that have been prevalent in that field.[118]

Buurtzorg's operating model is based on autonomous teams that are responsible for managing themselves, assessing patients' needs and providing comprehensive care. This structure reduces the number of intermediaries between decision-makers and care providers, so that those closest to the patients are able and empowered to make critical care decisions. Prioritizing the nurse-patient relationship effectively aligns healthcare delivery with the overarching purpose of improving patient outcomes and quality of life. This alignment is facilitated by a lean organizational support system, which rather than dictating practices provides nurses with the tools, resources, services and knowledge necessary to best serve their patients. This innovative approach has established Buurtzorg as a leader in home care in the Netherlands, and inspired healthcare organizations worldwide to reconsider their own organizational models in favour of more adaptable and patient-focused structures.

When the Customer Takes Centre Stage

Alibaba's success in the digital marketplace, Haier's innovative approach to product development and Buurtzorg's transformation of patient care all lead to important insights on the value of highly adaptable organizational structures. Each organization has shown in its unique way that this flexibility significantly enhances the ability to meet and exceed customer expectations. What also ties them together is the underlying priority of placing the evolving nature of customer needs at the forefront of decision-making. This strategy has enabled each organization to innovate continuously and maintain competitiveness in their respective fields.

The case studies clearly show how organizations can structurally align themselves around serving the customer, ensuring that every function and team is directed toward this goal. Their unique decentralized organizational structures are enabled by the interplay of organizational and technical capabilities. Teams can act independently and have the authority to make informed decisions that directly impact customer satisfaction and create a high degree of market responsiveness.

Adaptable organizational structures combine several principles discussed in Chapter 2. They allow for parts to easily be added, duplicated, removed, enhanced or replaced without disrupting the system or compromising efficiency. They enable the organization to quickly pivot teams, strategies and products around evolving customer expectations and emerging opportunities.

A strong digital backbone, as highlighted in Section 3.5, serves as the technical foundation for these organizational structures. It empowers them to operate with unparalleled efficiency and adaptability, providing a streamlined, secure and cost-effective means for the transfer of information, goods, data and money. This infrastructure is key to flexibly scaling operations, allowing rapid adjustment to market demands.[26]

Figure 3.8 shows the main elements and relationships of highly adaptive organizations: *Customers, Business Teams, Service Teams, External Partners, Alignment Framework & Capability Development.*

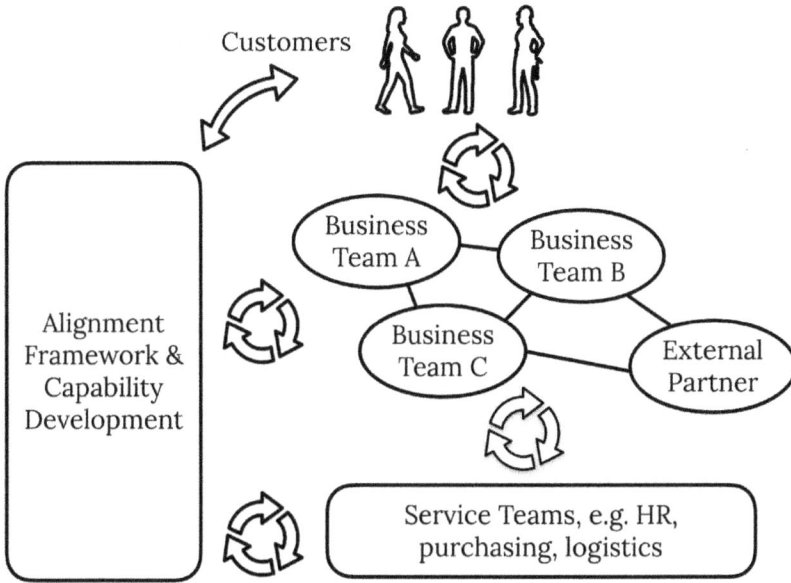

Figure 3.8
Adaptable and Customer-Centric Organization

Customers

Customers and their evolving needs take centre stage, with the entire organization's activities orbiting around them.

Business teams

Business teams work at the frontline, close to the customers. They are empowered to act autonomously and draw upon a rich set of capabilities to meet customer needs swiftly and effectively. These teams kick off by choosing which business opportunities to pursue and how to pursue them. Their task is to bring in the bulk of profits, fine-tuning their business model and operating its value streams. Each team aligns its operations with the business capabilities and resources required for the chosen opportunity. They can build up their own set of unique business capabilities and resources, but also acquire other capabilities and resources through supporting services. All business teams have full entrepreneurial responsibility and authority for their chosen opportunity, and can therefore be held accountable for their decisions. They determine strategies pertaining to their business, and are in charge of adapting and improving it. As part of this, teams can scale their business operations, implement their own supporting services, or spin off any part of their operations as a separate, fully independent business team.

Service Teams

The business teams rely on support services that provide them with specialized knowledge and capabilities, filling capability gaps in their business model and value chain. Support teams typically include back-office functions such as HR, IT support or purchasing, as well as front-office functions like prototyping and logistics. They serve as a support system for the customer-facing business teams, providing the essential resources and competencies required to maintain the fluidity of their operations. And while these service teams are not directly customer-facing, their role is just as critical. They operate with an understanding that their prompt and efficient service delivery is vital to the organization's ability to maintain its customer-centric focus.

The service teams also act as a reserve force, ensuring quick availability of slack resources required to act on upcoming opportunities or threats. Their task is to deliver their value-add capabilities on time, with the price and quality documented in their internal service contracts with individual business teams. They also need to be competitive with external, market-rate service providers. Supporting services thus operate their own business models and have full entrepreneurial responsibility and authority for offerings. They help ensure the scalability of their capabilities according to the requests of their clients, the business teams. This organizational construct allows the business teams to concentrate on innovation and customer service, knowing that the support functions are efficiently managed within the larger organizational framework, and sure to evolve and develop in alignment with the needs of business teams.

External Partners

Similarly, external partners can contribute specific services or business capabilities. These partners bring specialized expertise, resources or technology that complements the capabilities of the internal teams. The only difference is that they are legally independent from the organization, and have other owners. This has certain consequences for contracting procedures and the contracts themselves, such as intellectual property rights, licenses, sharing of profit and risks, or compliance with regulations. Partnerships extend strategic options and help ensure that the organization can quickly leverage external competencies, or flexibly scale capacity.

Alignment Framework and Capability Development

The alignment framework guides all teams in creating value and supporting each other. It sets the standards for efficient cooperation between teams and business operations. It enables the organization and all of its parts to collectively create value, and adjust and expand the capabilities according to the needs of its stakeholders, most notably customers and potential customers. And so, while each team operates with a high degree of autonomy, their actions are finely attuned to the organization's purpose and strategic goals.

The alignment framework also bridges the gap between evolving business environment trends and the organization's ability to capitalize on them. Larger strategic opportunities might be missed by business teams, or be beyond their capacity to prepare for them. The alignment framework can pick up on and fill these organizational gaps, initiating and financing development of new business capabilities. It is here, within this framework, that the true strength of an antifragile organization is realized. Each team is both a contributor to and a beneficiary of the alignment framework, ensuring that as customer needs shift, so too does the organization, seamlessly and cohesively.

The Digitalized Service Organization

If we further generalize this organizational setup, it turns out that the distinction between business teams and service or support teams is purely contextual. All customer-facing teams are business teams, and all other teams are supporting them. This leads us to the broad model of a digitalized service organization, where every business capability is organized as a service of its own, made available for other teams through the contracting and management functions of the digital backbone. This is typically in the form of a service catalogue (Figure 3.9). The service catalogue allows easy acquisition of all business capabilities — the competencies and resources that business teams need to act on an opportunity. They then combine the contracted business capabilities into a value stream that delivers services or products to customers.

Value Chain for a Business Opportunity

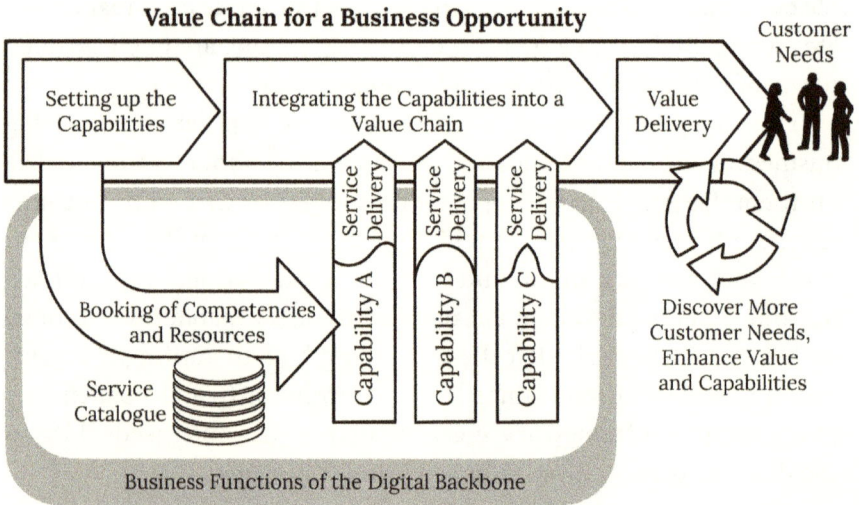

Figure 3.9
Digitalized Service Organization

It all comes down to an effective integration of different business capabilities with each other, and coordinating their efforts toward customers. Each value stream can be made available as a new service operation in the catalogue. That is the organizational concept that allowed AWS to grow the largest and most diverse digital service catalogue in the world. But the catalogue need not be limited to digital services. Any business capability can be organized and delivered in the form of a service operation, including design, programming, manufacturing, financing, logistics, controlling — virtually anything. It is a highly versatile organizational pattern, perfectly suited to flexibly manage complex and dynamic business needs.

In this model, each team is responsible for generating its own revenue and securing its own funding by actively seeking out customers in need of the teams' capabilities. Teams negotiate their own service contracts. The value of their contributions is reflected in the profits they are making. This encourages accountability and entrepreneurship, as service operations must continuously innovate and adapt to remain competitive and financially viable within the organization. Funding always flows from customers buying products and services to the involved teams, and from there to team members. The more a team earns, the more it can invest and expand. This allows the organization to fluidly adjust capacity to demand, without the need for centralized controls. By eliminating cumbersome budgeting practices such as fixed budgets, pay-as-you-go financing and yearly financial forecasts, and reducing the constraints of rigid contracting, the digital service organization minimizes bureaucratic barriers, allowing for faster approval processes and more flexible resource allocation. This makes it easier to fulfil the evolving needs of customers and discover new business opportunities.

A digitalized service organization can encompass a wide variety of capabilities. It can grow these without limitations, and expand the range of business opportunities within its reach. It becomes more capable, more versatile with every new service operation, competence and capability added to its service catalogue. One of the biggest benefits of this approach is that the individual service operations do not disturb each other. They are completely decoupled, each delivering value to different teams or customers. While some tried and tested operations bring in profits, others can be in an early stage of maturity, preparing to secure additional profits in the future. If an incumbent operation loses customers, becoming unprofitable, the team can safely decide to shut it down, sell it or turn the remaining valuable parts into a new service operation. Adapting an individual service operation to newly discovered client needs is equally easy, by cloning the operation, performing all required business upgrades and then making it available in the service catalogue as a new enhanced capability.

The many different service operations do not disturb but complement each other. They profit from their variety. They support each other. They can seamlessly transition between set-ups optimized for exploration, profit-orientation and supporting services. They can easily learn from each other and iteratively improve their individual services and collective portfolio. Together, they secure the long-term perspective of the entire organization.[26]

Conclusion

Our exploration reveals that by placing the customer at the centre, antifragile organizations are uniquely equipped to rapidly reconfigure resources and capabilities. They maintain strategic alignment and structural integrity while closely following the changing needs of customers and markets. This approach leverages collective expertise and emphasizes accountability and ownership, themes that have resonated throughout the discussions in Chapter 3, from processes to leadership to structural adaptations.

And with that, it becomes clear that the path to adaptability and responsiveness lies not merely in the fluidity of structures but also their alignment toward a shared purpose. As we transition into the next section, the limitations of traditional governance models in supporting and managing these organizational structures is evident. The dynamic nature of antifragile strategies, structures and processes calls for a framework that embodies organizational agility, capable of real-time adaptability.

3.9

From Forced Governance to Voluntary Commitment

The purpose of governance in an organization is to establish a framework that helps ensure accountability, transparency and effective decision-making, guiding the organization toward its strategic goals. Good governance provides the necessary oversight and direction to balance the interests of various stakeholders, including shareholders, employees, customers and the broader community. It provides the foundation for ethical behaviour, risk management, and compliance with laws and regulations. However, the emphasis on risk avoidance, often driven by government regulations and laws, has transformed governance in many companies into a bureaucratic and risk-averse system. Under this influence, decision-making processes are designed primarily to mitigate risk and help ensure compliance. While it is important to uphold legal and ethical standards, the chosen measures of conventional compliance systems stifle innovation and agility.

In many organizations, the focus on risk avoidance has led to a culture of excessive caution, where decision-making is bogged down by layers of approvals and documentation. This bureaucratic approach hinders responsiveness and slows down the ability to seize new opportunities or adapt to changing market conditions. Centralized rules for risk minimization and compliance primarily aim to avoid liability. Employees often become more concerned with adhering to rules and avoiding mistakes than with taking proactive, innovative, entrepreneurial actions.

The impact of this risk-averse mentality is particularly apparent and destructive in environments where rapid adaptation and creativity are critical for success. Rather than cultivating a culture that encourages risk-taking, experimentation and learning from failures, the emphasis on risk avoidance leads to a stifling of new ideas and a reluctance to deviate from established procedures. This limits the organization's potential for growth and reduces its ability to respond effectively to unforeseen challenges.

But these systems of rule-based compliance and centralized oversight have a much deeper flaw than adding bureaucracy. They create a highly problematic attitude of shifting responsibility for bad outcomes to proxies. This can take many forms: 'I just followed the rules,' 'This was not covered by the rules,' 'I am not certain what rules I should follow,' 'I do not have the authority,' 'The system requires it.' All of these attempts at justification show that people do not want to take responsibility for their own actions. The process becomes the proxy for responsibility and reasonable behaviour.[68]

Compliance-heavy governance systems infantilize employees. They better do as they are told, or face punishment. This teaches them to either abide by the rules, or at least not get caught sidestepping them. The risk of punishment incentivizes employees to get really creative in making others responsible for bad outcomes. Excellence in the blame game is required in the shark tank of senior management. These attitudes undermine the development of meaningful decision-making abilities, treating employees as if they are incapable of handling responsibility. They stifle people's growth, reduce their motivation, and inhibit the development of critical thinking and problem-solving skills. They also fail to deal effectively with new risks because they demand compliance with procedures that are irrelevant outside of their original context, or that are based on outdated best practices. Rule-based governance and compliance systems are always lagging behind in their ability to adapt. Their feedback loops are too long and sluggish, rendering them largely ineffective and unsuitable for dynamic business environments and innovation.

All these effects of conventional governance systems are incompatible with the principles of antifragile organizations, which require swift decisions, risk-taking, experimentation and unbiased evaluation of results. Conventional governance and compliance practices, if implemented in antifragile organizations, would slowly but surely kill them. Antifragile organizations use radically different strategies for appropriate governance.

Two Sides of a Coin:
Autonomy and Accountability

As we have discussed, decentralization of decision-making and autonomy are desirable characteristics of an antifragile setup. However, this must not come at the expense of responsibility. So, when an organization decentralizes decision-making and grants autonomy, it should treat employees as responsible and informed adults, not immature children. Otherwise, autonomous, decentralized decision-making is lacking a key ingredient: It must be clear who is responsible for the decisions made and the actions taken. The big question is who is accountable for the outcomes — the good and the bad, the intended and the unintended? Conventional governance ends up pointing to a few people in high positions. Consequently, these individuals try to protect themselves from personal risk. They install systems of oversight and control that funnel potentially big risks to their desks before giving the green light to related actions. The problem is that this risk management strategy is too slow for complex, dynamic environments. It creates a strategic bottleneck for organizations. It stifles innovation. However you try to mitigate these effects — and there are many proposed practices, such as OKRs (objectives and key results), regular performance reviews, detailed financial reporting or financial incentives — they just add bureaucracy and do not address the root cause of the problem. Namely, this strategy distributes accountability to only a fraction of all the people who are needed to take meaningful action. As a result, many people do not feel responsible, are not held accountable, and consequently are entrusted with very limited autonomy, if any at all. This lack of accountability and engagement has been a pervasive problem in the workplace for decades. According to Gallup's 2023 *State of the Global Workplace* report,[119] only 23% of employees are engaged at work, which means 77% are disengaged. This high level of disengagement has significant consequences. Inadequate management practices are a major contributor to this disengagement, as they fail to foster a sense of accountability and autonomy among employees.

Conversely, organizations that prioritize purpose over profit experience higher levels of employee satisfaction and engagement. Those who are actively engaged in the organization's purpose are more likely to feel passionate about and accountable for their work, and they perform at higher levels. Studies over an extended period of time have consistently reflected employees' desire for greater autonomy, recognition, and opportunities for growth and learning, underscoring the need for a paradigm shift.[119, 120, 121]

When greater autonomy depends on assuming accountability, there is only one way forward: Those who feel ownership of decisions and actions, and genuinely care about outcomes, can be entrusted with autonomy. Those who take pride in the good outcomes learn from bad results, overcome their shortcomings and grow in their abilities. To quote the longtime CEO of Haier, Zhang Ruimin, "The key to leadership is to transform your employees or workers into entrepreneurs."[31]

How does this work in practice? It all starts with a person's willingness and ability to make and keep commitments in the eyes of others. Over time, this accountability will earn them the trust of their clients and peers. They will grant these individuals increasing levels of autonomy. They can then act in certain roles without the need for approval from others, constrained only by the commitments they have made, their own abilities and the assets entrusted to them (see Section 3.7). Expertise, skills and accountability guide their actions, rather than a process or directive.[122]

But there are natural limits to what individuals can accomplish. Larger commitments require a team. The better this team keeps its commitments, the more trust its partners will place in their capabilities. With each challenge met, individuals and teams qualify for greater opportunities, which means greater autonomy. This is the natural way for it to grow. Autonomy can be gained by voluntarily taking on more responsibility, improving expertise and skills, and demonstrating a track record of accountability.

Voluntarily taking responsibility and the accountability that comes with it — as opposed to being 'held responsible' and accountable by others — is a key distinction in an antifragile organization. Such organizations therefore make accountability an integral, non-negotiable, inseparable and tamper-proof part of every action. Without clear accountability, every step of the way, autonomy cannot manifest. The more accountability is taken, and the better it is linked to the actions taken, the more autonomy can emerge.

This link between actions and accountability is relatively easy to make in scenarios where there is only one actor. However, organizations do not consist of a single actor. Most actions involve many players and contributors, which complicates the task of aligning their individual actions, and linking them to individual and collective accountability. Aligning actions and ensuring accountability of actors are key challenges that the governance of an antifragile organization must address.

Let us start with the challenge of aligning actions within a team. This is not as straightforward as you might expect. Remember, all actions must ideally be linked to voluntary commitments, without force or pressure. Each team member must feel accountable not only for their own individual commitments, but also for those made to the team and by the team.

Kickstarting Governance at Morning Star

The Morning Star Company is a prime example of how to build accountability into an organization. During its founding phase in 1990, it adopted two key principles: 'Don't Use Force' and 'Keep Commitments.' They became the foundation of the company's governance and operational strategy, emphasizing self-management and alignment of actions based on mutual, voluntary agreements. At Morning Star, all activities are organized around commitments documented in CLOUs, as described in Section 3.7. This helps ensure accountability and continuous adaptation, as everyone is held accountable for their commitments and actions. With this principle of non-coercion, decisions and actions are taken voluntarily and promote a sense of personal ownership. By not using force, Morning Star creates an environment where accountability is both personal and collective. Following through on commitments is equally important, as it holds individuals and teams accountable for their actions and cultivates reliability and trust.

This voluntary commitment model has a profound impact. Accountability is distributed throughout the organization, meaning that no management hierarchy is required to drive collective action. Each team member is responsible for fulfilling their commitments, ensuring accountability in every action and decision. The commitment-based approach also allows Morning Star to be highly adaptable, as teams and individuals are empowered to take initiative and respond quickly to changing conditions without bureaucratic delays or approvals from higher-ups.[110, 111]

Purpose-driven Alignment at Patagonia

Similarly, Patagonia demonstrates the power of a deep alignment between an organization's values, strategies and operations to catalyse remarkable success and adaptability. At Patagonia, this alignment is woven into the organization's culture, leadership and structure, becoming an integral part of its DNA. The company's core mission — to preserve the natural environment for future generations — drives sustainability and ethical practices in every decision and action. The shared purpose is the unifying thread that binds together all aspects of the organization, so every facet of the company's operations and strategies is in perfect harmony with its fundamental values and mission. This deep alignment enables Patagonia to meet challenges and opportunities with agility and integrity, driving continuous innovation and customer-centricity. Understanding and mastering these interconnected relationships is the cornerstone of the company's success, and its ability to inspire both loyalty and innovation.[30]

Aligned Autonomy as Enabler

Morning Star and Patagonia both exemplify frameworks that balance alignment and autonomy to improve organizational effectiveness and adaptability. They provide teams with the autonomy to make decisions and act independently, while ensuring that their actions are aligned with overall goals and strategy. Stephen Bungay, an authority on strategy execution and the author of *The Art of Action*,[123] argues that alignment is achieved not through detailed instructions and rigid control, but through a shared understanding of the mission and individuals' freedom to take initiative within that framework. This inspired Henrik Kniberg, a pioneer in agile and lean practices, to develop the *Aligned Autonomy* model,[124] which illustrates the benefits of aligning the efforts of autonomous teams toward a shared purpose. Both Bungay and Kniberg emphasize the need for clear goals, decentralized decision-making, alignment mechanisms, trust, accountability, continuous learning and supportive leadership in organizations. Kniberg's model becomes even more useful when we look at it through the lens of accountability. As we have discussed, accountability is a prerequisite for autonomy. Therefore, accountability and alignment of teams drive organizational performance. That performance depends on the level of alignment and accountability within it. Figure 3.10 illustrates the possible scenarios.

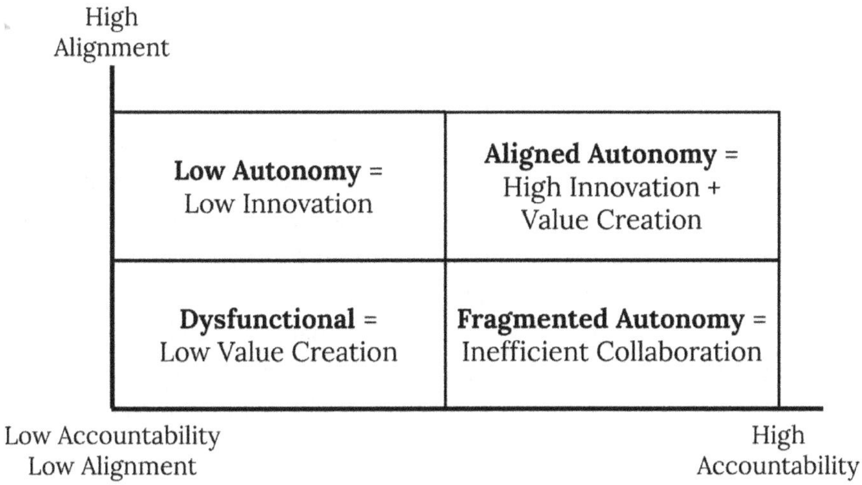

High
Alignment

Low Autonomy = Low Innovation	**Aligned Autonomy** = High Innovation + Value Creation
Dysfunctional = Low Value Creation	**Fragmented Autonomy** = Inefficient Collaboration

Low Accountability   High
  Low Alignment   Accountability

Figure 3.10
Impact of Alignment and Accountability
on Organizational Performance

Dysfunctional

When accountability and alignment are lacking, it is hard to imagine any meaningful autonomy. In such environments, accountability is being avoided and diluted top-down, which stifles initiative and engagement, leading to low productivity and innovation. The absence of both purpose-driven alignment and meaningful accountability creates bureaucratic hierarchies, characterized by excessive red tape and formalities that inhibit rapid decision-making and adaptability. This creates an environment where adherence to procedures is prioritized over achieving meaningful results, further contributing to organizational inefficiency. The result is a dysfunctional organization that creates minimal value.

Low Autonomy

Even with a strong alignment, low accountability will limit autonomy and innovation. Teams may understand and support the organization's purpose, but lack the earned trust and freedom to explore new ideas or take risks. This leads to a compliance-driven culture, where adherence to rules and processes is prioritized over creative problem-solving. Low accountability stifles innovation as employees focus on following established procedures rather than pursuing new solutions or improvements.

Fragmented Autonomy

When teams operate with high levels of accountability but lack alignment around a shared purpose, their efforts become fragmented. This fragmentation leads to inefficient collaboration and wasted resources, as teams may work at cross-purposes without a unifying direction. The lack of alignment leads to duplication of effort and suboptimal collaboration, causing teams or units to drift apart. The lack of cohesion can exacerbate inefficiencies and hinder overall organizational performance, especially when trying to address challenges that go beyond the capabilities of single teams.

Aligned Autonomy

The ideal scenario combines high accountability with high alignment. Clear goals, intrinsic motivation and voluntary commitments enable high value creation and innovation. Teams are free to innovate and take any action that contributes to their shared purpose, without having to wait for approval. They just need to make sure they stay aligned and deliver on their commitments. Ideally, the alignment of teams can adjust dynamically to new needs and opportunities, allowing organizations to evolve in close synchronization with their environment. This sort of dynamic alignment makes them highly adaptive.

Dynamically
Aligning Autonomy

When discussing alignment, there is a fundamental difference between antifragile organizations and traditional ones. People in traditional organizations typically define themselves by what they do. Alignment discussions there revolve around tasks, job titles or economic performance goals. When asked, few people there can describe why they work, beyond the notion of making money.

In stark contrast, antifragile organizations align around a core purpose that governs their strategies and actions. Ideally, their members feel deeply committed to this purpose. All meaningful actions seek to contribute to the purpose. A deeply embedded purpose not only drives effectiveness and performance, but also guides the direction of strategies and organizational development, especially when they need to be adjusted.[125] So, it all starts with purpose.

The purpose should resonate within the organization, down to each employee, so that they really feel accountable for contributing to it. This process of alignment starts with reflecting about oneself, and the purpose offered by an organization or collaborating team. What cause does one want to contribute to? What challenge aligns with the personal ambitions? This is the first step of accountability for individuals in an antifragile organization: Being true to themselves, aligning their actions with their heart, conscience and desires. And, with their individual capabilities, because they want to be able to keep their commitments. This step of individual alignment with an organization is so crucial that it should determine which organization one wishes to join or remain part of. And, it is entirely in the responsibility of each individual. In an antifragile organization, there is no manager telling them what to do and what purpose to support. It is their own responsibility: They must choose a cause worthy of their precious time on earth.

Once a purpose is backed by several people, they naturally feel the urge to bring it to life, to move it from vision to reality. This results in strategies and actions that are all aligned around the same driving purpose. Strategies and actions can then change dynamically at any time, as long as they still contribute to the same purpose. A clear purpose is therefore a powerful enabler for dynamically and autonomously adjusting strategies and actions. Any member of a team with a shared purpose can adjust or change strategies and actions after aligning them with the rest of the team. Once the team is convinced of a better course of action, it can pursue it immediately, without the need for approvals or other bureaucratic delays.[122]

Dynamic Autonomy in Haier's Internet of Food

Again, Haier provides a prime example of the dynamic alignment of multiple autonomous teams. Its *Internet of Food* is a business ecosystem in which diverse micro-enterprises collaborate to meet consumer needs for food storage, management and consumption. Participating micro-enterprises align their contributions through the shared purpose of the ecosystem micro-community (EMC). The purpose gives them a specific reason to work together and provides a shared strategy for this ecosystem. Together, these form the framework that aligns the specific business purpose of each micro-enterprise, enabling each team to develop and dynamically adjust their own strategies in response to new needs and opportunities. This is always done in close alignment with the shared purpose and shared strategy of the ecosystem micro-community (Figure 3.11).

For example, the Smart Cooking EMC wanted to help users prepare complicated, restaurant-quality dishes. As Michael Y. Lee, an expert in organizational design and innovation, and his colleagues[126] describe in their case study, the ecosystem launched its mission with the iconic Beijing Roast Duck as its first product. Through Haier's unique bidding and revenue sharing system (see Section 3.5), it then attracted micro-enterprises to develop the necessary smart kitchen appliances, external partners to develop the recipe, a duck farm for food supply, a food processing company and others. For example, one micro-enterprise developed the programmable oven to roast the duck with the single press of a button. Each partner and micro-enterprise shared the same overall purpose: achieving simple, homemade, restaurant-quality dishes. And each partner shared the same strategy: start with Beijing Roast Duck, and then expand the portfolio. From this strategy, each partner derived its specific contributing actions, aligned them within their own team,

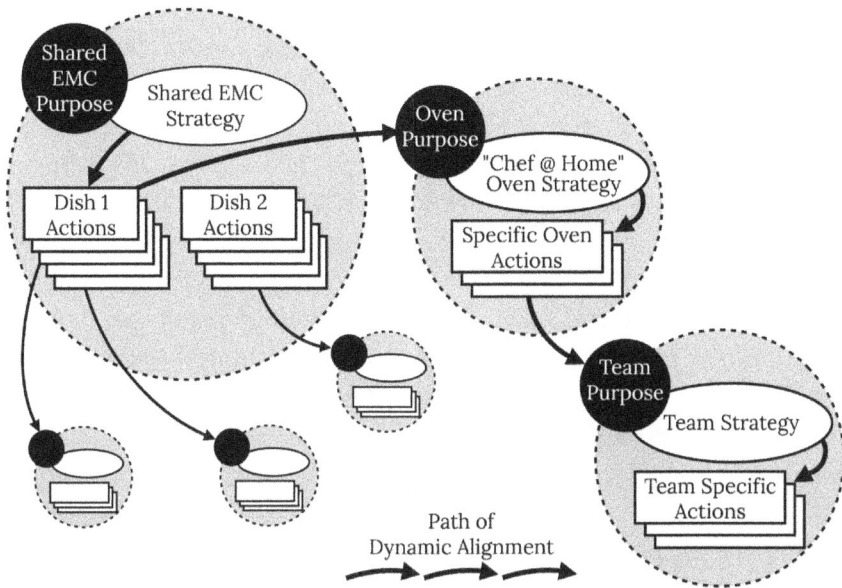

Figure 3.11
Shared and Dynamic System of Aligned Accountability
in Haier's Ecosystem Micro-Communities

and also coordinated with the interdependent actions of the other partners. After successfully launching the first product and selling 20,000 ducks within six months, more products were added to the portfolio, and more external companies and micro-enterprises joined the Smart Cooking EMC. Within months, it had successfully launched 16 additional restaurant-quality dishes.[126] At the time of this writing, Haier's smart home app offers more than 300 recipes, with step-by-step instructions for the users and automated programming of the required smart cooking appliances.

By examining the alignment of actions within an ecosystem micro-community (as shown in Figure 3.11), it becomes clear how this approach differs from traditional work breakdown structures. In a typical work breakdown structure, decisions are centralized, whereas in this ecosystem model, decisions are made at the level of, and by the team, that is best able to implement them. This model enables self-management of actions within each level and team, eliminating the need for centralized management. Actions can move fluidly between levels and teams, depending on where they can be most effectively decided and implemented. This flexibility is particularly beneficial as teams discover interdependencies between their actions and those of other teams. They can easily move required actions across teams, until actions are located in appropriate teams, and at a level appropriate for implementation. Such a system avoids the pitfalls of setting up special cross-team coordination efforts, which inevitably result in complex coordination structures that cripple decision-making speed across all teams, without adding value. Instead, interdependent actions are coordinated within the team that is best suited to solve the dependency issues, shielding the other teams from distractions and issues that do not affect them. In this way, teams evolve naturally based on the interdependencies that arise from their strategies and actions. Each team can contribute to higher-level decisions and actions by dispatching one of its members part-time into higher-level teams, for efficient coordination at higher levels without sacrificing insights and intelligence from lower levels.

Of course, this flexibility requires transparent strategies and actions, to help identify dependencies. And it is transparency that facilitates rapid adjustments, because it is then clear who to align with before implementing actions that affect others. Every team and team member has the right to be involved in decisions that affect their commitments and investments. After ensuring that the interests of contributing parties are aligned, adjustments can flow dynamically, both top-down and bottom-up, at any time. The dynamic flow eliminates the need for time-boxed synchronization events that are common in agile methodologies, such as the *Scrum* approach we described earlier. With dynamically aligned autonomy, there is no need to wait for synchronization events, such as a 'sprint' planning session, before adjusting cross-team actions.

In essence, dynamically aligned autonomy creates a fluid and adaptive environment where teams self-manage, coordinate their actions and evolve based on real-time interdependencies, ensuring agile and effective decision-making.

The Role of the
Digital Backbone

Without technology to support the implementation of aligned accountability, the governance of decentralized units would be far too costly, cumbersome, inefficient and ineffective, rendering it pointless. As discussed earlier, the digital backbone plays a critical role as an enabler of a new decentralized governance. Through automation, it can provide an uninterrupted, unambiguous and transparent path of aligned autonomy for every activity, with decision-making automatically logged and securely tracked. With this transparency of accountability pathways, everyone in the organization is able to identify and change alignment deficiencies, inappropriate decisions and strategies. The digital backbone supports these interventions by providing the appropriate tools and automating key procedures. It thus preserves the integrity of commitments, and helps ensure that dynamic alignment processes always involve all necessary stakeholders, regardless of where they start. In this way, dynamic alignment processes can be initiated anywhere, not necessarily at the top of collaboration structures. As a result, governance is conducted on the broadest possible personnel basis and becomes more or less democratized. A well-designed digital backbone can act as an enabler for dynamically aligned autonomy. We are already seeing the first promising steps of such software-enabled governance systems, and their great potential to support the development of dynamic capabilities in organizations, regardless of their size.

Conclusion

Apart from training employees in ethical and lawful behaviour, governance in antifragile organizations fundamentally differs from that in traditional enterprises. Antifragile organizations embrace a governance model that emphasizes autonomy and accountability of its members around their commitment to a core purpose. Unlike traditional organizations, which often rely on centralized control and rule-based compliance systems that stifle innovation and responsiveness, antifragile ones encourage risk-taking, experimentation and learning from failure. This allows them to quickly adapt to changing environments and seize new opportunities. Antifragile organizations accomplish this by embedding accountability into every action and decision, ensuring alignment with the organization's purpose. This kind of governance is a prerequisite for successfully participating in or trying to build multi-organization ecosystems.

3.10

Progressing to Ecosystems

As our examination of the characteristics of dynamic business systems makes evident, antifragile companies excel due to exceptional synergy in their organizational capabilities. The design of internal business processes, structures and strategies in those organizations are driven by the needs of external customers and markets. This *outside-in* approach determines the speed of adaptation, ensuring that internal speed always aligns with the market speed.

Customer-centricity thus is the focal point around which antifragile organizations are constructed. It helps ensure that every decision, innovation and strategy is designed to meet, and even anticipate, the evolving needs of customers. Internally, the shared interest of increasing value for customers aligns the collaboration efforts of teams. In order to be particularly flexible and fast, antifragile organizations move to modular, autonomous teams, which co-create value in networked, fluid structures. Through the service alignment pattern (see Section 3.8), each team in these structures contributes specific business capabilities to one or more co-created value chains.

From a macro perspective, the amount of available business capabilities determines the range and number of opportunities that can be pursued simultaneously. As we have discussed, an antifragile organization tries to maximize this number of business opportunities. It therefore aims to increase the diversity of its capabilities, along with their operational processing capacity.

One way of doing this is to organically build up the required capacities and develop new capabilities with a company's own resources. This is a slow growth strategy, applicable especially when those resources are needed in the long run. It has some benefits, particularly regarding the level of control and governance that can be exerted, and the quality of services and products, because value creation chains and their governance can be tightly integrated for specific business needs. However, the downsides of this approach are significant:

- **High costs**: Developing internal capabilities often requires sizeable financial investment in infrastructure, technology, training and hiring skilled personnel. This can strain company resources, especially for smaller businesses.

- **Time consuming**: Building internal capabilities is a time-intensive process. It takes considerable time to develop the necessary skills, processes and systems, which might delay the company's ability to respond to important market changes.

- **Limited flexibility**: The portfolio of available internal capabilities limits problem-solving capacity. Problems that require developing specific new skills are out of reach for business, or may require insourcing of new capabilities, which can be a disadvantage in fast-evolving industries.

- **Focus diversion**: Developing internal capabilities can divert focus and resources from core business activities. This can lead to a loss of efficiency and effectiveness in areas that are critical to the company's primary objectives.

- **Resource allocation**: Internal resources and budgets are always limited. This makes every decision to develop new capabilities a challenging one. The allocation of resources to build one specific internal capability may, in fact, take away valuable assets from other opportunities. The general scarcity of resources constrains the company's capacity to invest extensively and expand rapidly.

- **Missed collaboration opportunities**: Investing heavily in internal capabilities may result in missed opportunities to collaborate with external partners who could provide complementary capabilities, technologies or market access. The build-up of internal capabilities competing with external vendors can have a negative impact on strategic positions.

- **Innovation stagnation**: Over-reliance on internal capabilities can lead to a closed mindset, where the company becomes insular and resistant to external ideas and innovations. This can stifle creativity and hinder competitive advantage.

- **Scaling issues**: Scaling internal capabilities can be difficult and costly. As the company grows, the complexity and cost of maintaining and expanding these capabilities can escalate.

In hyper-dynamic market environments, the time available for developing internal capabilities shrinks, and the period during which these capabilities are needed is highly uncertain. Antifragile organizations have better options to grow their business capabilities, and to unlock more business opportunities. Taking advantage of their flexible cooperation capabilities, they can evolve into business ecosystems.

Pushing Boundaries and Limitations

The composition of antifragile organizations is quite similar to that of ecosystems, except for one important difference: They still rely on their own resources to create value. Removing this limitation means evolving into an open business ecosystem. Such an ecosystem brings the resources of different organizations together. Each can bring specific competencies and capabilities into shared value chains (Figure 3.12). The transition from operating in isolation to embracing external collaboration unlocks new business potential. By forming strategic partnerships, alliances and joint ventures, organizations extend their capabilities beyond their internal boundaries. This external collaboration broadens their problem-solving abilities and opens new avenues for innovation and growth.

As collaboration intensifies, a natural evolution occurs, leading to the formation of interconnected networks and the emergence of practices that facilitate co-creation. These networks drive the exchange of data, expertise, goods and payments for the purpose of shared value creation.

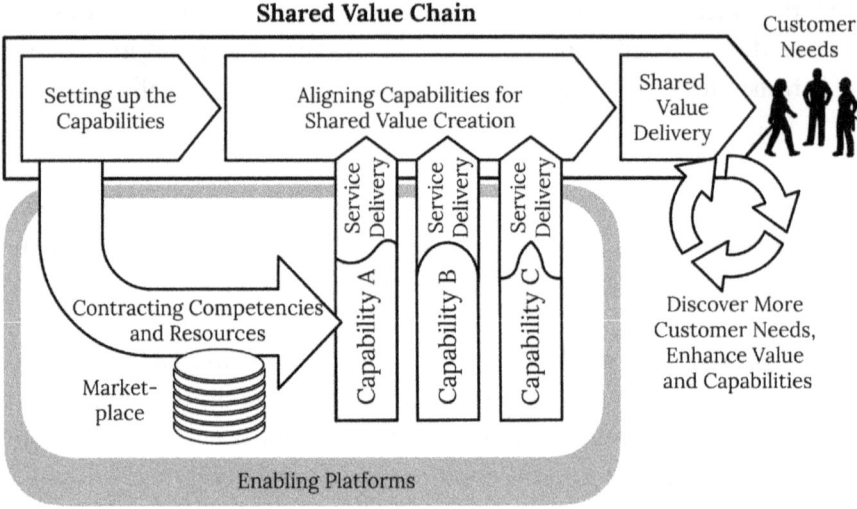

Figure 3.12
Co-Creation Ecosystems

Platforms for co-creation capture these practices, making them an integral part of working in shared value chains. The internal service catalogues of antifragile organizations (compare with Figure 3.9) now evolve into marketplaces of services. These services can be offered by many different participants. Each service is organized as its own business operation, delivering value to its customers, regardless of their organizational affiliation. Services competition in the marketplace drives value creation and innovation. The market's attractiveness for entrepreneurs and customers determines the speed of growth of the ecosystem. Both sides are attracted by secure, fair and favourable conditions for co-creating, delivering and capturing value, which requires a balanced approach of governance in the ecosystem. Without this balanced approach, growth of the ecosystem remains limited. But growth is critical for its success; only growth leads to a broader range of business capabilities in the ecosystem. The broader the portfolio of capabilities — the greater the range of opportunities for its participants — the more customers it can serve. The ecosystem reinforces itself through growth. Over time, it adjusts its business capabilities to changing customer and market needs. It naturally gets rid of resources and capabilities that have become irrelevant due to a lack of customers. Thus, all value chains and organizational structures in ecosystems are temporary interaction networks, relevant only as long as they provide value. Their inevitable obsolescence enables a fluid and fast response to changing needs, because it automatically allocates resources to where they provide the most value. Ecosystems naturally evolve and adapt to new business needs and opportunities.

The Smart Cooking community, introduced in Section 3.9, exemplifies co-creation within ecosystems. Initially comprising a small group of internal teams and external partners intent on bringing restaurant-quality Beijing Roast Duck to home kitchens, the community has since grown to encompass more than 70 collaborators, further extending their offerings to the customer. The value of the ecosystem hinges on the value-add it continues to provide for the participants and their customers. Should it cease to do so, it will naturally dissolve, reflecting the ecosystem's inherent capability to quickly shed what becomes irrelevant. This example demonstrates the ecosystem's capacity for self-reinforcement and adaptation. It also highlights the transient nature of its constituent elements and their alignment with a company's core purpose.

As detailed earlier, AWS is another example of an open ecosystem. It offers a wide range of cloud computing services, including third-party applications and development tools to support diverse workloads and business needs. Every new third-party service provider enhances the overall capabilities, reach and attractiveness of the ecosystem. This then draws more customers and businesses into the space, creating a cycle of growth and continuous innovation. AWS's balanced governance helps ensure security, reliability and fairness, cultivating an environment conducive to mutual growth and innovation.

Similarly, the Linux Foundation supports the creation of sustainable open-source ecosystems by providing a secure and fair governance model for collaborative development. Conceived by Linus Torvalds in 1991, Linux has evolved far beyond its initial scope as a free computer operating system. The foundation's projects, such as *Kubernetes*, benefit from the contributions of a wide array of companies and individuals, driving innovation and growth. The open nature of these projects helps ensure that they can adapt quickly to changing needs, maintaining their relevance and continuously attracting more contributors and users.[127, 128]

Successfully handling complex challenges requires a solution system that matches the scope and variability of the problems it faces, as suggested by cyberneticist W. Ross Ashby (*Ashby's Law*).[129] In a globally interconnected world, networks and ecosystems are the logical organizational form to meet these demands. They allow organizations to harness a much wider range of capabilities and solutions, enhancing their ability to effectively respond to a wide range of challenges.

Ecosystem Governance

The very characteristics that make ecosystems so powerful — diversity, autonomy and interconnectivity — also pose significant challenges to a governance framework. Unlike the governance of a single organization, which typically focuses on aligning the interests and perspectives of its internal units, an ecosystem encompasses a multitude of diverse, independent organizations, communities and stakeholders, each with their own internal governance. These different levels of governance need to be compatible and resonant with each other, to provide effective and efficient collaboration. This requires weaving a variety of perspectives and interests into a cohesive framework, without stifling the unique qualities and contributions each partner brings to the table. Moreover, these governance mechanisms must be at least as dynamic and adaptable as the ecosystem they aim to steer.

Challenges of Ecosystem Governance

Ecosystem governance comes with a unique set of challenges that necessitates a delicate balancing act. These are not just matters of scaling governance, but about preserving the essence of what makes ecosystems dynamic and innovative.

- **Aligning diverse interests**: Ecosystems are a collective of disparate entities and stakeholders, each with its agenda, culture and goals. Aligning these diverse interests requires a governance model that can synthesize these differences into a cohesive strategy. The challenge lies in crafting a common purpose that resonates with all participants, without diluting their individual autonomy. Governance structures must serve as a harmonizing force that cultivates collective direction while allowing for the individuality that fuels innovation and competitiveness.

- **Maintaining openness, flexibility and adaptability**: One of the primary advantages of ecosystems is their inherent openness and flexibility, which enables rapid adaptation and evolution. However, this does not eliminate the need for a stable core of governance that helps ensure coherence and continuity. The governance framework must strike a delicate balance, providing enough structure to prevent chaos but not so much as to constrict the flow of ideas and the ability to pivot when necessary. It is about establishing a flexible backbone that supports growth and change.

- **Managing complexity**: Ecosystems can be dizzyingly complex, with a web of interactions, dependencies and transactions that are often nonlinear and emergent. Governance systems are tasked with making sense of this complexity, providing clarity and direction amid the potential for confusion. They must do so without becoming overly prescriptive, allowing the ecosystem to breathe and self-organize within a light-touch framework that guides rather than dictates.

- **Ethical and legal considerations**: As digital ecosystems become more prevalent, ethical and legal considerations become increasingly important. Fairness, transparency and ethical business practices are key. Governance must help ensure that all activities within the ecosystem adhere to ethical standards and comply with legal regulations. This involves cultivating an environment where innovation is encouraged without compromising ethical boundaries or legal requirements. Ecosystem governance models must navigate the dual imperatives of promoting growth while upholding principles of justice and accountability.

- **Aligning short- and long-term interests**: By balancing immediate objectives with future-oriented goals, a business ecosystem ensures its viability over time, thriving in the years ahead without compromising current success. In hyper-dynamic environments, it becomes especially critical to continuously and rapidly realign stakeholder interests through governance interventions. The different temporal horizons of such interventions, combined with the evolving conditions in the ecosystem only add to the complexity of achieving a sustainable balance.

These challenges require ecosystem governance to be adaptable, yielding a dynamic, evolving system. It must be agile enough to adapt to the continuous changes within the ecosystem, while providing a stable framework that upholds the collective vision and ethical standards. The governance of ecosystems is therefore not a destination, but a journey of constant negotiation, learning and adaptation.

Two Distinct Ways of Governance

Depending on the ecosystem's setting, governance can be broadly categorized into two distinct approaches: centralized and participative. Each method offers unique advantages and challenges, shaping the ecosystem's ability to align short- and long-term interests effectively.

Centralized Governance
Centralized governance is characterized by a single leading entity that oversees and directs the activities within the ecosystem. Often, this happens as

a result of one organization evolving into an ecosystem, while providing the company's own backbone for cross-enterprise collaboration with partners and suppliers. The centralized approach often results in a minority of stakeholders dominating the governance processes and decisions. This is often tied to the financing mechanisms of the governing body — when it is dependent on the financial contributions of big stakeholders to finance governance operations. The financial contributions then gain influence over the bargaining power of stakeholders within the governing body. This usually leads to the wealthiest participant setting strategic directions, establishing rules and possibly securing unfair advantages over other stakeholders in the ecosystem.

The centralized governance model can be set up relatively quickly, and is effective in scenarios where rapid growth is necessary and close control over the ecosystem is essential. It provides a clear, unified direction and can streamline operations, making it easier to implement cohesive strategies, establish compliance and maintain control over the ecosystem's resources. The majority of business ecosystems are formed according to this model.[130]

However, centralized governance also has its drawbacks. It can stifle innovation and creativity, as the dominant organization's decisions may not always reflect the diverse perspectives and expertise within the ecosystem. Moreover, it can create dependency, where smaller participants rely heavily on the leading entity, potentially limiting their growth and autonomy.

Participative Governance

Participative governance, on the other hand, emphasizes inclusivity and shared decision-making. This construct often emerges in contexts with a wide range of stakeholders with very diverse interests, and when all stakeholders are similarly important for the ecosystem, as in urban communities, open-source initiatives or innovation clusters.

In this model, various stakeholders, including companies, communities, public administration and individuals, have a voice in governance. Responsibilities for each governance area are transparently distributed throughout the ecosystem according to the principle of subsidiarity, and these responsibilities can be periodically reorganized, redistributed and adjusted to keep governance itself aligned with the environmental dynamic. Decision-making is largely decentralized, with a focus on collaboration and consensus-building, or consent if consensus cannot be achieved in a reasonable amount of time. These mechanisms cultivate an environment of trust and cooperation, encouraging innovation and allowing the ecosystem to take advantage of a wide range of ideas and solutions. To protect itself against unfair influence, participative governance establishes several counter-mechanisms, such as financing governance operations independently from sponsoring members, periodical rotation of influential positions, voting procedures and sanctioning for unfair practices.

The participative model excels in adapting to complex and dynamic environments. It ensures that governance can establish a framework for the operations within the ecosystem that represents a balance of interests of all participants and affected parties. This enhances the ecosystem's adaptability and ability to innovate. However, this approach can also present challenges. It may lead to slower decision-making due to the need for consensus-building and negotiation. Additionally, maintaining coherence and direction is more difficult when multiple stakeholders have a say in governance.

Effective ecosystem governance often requires balancing elements of both centralized and participative approaches. Centralized structures can provide the necessary continuity and stability, while participative elements bring inclusivity and adaptability. By integrating these models, ecosystems can harness the strengths of both, aligning short- and long-term interests. Understanding and implementing an appropriate governance model is a necessity for the success of business ecosystems.

Barcelona's Smart City Ecosystem

Barcelona's Smart City initiative exemplifies how an ecosystemic approach can transform urban living by integrating technology, sustainability and community engagement. The Spanish metropolis of 1.6 million inhabitants exemplifies a successful approach to smart city development, serving as a valuable case study for understanding effective ecosystem governance in urban settings. The initiative is centred around a strong purpose of improving the quality of life for residents and boosting economic progress.[131] Barcelona has successfully integrated a range of advanced technologies into its urban infrastructure, including IoT devices, big data analytics and smart sensors across various sectors, including energy, waste management and transportation. Its Sentilo platform, an open-source IoT sensor network, enables the collection and analysis of real-time data on environmental parameters such as noise levels and air quality.[132] This allows the city to take immediate action for complex challenges like traffic management, by temporarily diverting vehicles from heavily affected areas or even completely redesigning these areas.

Barcelona places a strong emphasis on citizen participation and has established digital platforms and mobile apps to better involve residents in decision-making processes. This approach helps align public services with the needs of the community. Projects like the Barcelona City OS provide an open data infrastructure that allows for efficient resource distribution and new data-driven services tailored to citizens' needs.[133] Central to this is technological sovereignty, which democratizes the governance of data and technology infrastructure. The city's open data policy invites stakeholders, from local residents to global researchers, to innovate and contribute to its growth. This approach enhances transparency and accountability while confronting privacy and security challenges through stringent measures that adhere to privacy-by-design principles.[132, 134]

Barcelona's emphasis on e-government, powered by open-source technologies, streamlines and enhances public services. This champions technological sovereignty and avoids over-reliance on proprietary systems, fostering knowledge sharing and collective problem-solving. The approach involves user-centred design and agile methodologies, which provide flexibility and accelerate service development and delivery. It also implements open public procurement practices, making it easier for a broader range of vendors to participate, increasing transparency in awarding contracts, and ensuring that solutions adhere to open standards — ultimately establishing a more inclusive and innovation-friendly procurement environment.[131, 133]

Barcelona's Smart City projects have significantly boosted economic growth and innovation. The city has become a hub for startups and tech companies, attracting substantial investment and generating many job opportunities, as in the 22@Barcelona innovation district, which provides a dedicated space for research and development.[135, 136] Public-private partnerships have been important in this ecosystem, with collaborations involving companies like Cisco, Schneider and Philips contributing to the city's technological infrastructure.[132]

All initiatives are seamlessly integrated into the broader urban planning framework. The city's approach includes the development of smart districts and the incorporation of sustainable practices into urban regeneration projects.[137] This integration helps ensure that urban growth and environmental sustainability are optimally supported by technological advancements.[134, 138]

The city's ecosystem governance model emphasizes collaboration among various stakeholders, including government agencies, private companies, research institutions and citizens.[139] With this multi-stakeholder approach, all parties are effectively aligned and working toward shared objectives. Key aspects of the ecosystem governance are as follows:

- Collaborative frameworks bring together public and private entities, facilitating the sharing of resources and expertise necessary for implementing complex smart city projects.[133]

- Regulatory frameworks support innovation and the adoption of new technologies, encouraging experimentation and accelerating the deployment of smart solutions that contribute to the overall purpose.[132]

- Data accessibility to the public promotes transparency, stimulates innovation, and empowers residents to contribute to urban development.[135, 140]

- Mechanisms for continuous feedback and improvement help ensure that single initiatives remain aligned with the purpose, and stay relevant and effective.[134]

The Barcelona example clearly demonstrates that success of ecosystems relies on the continuous alignment of individual initiatives and governance of the ecosystem with overarching values and a clear shared purpose. This gives meaning to each and every effort that is taken. It also demonstrates how the purposeful adoption of advanced technologies enables effective governance for creating frameworks that support innovation, transparency and citizen engagement.

The role of the Digital Backbone in Ecosystems

Similar to its role in antifragile organizations (see Section 3.8), the digital backbone facilitates and enables a multitude of different transactions in ecosystems. In doing so, it establishes clear paths of traceability, and helps ensure that important standards of creating, delivering, capturing and sharing of value are met. As such, the digital backbone supports various functions essential for ecosystem operations and governance.

Constituting Role

The digital backbone forms the foundation upon which ecosystems are built, integrating diverse components into a cohesive system. It establishes seamless connectivity and interoperability across different entities, enabling them to function as a unified whole. This integration is vital for the automation of governance tasks, where routine administrative and regulatory functions can be efficiently managed through sophisticated algorithms and AI, reducing human intervention and minimizing errors.

Compliance Role

In the realm of compliance, the digital backbone is indispensable for establishing and ensuring transaction standards. It enforces protocols and regulations uniformly across the ecosystem, so that all participants adhere to predefined norms. This standardization is essential for maintaining the integrity and reliability of transactions, which is further bolstered by the transparency and traceability features inherent in the digital backbone. Every transaction can be recorded and audited in real time, providing a clear and indisputable trail that enhances accountability. This automation of documentation tasks relieves the governing body of much of the bureaucracy associated with compliance management.

Transparency of Governance

The digital backbone significantly enhances the transparency of governance by making information accessible and verifiable. This transparency is essential for ensuring that governance decisions are perceived as fair and just by all stakeholders. The ability to audit and review decisions in an open manner helps build trust and confidence among participants, ensuring that the governance framework is respected and adhered to.

Facilitating Participation

The digital backbone can facilitate processes essential for participative governance, such as the provision of multi-sided feedback, open discussion and voting channels, as exemplified in concepts like *liquid democracy*, where everyone can have a say on all policy proposals. In this role, the digital backbone enables governance decisions to be directly influenced by affected parties, ideally transforming the governance system into an inclusive, dynamic and balanced representation of stakeholders and their interests.

Conclusion

Progressing to ecosystems represents a logical evolutionary step for antifragile organizations. These organizations excel by swiftly aligning internal operations with external market needs, but transitioning into an open business ecosystem unlocks even greater potential. In this context, ecosystem governance is essential to help ensure the effective management of intricate relationships and co-dependencies. It requires a dynamic and adaptive approach to the balancing of a multitude of different, evolving interests of different stakeholder groups. Successful governance strikes a dynamic balance between short- and long-term needs, providing a stable yet adaptable framework that supports continuous growth and innovation.

In summary, the evolution from antifragile organizations to thriving ecosystems marks a profound shift that requires managers and leaders to look far beyond their own immediate agendas.

3.11

Reflection

Reflect on these questions about how your organization can integrate the capabilities discussed throughout this chapter to become more adaptable, dynamic and customer centric.

- How effectively does your organization gather and utilize customer feedback? What improvements can be made to better understand and meet customer needs?

- How easy is it for any employee to bring in a new idea and pursue it? What systems or processes support this?

- Identify specific operational processes that are less adaptable. What steps could be taken to enhance their flexibility and responsiveness?

- How flexible are your organizational structures in supporting newly emerging business needs?

- How mature is your digital backbone in supporting highly adaptable processes, organizational structures and governance frameworks?

- How flexible is your governance framework? How does it promote accountability?

- Which capabilities does your organization need to develop to be able to participate in business ecosystems?

Chapter 4

Building Antifragile Organizations

Agility, flexibility and adaptability emerge from well-shaped strategic pathways.

"Never stop learning because life never stops teaching."

– **Buddha**

As we have discussed, an antifragile approach offers a valuable framework for developing organizational capabilities that can adapt and evolve in response to the dynamic external environment. Looking at the previous chapters, one might be overwhelmed by the sheer amount of change that is necessary to build such an organization, and the complexity of leading such a task.

It requires a radical shift from closed, vertically-integrated models to open, ecosystem-based collaboration. Despite its radical ambitions and unconventional strategies, this evolution is still a gradual process, with organizations learning more during each change they undergo, refining their next steps, continuously improving and adapting.

In this chapter, we will delve into the practical strategies and approaches that have proven successful in building antifragile organizations. Drawing upon hands-on experiences and real-world examples, we will provide insights and guidance for those seeking to transform their organizations and create lasting success in an unpredictable world.

4.1

Build, Change or Transform?

Building an antifragile organization is a challenging task. The operational and functional characteristics of such companies, as discussed in Chapter 3, are fundamentally contrary to the conventional norms observed in most businesses. Antifragile organizations follow different principles and a different logic. Incrementally changing established organizations, that have been built according to different principles and with a radically different logic in mind, will inevitably cause big problems and organizational pain. This will occur to such an extent that it risks large groups of stakeholders abandoning ship or, more likely, the whole effort disintegrating in a clash of new organizational elements versus 'the incumbents.'

Therefore, building an antifragile organization from scratch may seem to be the easiest way. It helps ensure that all systems and processes are designed with antifragility in mind from the outset, makes it possible to onboard only those people attracted by the new organizational system, and avoids the additional painful efforts of redirecting and changing a well-established organization. However, this approach is fraught with challenges and not without risk. There will be a high degree of initial uncertainty, significant resource requirements, the difficulty of building a culture from scratch, and the need to establish a market presence from the ground up. Moreover, whatever organization results from this startup phase, it still needs to prove that it has developed the required adaptive capabilities for the long run ahead. Are these organizational capabilities sufficiently strong for the coming challenges, especially when the organization starts settling into favourable market niches?

Let's be clear here: Succeeding one time with adaptation efforts is not enough to prove that an organization is antifragile. One-time adaptation may solve an immediate challenge, but it does not necessarily prepare the organization for future, unforeseen disruptions. An antifragile organization must be capable of learning, evolving and improving continuously to handle new and emerging challenges. Only when it has repeatedly demonstrated its adaptiveness can we assume that it has developed the antifragile capabilities of evolving in synchronicity with its environment and whatever unforeseen situations arise.

When bootstrapping organizations for specific environments is not the most viable solution, and incrementally changing established ones is too difficult, what else can be done to build antifragile organizations?

We believe there is a third way that combines the strong points of both approaches and minimizes the downsides. We call it *antifragile transformation*. In the next section, we take a closer look at two real-world examples and the lessons they teach.

4.2

Antifragile Transformation

Before jumping into transformational activities, some pre-considerations and groundwork are required. Organizations need to first achieve clarity about the full extent of their intended transformation and what it means for them. Evolving into an antifragile organization in general means that:

- Value can be created, delivered and captured in new ways.

- Delivery on new customer expectations can be done at a speed similar to their emergence.

- Individual operations can connect to their customers in new ways.

- Work and people can be organized in new ways.

- All these new, formerly unthinkable ways of operation will continue to change and evolve.

- This transformation will be led by a shared purpose.

- The new modes of operation will be aligned through largely decentralized governance mechanisms of direction-setting and organizational learning.

When embarking on this journey, organizations need to crystallize their thinking on the goals of transformation, and receive adamant commitment among all relevant stakeholders. This is the only useful guiding star, as all other intentions and plans will inevitably be subjected to uncertainty and change along the way.

To get a sense of what such a transformation might look like, Haier's RenDanHeYi management model provides an excellent example. The book *Reinventing Giants*,[13] discussed in Chapter 2, serves as a valuable resource for understanding the context, implementation and impact of this approach. Thanks to further analysis by Danah Zohar,[72] a pioneer in quantum leadership and organizational transformation, and Yang-feng Cao,[75] a professor and strategic consultant who has collaborated with Haier for over a decade, one can follow Haier's journey in great detail. We will look at aspects of its transformation below, with a focus on how to successfully kickstart major strategic moves.

Haier's Transformation into a Business Ecosystem

Haier has gone through a remarkable transformation over the decades. This evolution has transitioned the company from a conventional organizational structure to an antifragile ecosystem, with an unwavering focus on delivering exceptional customer experiences.

In 2004, after years of successfully implementing an efficient management system, Haier operated like most of its Western counterparts, with a hierarchical structure and centralized decision-making processes. Long-time CEO Zhang Ruimin felt that this achievement was not sufficient, as there were still many *invisible walls* hampering the organization from effectively and rapidly meeting customer needs. The urgency to transform was high because Zhang recognized that in a rapidly changing global market, Haier needed to become more responsive to customer needs and more innovative in its operations. He believed that the traditional hierarchical structure stifled employee initiative and hindered the company's ability to adapt quickly to market changes.[13]

This led to the development of the **RenDanHeYi** model in 2005, which aimed to empower employees, decentralize decision-making, closely align individual and organizational goals to better meet the demands of the market, and ignite a more entrepreneurial spirit within the company. It began as a pilot program in one of the company's business units. The results allowed Haier to refine and adapt the model based on practical insights and real-world challenges. The success of this pilot implementation provided the confidence and framework necessary to apply it more broadly, and by 2007 Haier was expanding the approach throughout its organization. It took about seven years, with significant milestones reached by 2012, to fully integrate the RenDanHeYi model across the entire company.[13, 72]

This phase was characterized by the dismantling of traditional hierarchical structures, replaced with self-organized teams that operated with high autonomy. These teams were empowered to make decisions and take actions that directly impacted customer satisfaction and business outcomes. The decentralization allowed for increased agility and innovation, as decisions were made closer to the customer and market needs. The company began to function like a marketplace where internal capabilities could be easily integrated into the value stream. This new business system gave employees strong opportunities and incentives to develop their entrepreneurial skills.[26]

During this phase, Haier started building the foundations for a platform-based, networked enterprise. More than 2,000 business processes were reengineered, creating a more cohesive and efficient operational framework where information and resources move seamlessly across teams, reducing bottlenecks and enhancing the overall responsiveness to market demands. Haier implemented a global IT integration platform to support end-to-end business processes, from order acquisition through delivery. This digital backbone included visual data analysis tools and systems to support cross-border operations, ensuring that local adaptations could be made in accordance with regional laws and market conditions. Establishing new organizational capabilities together with the digital backbone was a prerequisite for Haier's further transformation.[13, 72, 141]

By 2012, after learning from several pilots, Haier was ready to advance to the '**Networking Strategy Stage**' of its RenDanHeYi model.

The interconnected platform could now enhance collaboration, resource sharing and customer-centric value creation across micro-enterprises, within the company and with external partners. The transformation focus shifted to creating an open platform where micro-enterprises could leverage external resources and capabilities to further boost innovation and responsiveness. This removed the bottleneck of resource scarcity, allowing flexible scaling of business operations. Many contributors became self-employed or part-time, blending seamlessly into the Haier ecosystem. During this transformation phase, the company seamlessly integrated its innovation ecosystem HOPE (detailed in Section 3.3), into business operations. This platform provided extensive support to entrepreneurs, drawing on the expertise of thousands of researchers and institutions worldwide. By leveraging the HOPE platform, Haier could interact deeply with customers, understanding their needs and rapidly acting on their feedback, especially during early stages of product development. The platform enabled micro-enterprises to collaborate internationally with thousands of academic researchers, freelancers and innovators. As a result, Haier significantly reduced the time to market for new products, by up to 70%.[75, 142]

Overall, the transformation into a co-creation platform allowed employees to act as entrepreneurs, managing their own micro-enterprises while benefiting from the strong network of internal and external partners and services.[13, 72, 143]

By 2019, Haier entered its '**Ecosystem Brand Strategy Stage**,' a stage focused on aligning the micro-enterprises into Ecosystem Micro-Communities (EMC) with a shared purpose. This alignment was meant to cultivate a deeper sense of collaboration and coherence among the various units, enabling them to work toward broader customer scenarios more effectively. This evolution also marks the beginning of ecosystem-centric strategies, where Haier started to build a comprehensive network of interconnected services and products around customer scenarios, such as the *Internet of Food*. The goal is to create a seamless, integrated experience for customers, where the ecosystem is able to anticipate and respond to their needs proactively.[32, 35]

With each new stage, Haier unlocked new capabilities and was able to implement more advanced strategies, clearly demonstrating the qualities of an antifragile organization. Its impressive financial track record and performance underline the effectiveness and adaptiveness of Haier's organizational system (see Section 2.4).

Haier's evolution provides us with two important lessons. First, an antifragile transformation is a journey into the unknown, and can take a very long time. Second, transformation activities require an uninterrupted, continuous force driving them forward during this whole time, especially when the going gets tough. Having a powerful and committed CEO like Zhang Ruimin at the helm for many decades is a rare occurrence, and possibly one of the reasons large-scale organizational transformation is so uncommon. Most organizations simply lack this stable leadership or cannot sustain such a sweeping reinvention over the long haul. We will look at another successful transformation below that confirms the importance of this organizational grit.

The Transformation of Klöckner & Co SE

Klöckner & Co SE, one of the world's largest steel distributors, took a distinctly different path than Haier's in its transformation. While both aimed to become adaptable, digital-first enterprises, their strategies and transformation speeds differed significantly.

Founded in 1906 in Duisburg, Germany, Klöckner has a long history of supplying steel and metal products to various industries. By the early 2010s, the company faced increasing pressure from global competition, fluctuating demand, and the need for more efficient and customer-centric operations. Traditional business models and processes were no longer sufficient to sustain growth and profitability.

Under the leadership of CEO Gisbert Rühl, Klöckner recognized that merely optimizing existing processes was not enough. The company needed to fundamentally rethink its business model if it was to remain competitive. This realization led to the development of its *Klöckner & Co 2022* strategy, aimed at transforming the company into a leading digital platform in the steel and metals industry.

A key opportunity was to address the fragmented, opaque nature of the market, providing a more streamlined, transparent, personalized experience for customers. Rühl envisioned Klöckner as 'the Amazon of the steel trade,' using digital platforms to disrupt the traditionally resistant materials market.[144]

Central to this transformation was the development of the Kloeckner.i organizational entity, based in Berlin, in 2014. This was a separate legal entity that allowed for rapid development and scaling of solutions, such as an online marketplace, order management systems and data analytics capabilities. Born digital, Kloeckner.i could operate without the restrictions of the core business, quickly attracting innovative, entrepreneurial employees from the creative, digital business environment in Berlin. By 2017, Kloeckner.i had already started showing significant results, contributing to the company's overall efficiency and cost reduction efforts. The platform became open for third-party distributors that offered complementary products, further enhancing its value-add for customers. The rapid integration of digital solutions into Klöckner's core operations and the focus on digital sales channels led to substantial financial gains within a few years.[145, 146]

Kloeckner.i exemplified proof of concept for the digital platform business, and became the nucleus of a new organization that acted faster and was more adaptive than the incumbent business. A key strategic move of Rühl's was to, slowly but surely, moving Kloeckner.i and the legacy organization into more and more collaboration and co-creation projects. Any employee who wanted to acquire new digital skills had free access to online education and training, and could pursue this during regular working hours. Moreover, any employee of the old-line business could self-apply to temporarily join Kloeckner.i, for first-hand experience in the different way of operations in their Berlin office. This proved to be an invaluable move, as these employees were immersed in the logic of the new organizational system and could see how and why it worked so well. They could also develop the skills required for this organizational system much faster than in the other parts of the company that were not reliant on these skills in the way Kloeckner.i was. And, they made friends with their new colleagues in Berlin, which proved to be vital once they returned to their home office. These personal relationships with Kloeckner.i, based on trust and mutual respect, were essential for cross-collaboration and innovation efforts in all of the company's operations.

But Rühl had in mind even more than that. By making the new platform indispensable for future business operations across the company, he saw to it that the innovative nucleus Kloeckner.i could grow and expand inside Klöckner without having to fight its way through. Instead, it was a process of assimilation: The incumbent systems and processes gradually transitioned to a new logic. They still retained sufficient freedom to adapt new practices to their own context, and at a manageable pace, thus avoiding major pitfalls that could easily lead to frustration and resistance. The skillfully managed integration compelled the incumbent organization to incrementally shift more business to the new enterprise platform, and acquire the necessary new ways of operation and required digital skills, along the way.

In addition, the new platform allowed Klöckner to enhance its customer-centricity. The company introduced personalized services and flexible delivery options to meet a wide range of customer needs. For example, various customers used different designations for the same steel grade and different units of measurement. They also had individual preferences regarding procurement and invoicing channels, ranging from telephone conversations, voice or fax messages to digital procurement platforms. In essence, each customer had its own unique language and protocols for interaction. The digital platform Kloeckner.i had to mirror this variety, providing each customer and supplier with customized ways of interaction at the front-end, while reliably performing standardized platform transactions in the background. The transparency and ease of access significantly improved the customer experience in an otherwise opaque market.

Understanding the importance of collaboration in the digital age, Rühl went on to form strategic partnerships with technology providers, startups and industry peers to co-develop novel solutions. This ecosystem enhanced Klöckner's ability to innovate and respond to market changes swiftly. It led to Klöckner's further expansion of its platform business through its open industry platform XOM Materials in 2018. This provides an open marketplace for suppliers and buyers of all kinds of products in the materials industry, not only steel products. Unlike Kloeckner.i, which was developed as an internal innovation hub, XOM Materials operates independently of Klöckner, jointly governed by its co-creation partners, and aiming to revolutionize the broader sector by providing a transparent and efficient procurement solution.[146]

The transformation of Klöckner, much like Haier's, reflects the significant shifts organizations must undergo: Old norms and structures dissolve, and new ways of operating must take their place.

WHY: The Driving Force Behind Transformation

A well-defined purpose provides coherence and unity amid the complexities and uncertainties of this journey, shaping and sustaining the transformational efforts. In the case of Haier, it was the CEO's idea of organizing value chains around customer needs to become a truly customer-oriented organization. Similarly, Klöckner's transformation was driven by the need to reinvent its business model to remain competitive in a rapidly changing market. The company's CEO recognized the importance of digital innovation and customer-centricity, which became the cornerstone of Klöckner's transformation.

Both examples demonstrate how a visionary purpose acts as the guiding force during the transformation, providing clear direction amid all the ensuing complexity, uncertainty and inevitable setbacks. Purpose aligns individual efforts with the overall goals of the transformation. When employees understand the purpose, they are more motivated and engaged. They can contribute to the transformation with a sense of ownership, sharing their insights and additional voluntary efforts. A clear purpose helps to identify and evaluate new options and make consistent choices. It reduces ambiguity and provides a reference point for navigating challenges and opportunities.

The clarity of *why* enabled both companies to adapt dynamically, changing and refining specific transformation activities, but always staying true to their core mission.

Preparing for a Journey
into the Unknown

After having clarity about why, the next question is *how* to move forward. As we have seen with Haier and Klöckner, in hindsight both organizations took distinct evolutionary steps. After each step, they took inventory of their newly acquired capabilities, and progressed into more challenging territory only when sure that these enabling capabilities were firmly embedded in their organizational culture and routines. All this took time — especially the first steps, when old ways of operating still dominated, and the replacements yet had to prove their effectiveness. At that time, there was no way of knowing how each new idea would work out in the end. The companies simply had to explore different options and learn fast, abandoning ill-fitting approaches and carefully considering ideas with more growth potential.

Both examples highlight that while the transformation might be similar, the execution is always unique. Factors such as existing organizational structure, market conditions and technological capabilities all influence the specific approach and pace of transformation. For effective transformation, organizations need to take some pre-considerations into account to achieve clarity about the following:

- **Purpose-driven alignment**: All actions need to support the purpose and overarching transformation goals, creating synergistic effects within the organization. As discussed before, this alignment drives coherence and unity in achieving the desired outcomes.

- **Outside-in approach**: New customer needs are a natural guiding force, presenting rich opportunities for adaptation and innovation. Customer benefit is a reliable yardstick to assess the relevance and value of all transformation activities. They need to be clearly linked to it.

- **Learning journey**: Antifragility is not a one-time event, but an ongoing evolution. The organization needs to establish a highly effective system to effectively acquire, integrate and grow new capabilities, using transformation activities as pacesetters for greater adaptivity and faster learning cycles.

- **Speed of action**: Individual transformation activities need to be of short duration and contribute to overall momentum, especially in a highly dynamic environment. Otherwise, progress and value cannot be determined, and the risk of losing traction and getting off track is significant, possibly derailing important strategic efforts.

- **Tailored strategy**: Successful organizational transformation necessitates a tailored approach that considers the organization's current status, its distinctive dynamics within its environment and the state it is heading toward. All of this determines where the *Learning Journey* can start, which options are likely to lead in the desired direction, and how to activate the organization to contribute to the transformation activities.

Since each organization has its own unique configuration of governance, business processes, structures and culture, successful transformation necessitates a tailored approach. What works in one context may not translate effectively to another. Specific challenges or opportunities encountered along the way can have a real impact on the path of transformation. And, these external factors are largely outside of the control of the organization itself, especially in an environment of rapid technological change, shifting market dynamics and evolving customer needs. The following chapter covers all of these requirements in a powerful, yet simple-to-understand, systemic approach.

4.3

The Learning Journey

At the heart of the transformation journey lies an iterative cycle of learning and adaptation (Figure 4.1). The findings, challenges and practices of specific teams, especially those dealing with new customer needs, can offer a magnified view into possibly organization-wide shortcomings, learning and adaptation potential. Whenever teams identify improvement opportunities or restrictions in structures, processes and regulations they cannot handle alone, the organization can quickly step in and strategize to formulate and pilot possible solutions, derive lessons learnt and rapidly incorporate better, more flexible practices in its operations. This flexible approach guarantees that the organization stays responsive to emerging challenges while moving ahead in the desired overall direction.

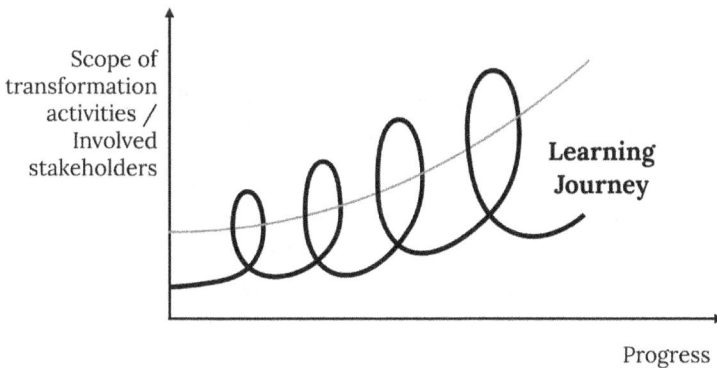

Figure 4.1
The Learning Journey

At the core of this dynamic approach is the concept of initiating change through small, targeted efforts. These pilot teams become catalysts for innovation, rapidly identifying and helping dismantle barriers that hinder appropriate organizational response to market, customer and stakeholder demands. As these insights emerge, the *Joint Action Model,* which we will discuss in Section 4.4, provides a systematic framework for enacting changes across the organization, so agility and adaptability are woven into the fabric of business operations. The steps in the *Learning Journey* unfold as follows:

- **Start with pilot teams**: Transformation begins with a few selected teams, each focusing on critical areas where responsiveness to new needs, external and internal, can be enhanced.

- **Rapid learning and adapting**: The pilot team's mission is to quickly try out new solutions, identify obstacles in their way and spotlight possible paths for organizational improvement. The teams progress by closely observing and analysing organizational responses to actions that were initiated in the search for new solutions.

- **Apply and scale**: Solutions can manifest in new practices on team level, in new processes, or at the level of the whole organization. Valuable solutions, practices or strategies identified by pilot teams can be refined and hardened on a larger scale, and ultimately made available organization-wide. Each application needs to be complemented with a feedback loop for further refinement and adaptation.

- **Disseminate organizational learning**: The new solutions are widely communicated, and their adoption facilitated throughout the organization. This ensures that they reach all relevant areas and that feedback contributes to their enhancement, or their abandonment when circumstances change or better solutions emerge. Thus, organizational feedback loops facilitate organizational learning and unlearning.

By embedding this cycle of iterative adaptation within the organization, transformation becomes an ongoing journey of learning, evolution and enhancement. This strategic approach helps the organization remain dynamic, capable of swift and substantial transformation, making learning a core competency for sustained success. The strength of the *Learning Journey* lies in its scalability. Organizations can expand the scope of their transformation efforts as they iterate, learn and adapt. This is an organic growth, driven by real insights and tangible results. As growth occurs, new challenges arise. However, the *Learning Journey's* inherent ability to recalibrate, adapt and forge ahead helps ensure that transformation can be proactive and not merely reactive. Through rapid cycles of iterative learning and the promotion of emergent practices, organizations can effectively transform collaboration systems and culture. This makes room for an environment that celebrates experimentation, sees risks as opportunities, and instills innovation and learning into the very essence of the organization.

Importantly, this approach empowers organizations to chart their own course in the transformation process, allowing them to determine where to begin and at what pace to proceed. It recognizes the unique characteristics and readiness of each organization, ensuring that the path of transformation is both effective and sustainable, aligned with an organization's unique context and goals.

The *Learning Journey* never ends. Antifragile organizations either establish rapid organizational learning and effective adaptation as a permanent habit — learning to deal with the inherent variety and non-stable nature of organizational practices and solutions — or they will face an inevitable decline.

Turning Constraints into Enablers

The *Learning Journey* is particularly effective when addressing the constraints hindering organizational progress. Every organization has its set of invisible chains: constraints that hinder growth, stifle innovation and impede change. However, by adopting the iterative nature and emphasis on emergent practices of the *Learning Journey*, these impediments can be transformed into enablers. This helps in quickly identifying constraints and taking decisive actions to overcome them.

Removing such roadblocks is not rocket science. The *Theory of Constraints* management methodology was developed to remove capacity bottlenecks in production lines. It views any manageable system as being limited in achieving its goals by a small number of constraints. It focuses on identifying and addressing the most critical limiting factor that stands in the way of achieving an objective, typically a higher throughput. The intention is to look at the system as a whole rather than optimizing individual components without considering their impact on the entire system.[147]

Antifragile organizations take this idea to a higher level: Here, constraints are seen as not just capacity bottlenecks, but limitations on the organization's ability to act in different ways. By removing these constraints, an antifragile organization seeks to increase its degrees of freedom. This broader approach emphasizes removal of constraints not just as a means of increasing efficiency, but as a fundamental strategy for unlocking new potential and increasing adaptability. It encourages organizations to rethink and redesign their structures, processes, governance and culture as critical enablers of new capabilities.

In summary, the *Learning Journey* bridges intention and realization in the transformation. Its role is critical in ensuring that the transformation is a calculated journey, not a blind leap. By embedding learning and building new capabilities at its core, it helps make organizations ready for the future, poised to thrive in an ever-changing business landscape. As they advance on their *Learning Journey*, it is essential to gain a better understanding of organizational constraints and their systemic interactions. While the iterative approach provides a dynamic route, a thorough framework is necessary to navigate the intricate web of interconnected action fields that propel organizational change. This is where the *Joint Action Model* comes in to help.

4.4

The Joint Action Model

As we have said, antifragility cannot be achieved through a one-size-fits-all approach. The path to success is as varied as the organizations that pursue it. Each organization's journey hinges on how effectively it addresses various *action fields* — distinct but interconnected domains of organizational activity (e.g., strategy, culture, processes or technology) — that collectively influence its capacity to adapt, innovate and thrive. Each organization's path is characterized by its unique ability to eliminate internal barriers to change, regardless of whether they are structural, process, cultural or strategic. Interdependencies across organizational action fields present both a challenge and an opportunity. A change initiated in one field does not occur in isolation. Instead, it sets off a chain reaction that triggers further adjustments across the organization. This cascading effect uncovers new dependencies, reveals hidden barriers and highlights fresh opportunities, all illustrating that the path toward hyperadaptation and antifragility is iterative and emergent.

The *Joint Action Model*, as shown in Figure 4.2, can serve as a strategic compass for organizations embarking on this complex transformation journey. It advocates for a comprehensive perspective that acknowledges the interconnectedness of major action fields. Moreover, it emphasizes that transformation is not a linear sequence of isolated changes, but a harmonized, synergy-driven endeavour. Every field of action has the potential to significantly impact others, creating a complex network of effects that can either strengthen or weaken the overall antifragility of the organization. It is critical to embrace the complexity of this interconnected system. By encouraging exploration, collaboration and learning, organizations recognize that every action contributes to the broader transformation.

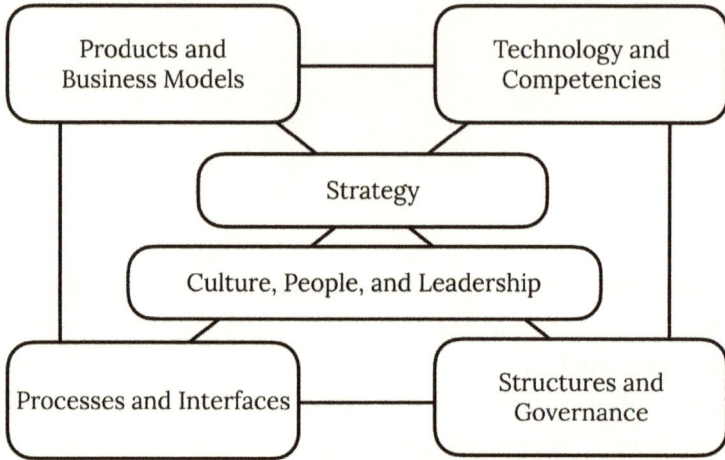

Figure 4.2
The Joint Action Model

With this overarching perspective in mind, we will further examine the unique action fields — their role in transformation, how each can cause constraints, how they can act as enablers of transformation, and how actions in one field can have ripple effects that impact others.

The Action Fields of Transformation

The fields of action build on the key elements of antifragile organizations discussed in Chapter 3. Therefore, we will focus here on the transformational aspects and constraints of each field, as well as the interdependencies between them. For working with this framework, we also provide a baseline questionnaire in the *Appendix* to address its six distinct fields.

Products and Business Models

The action field *Products and Business Models* is critical in shaping how an organization creates value for its customers and sustains its competitive edge. It involves developing innovative products and business models that evolve in close alignment with market needs and technological advancements.

Antifragile organizations maintain a relentless focus on delivering value for customers in their product development and business model strategies. To this end, they foster a highly flexible framework of value creation, together with a culture that embraces exploration and rapid learning. This allows all parts of the organization to quickly pivot and adapt to new market demands and opportunities (Sections 3.2 and 3.3).

Deficiencies in this action field constrain the responsiveness to market changes, reducing the value the organization can deliver to customers. Without this customer-centric innovation focus, the organization risks losing relevance, and consequently faces decline. A rigid process landscape and inflexible governance pathways exacerbate this constraint, hindering its ability to pivot or scale new initiatives effectively.

Strategy

The action field *Strategy* is a key driver to promote the continuous adaptation and matchmaking of resources and capabilities with the opportunities. It must fit both internal and external conditions, or it is sure to fail. Therefore, a top priority for any organization is designing a clear, concise and adjustable strategy that aligns with both internal capabilities and the external landscape.

In antifragile organizations, strategy is aligned with the organization's purpose and focuses on flexibility and responsiveness to changes in its environment, as discussed in Sections 3.1 and 3.2.

Deficiencies in strategy can constrain not only an organization's strategic progress but also its adaptability, organizational clarity and coherence. More specifically, unclear, contradictory or missing long-term vision and purpose create misalignments, making it difficult to adapt to changing market conditions and emerging opportunities in a sufficiently timely manner. Without frequent strategic process reviews and broad involvement of various organizational levels, the strategy can become stagnant and disconnected from operational realities. A poor Strategic Fit between the organization's capabilities and market demands leads to inefficiencies and missed opportunities. Tolerating actions that contradict the company's purpose can undermine strategic goals and transformation efforts. Siloed thinking and clinging to past successes impede strategic agility.

Culture, People and Leadership

Culture, People and Leadership brings together the critical people-centric factors that have major influence on an organization's ability to adapt to its environment. This action field sets the stage by giving teams the support and autonomy necessary to explore new ideas and innovate in an environment where trust, transparency and open communication are prioritized. Flat organizational structures with flexible resources, decentralized governance and transparent, inclusive decision-making practices contribute to and nurture this action field.

For antifragile organizations, this is the source of their adaptation power. It is here where they establish a remarkable balance of entrepreneurial autonomy and accountability, together with a thirst for innovation. Here, leadership is seen as a shared capability where everyone aligns their contributions toward shared goals, fostering a collaborative culture (Section 3.7).

Deficiencies in this action field can constrain an organization's ability to foster an innovative working environment. Rigid leadership models and poor communication practices stifle creativity and collaboration. An organizational culture that is risk-averse and lacks trust, accountability and openness leads to employee disengagement, resistance to change and lack of innovation. This ultimately prevents transformation initiatives from enduring beyond initial pilot projects.

Processes and Interfaces

The action field *Processes and Interfaces* largely determines the responsiveness and flexibility of operations regarding emerging opportunities and new stakeholder needs.

Antifragile organizations prioritize variety, speed and collaboration in their processes and interfaces. They systematically develop process competence and technological skills on all levels, carefully architecting standards that promote flexibility and efficiency of cross-collaboration efforts. By doing so, they are better equipped to respond quickly and effectively to new challenges and opportunities (Section 3.4).

Deficiencies in this action field limit operational efficiency and effectiveness. Rigid, hard-to-change processes create bottlenecks, slowing the implementation of innovative ideas. They severely limit an organization's ability to respond appropriately and rapidly to unexpected events. This rigidity limits strategic flexibility, and hinders the speed of evolution and innovation, especially regarding new business models. Missing process competency at the executive level limits the transformation potential of an organization, as leaders may not fully understand or support the necessary changes in the process management framework.

Structures and Governance

The action field *Structures and Governance* addresses the overall framework of internal structures and the system of governance of an organization. It lays the groundwork for autonomy, flexibility and speed in all other action fields. This plays a pivotal role for agility and adaptability, as it determines how fast and effective an organization can recalibrate its operations and responsibilities in the face of new opportunities and threats.

Antifragile organizations allow structures to emerge in direct response to opportunities, quickly aligning teams and organizational capabilities around the challenge at hand. Their related governance frameworks perfectly balance autonomy and accountability. They provide strong incentives for customer-orientation and effective collaboration, while ensuring the fair sharing of risks and rewards among contributing teams. Transparent and decentralized governance lays the groundwork for antifragile transformation efforts (Sections 3.8 and 3.9).

Deficiencies in the action field *Structures and Governance* constrain a company's organizational adaptability. Siloed and deeply nested structures with an inward focus limit cross-functional collaboration and slow down decision-making processes. Hierarchical reporting lines and outdated governance models reduce the organization's ability to respond appropriately and quickly to new challenges. They are often unsuitable for guiding transformation efforts, which contributes to delaying, shying away from or preventing them from gaining momentum.

This field of action strongly determines the possible modes of operation of an organization in many other action fields. Change efforts here are particularly difficult, but when successful they can generate exceptionally strong and fast follow-up transformation actions in other fields.

Technology and Competencies

The action field *Technology and Competencies* encompasses the infrastructure and skills required to effectively leverage cutting-edge technology for both product innovation and enhanced operational efficiency and effectiveness. This includes the development, implementation and management of technologies that support aligning the organization's purpose, strategic goals and operational needs, enhancing its capabilities for sensing and acting on new challenges and opportunities.

Antifragile organizations use technology to continuously enhance their ability to sense and act on new challenges and opportunities. They focus on speed, flexibility and seamless workforce collaboration skills. By ensuring smooth information flow and dynamic coordination of efforts, technology supports better decision-making and improved project outcomes. It facilitates continuous learning and adaptation, keeping employees equipped with the latest skills and helping them easily connect with customers and outside expertise. Advanced technologies, such as data analytics and AI, help them better understand and serve marketplace needs and personalize experiences (Sections 3.5 and 3.6).

Deficiencies in this action field constrain an organization's ability to enhance its flexible value creation and collaboration capabilities. Outdated IT infrastructure and insufficient technology management skills significantly delay strengthening these abilities. Shortsighted strategies with insufficient budgets for tech and organizational innovation further hinder development. Information technology is a catalyst for enabling quick adaptation, seamless collaboration and proactive risk management. Without it, the organization cannot maintain the speed, flexibility and innovation required to thrive in a constantly changing environment.

Challenges and Overcoming Them

As preliminarily discussed in the description of each action field, they mutually influence each other, demonstrating a complex network of interdependencies. They are rooted in the natural evolution of these fields within an organization as it grows (Section 3.7). The characteristics of each are closely linked to the history of the organization and evolve in concert with the other fields of action. As the organization develops, the synergy between these fields becomes more pronounced, with improvements or deficiencies in one having a significant impact on the others. For example, advancements in technology and competencies can drive innovation in products and business models, while a strong strategic direction can align and enhance the effectiveness of processes and interfaces. Small innovations in one action field usually cause only limited effects on others, giving them sufficient time to adapt, if necessary. Deficiencies in one action field, on the other hand, can limit the degree of freedom in another, sometimes even forcing them to compensate for shortcomings. For instance, weak leadership skills of middle managers are often compensated for and hidden by extensive regulation and bureaucracy, creating additional challenges for transformation efforts.

A transformation, independent of where it starts, over time always affects all action fields, as the fine-tuned interplay needs to be recalibrated. The sequence is difficult to predict, because some action fields have direct dependencies, while being linked to others indirectly. In addition, some action fields are more responsive to interventions. They can be changed faster and in a more manageable way. Others require more time and elude directly managed change efforts. For example, a minor product facelift will affect solely the *Products and Business Models* field. It will not impact any others. It is a quick and manageable change, as this action field can respond quickly to market needs.

The action fields *Products and Business Models* and *Strategy* are closely linked to value creation, and are therefore usually the most adaptable. Starting a transformation in these action fields allows for an easy entry into it, because the organization can focus on a clear set of known challenges and well-manageable activities. This approach keeps initial transformation efforts on a clear track. It can quickly identify barriers to progress in other action fields that require additional adaptation activities. In this way, transformation activities slowly begin encompassing more action fields, until the organization has developed advanced capabilities that allow it to perform on a higher level. However, transforming an organization with this approach takes an unpredictable amount of time, as barriers keep popping up sequentially. It is not unlikely that transformation efforts will run into roadblocks, requiring changes in action fields that the organization is not ready to touch yet. Or, this can occur when the gap between existing and required capabilities is simply too big to be closed in time or seen as too risky or expensive.

Starting in the action fields *Products and Business Models* or *Strategy* may therefore enable a quick start and tangible results. Yet, it runs the risks of falling short, declaring success prematurely, and losing momentum and enthusiasm before making sufficient progress in more difficult but critically important action fields, such as *Structures and Governance* or *Culture, People and Leadership*. We will look at their role in transformation efforts shortly. But first, we need to briefly analyse the transformative potential of two other action fields, both of which require highly specialized knowledge and skills: *Processes and Interfaces* and *Technology and Competencies*.

The adaptation speed of the *Processes and Interfaces* and *Technology and Competencies* fields is usually moderate, because they naturally change at a slower pace. They typically adapt only after driven by the new needs of the more dynamic front-end action field *Products and Business Models*. Such adaptations can improve operational efficiency and expand the tech competence and product lines of the organization, but they often lack the urgency and aspiration needed to move beyond immediate market needs into uncharted territories. This might extend to a complete reimagining of how and for whom the organization should create value.

Therefore, the action field *Processes and Interfaces* has tremendous potential for transforming organizations, as discussed in Section 3.4. However, it is unlikely to be the starting point of a transformation. The risk of disrupting existing workflows and the potential for operational downtime makes managers in these areas more cautious. They are unlikely to implement changes that go beyond immediate business needs. The potential benefits of difficult changes, such as implementing a modular process management framework, might not be immediately apparent, and there is always a risk that such changes may not deliver the expected improvements. Unlike new products or market expansions, improvements in *Processes and Interfaces* usually do not receive much top management attention. Achievements are less visible and require a long period of highly focused collaboration efforts and special coordination skills. As a consequence, few organizations have leveraged the transformative potential of this action field, and none without strong interventions and continuous support by executive management.

The action field *Structures and Governance* adapts even more slowly due to its foundational role in establishing the framework within which the organization operates. Adaptations in this field are highly impactful, but also highly complex, as they affect decision-making processes, reporting lines and accountability mechanisms. Starting a transformation here therefore runs into issues similar to those we see in *Processes and Interfaces*. And so, it takes a leap of faith. On the positive side, only a few people, usually those leading an organization, are required to take it. All others will either fall in line or leave the company if outcomes develop unfavourably for them. Given sufficient power, any change — even a long-lasting and radical overhaul like that carried out by Haier (see Section 4.2) — is possible. And the rewards of starting in this action field can be enormous. As soon as a new governance framework is in place and embedded in the business processes, changes in all other action fields are much easier and quicker to implement. By forcing radically decentralized structures and a new system of governance into the organization, business processes quickly enable cross-team operations, powered by improved technology for seamless collaboration on shared data. Throughout such transformation, culture and leadership undergo significant change, advancing entrepreneurial behaviour in every part of the organization.

However, if not managed appropriately, or driven by flawed ideas, starting a transformation in *Structures and Governance* risks alienating the whole organization from its leadership, likely leading to its downfall. Starting here is therefore best done in combination with founding a new organization, as demonstrated by Klöckner (see Section 4.2). New business entities can be created with a radically different system of governance, and a fluid organizational structure, from the start. This greatly limits risks, as the new organization, with its radically new framework, can prove its worth without disturbing established value chains. If successful, it can then continue to grow in close, skillfully managed collaboration with older organizational entities. This collaboration prepares the legacy body for new ways of creating value, until it has acquired the skills required in the new framework, and ultimately become a part of it.

The action field *Culture, People and Leadership* usually adapts very slowly to changes, as it requires altering people's habits and deeply ingrained organizational behaviours, assumptions, values and beliefs. This takes time, sometimes generations. Organizations can change their cultural norms quickly only in the case of significant, severe events, such as the COVID-19 pandemic or a major corporate crisis. These events then force immediate and widespread shifts in this action field. Cultural adaptation underpins the success of all transformation efforts, as it requires creating an environment where innovation, collaboration and adaptability can thrive. This field evolves continuously and is reinforced by all changes and adaptations in the organization. Transforming it takes time, and persistent effort in all other action fields, since it can only be changed indirectly by creating new organizational learning experiences. That makes it one of the slowest, but most impactful, fields to influence. Once people have adopted and value a new culture, they will strive to preserve it.

And this is precisely the mechanism that can be used to speed up the rate of change in this action field. Individuals are much more adaptable than established groups. Groups already have their own culture and try to uphold it. They have to change their cultural norms and behaviour as a collective, and this takes time, as all members have to support and embrace the new culture. The slowest and fastest to adapt set the pace for the whole group. The larger the group, the slower cultural norms tend to change.

Conversely, individuals pick up new cultural norms much quicker when they are immersed in a group with a different culture. Immersion is the key factor: Block out the old norms, and people will pick up a new culture really quickly. This is driven by an inherent human need to be part of a social environment and belong to a group that provides support and protection. This behaviour is deeply ingrained in our DNA. Being part of a team with a different culture for a period of time allows an individual to immerse in and acclimate to a new setting. They experience the new culture firsthand and adopt new cultural norms much quicker than by merely hearing about them in a classroom or off a corporate campaign poster. After their immersive tour, they are much more likely to have adopted new perspectives and ways of working. They are apt to bring innovative practices and a new mindset back to their original organization, contributing to its push toward a new culture. Organizations can use this mechanism not only in leadership development programs, but also in innovation and knowledge transfer programs that are broadly accessible for large parts of the organization. The more people value and contribute to new cultural norms, the faster they become accepted. Organizational exchange programs can foster skill development and cross-functional knowledge transfer while effectively accelerating cultural change.

4.5

Conclusion

In this chapter, we have explored the framework necessary to cultivate antifragility within organizations. This requires a fundamental reevaluation and restructuring of conventional organizational norms — from leadership styles and operational models to employee empowerment and culture.

Building or transforming an organization into an antifragile one demands a willingness to embrace radical change, a powerful purpose, and an unwavering commitment to continuous learning and adaptation. The transformative paths exemplified by Haier and Klöckner show that while the journey toward antifragility can be daunting and fraught with challenges, it is also replete with opportunities for innovation, entrepreneurship and enduring success.

Each organization needs to find its own path, which can only be forged by moving forward with a determined yet open mind, learning and evolving together, taking pride and joy from every discovery along the way.

4.6

Reflection

As we conclude our exploration of how to build and grow antifragility in organizations, we invite you to reflect on your insights and apply them to your organization.

- What are key factors in your organization that could facilitate its first steps toward transformation?

- Which action fields would have the biggest impact on transformational efforts in the short term?

- Which ones limit the organization's long-term transformation potential?

- What aspects of governance and culture need to change to enable or accelerate transformation efforts?

- Which technologies could your organization adopt to accelerate learning cycles, and to effectively include all parts of the organization?

- How could the organization integrate the *Learning Journey* in its long-term strategy, and how could it be fostered in an inclusive manner?

Embracing Opportunity

"The future belongs to those who give the next generation reason for hope."

– Pierre Teilhard de Chardin

In our rapidly evolving world, marked by complexity and change, the imperative for organizations to swiftly adapt has never been more urgent. By embracing the principles of antifragility, organizations can overcome challenges and actually transform them into rich opportunities for human progress, responding to the need for a more sustainable and inclusive system of fair value creation.

Because of their enormous economic potential, large companies in particular have an obligation to act as stewards of their environment and the communities in which they operate. This responsibility goes beyond corporate social responsibility, embedding sustainability and ethical considerations at the core of their business strategies. By doing so, companies can see to it that their growth contributes positively to society and the wider environment, creating a virtuous cycle of value creation that benefits all stakeholders and the world around us.

The industrial age developed highly efficient organizations and social contracts that improved the wealth and well-being of societies. But this progress was largely built on the unsustainable economic practices of capitalism. No system can survive in the long term if it continues to drain the pool of its resources. Current economic systems create misguided incentives for growth, placing the needs of a few above those of all others, jeopardizing the natural environment, and limiting the development opportunities of large segments of society and future generations. There is nothing sustainable about this behaviour. It has only worked for so long because it has always been able to find new resources to drain, without adequately giving back in return. Our current economic systems have a long history of exploitation and oppression — from feudalism, colonialism, slavery, the suppression of workers' rights, oppression of women and child labour, to continuing environmental degradation.[148]

These exploitative practices are now at a crossroads. They are incapable of solving the complex challenges of our time. They are beginning to cast increasingly dark shadows over the economic outlook of many people, our natural environment and future generations. They deepen social inequalities, contribute to civil unrest and war, and jeopardize the long-term prospects of humanity. In its *Davos Manifesto 2020*, the World Economic Forum called on companies to adopt a new business ethic.[149] It was a clarion call for humanity to urgently develop new systems of shared, fair, inclusive and sustainable value creation that enhance our collective capacity to solve complex challenges.

Antifragile organizations, together with their ecosystems, can play an important role in this push toward more sustainable and inclusive systems of shared and fair value creation. Their fundamentally higher adaptability and innovative ways of creating value, and the inclusive nature of their open business ecosystems, can reshape economic frameworks and hopefully contribute to a more equitable distribution of wealth. This is essential for maintaining social stability, civil rights and freedom.

By embracing opportunity, antifragile organizations create a lot more than just economic value. They give us hope for the future.

Appendix

Joint Action Fields – Questionnaire

Products and Business Models

Innovative products and business models can help kickstart transformation, especially when the challenge at hand cannot be solved with established ways of working. Finding new ways to create value initiates a learning cycle that requires building the new skills and capabilities that characterize antifragile organizations. However, a lack of innovation in products and rigidity in business models can lead to obsolescence and a decline in market relevance. These are major obstacles in an organization's path to becoming antifragile, carrying the risk that organizational capabilities are not diversified and insufficiently adaptable to new market requirements. To assess the effectiveness of an organization's approach in this action field, consider the following:

- What promising market opportunities has the organization failed to capitalize on?
- How does its product development process encourage innovation and responsiveness?
- How easy is it for an employee to start exploring a new idea? How easy is it to gain entry to the innovation process?
- How responsive and adaptable are the current business models to market changes?
- What mechanisms are in place for continual assessment of new customer needs?

Strategy

A clear and well-designed strategy can enable significant transformation by providing a roadmap and allocating resources for innovation and adaptation. This creates an environment where quick responses to market changes are both possible and encouraged. At the same time, an outdated or rigid strategy can severely hinder an organization's ability to transform, trapping it in inefficient practices and preventing it from seizing new opportunities. In order to assess the effectiveness of a strategy, the analysis should consider:

- How frequently is the strategy reviewed and adapted, to keep it aligned with market and organizational changes?
- Does the strategy facilitate quick adaptation to market changes and disruptions?
- How effectively is innovation and risk-taking encouraged and endorsed in strategic planning?
- How well does the strategy integrate with other organizational aspects, such as technology, operations and culture?
- What measures are implemented to ensure the strategy's execution and ongoing enhancement?

Culture, People and Leadership

A strong and adaptive culture, coupled with effective leadership, can drive transformation by creating an environment where new ideas fall on fertile ground. This encourages employees to embrace change, explore new ways of creating value and collaboratively solve problems, propelling the organization forward. Conversely, a timid and risk-averse culture can significantly undermine transformation efforts. To evaluate how well culture, people and leadership enable transformation, consider the following baseline questions:

- To what extent does the organization promote open and transparent communication across all levels?
- How does it encourage and support innovation and risk-taking?
- In what ways does the organization provide continuous learning and development opportunities?
- How transparently and inclusively are decisions made?
- How compellingly do leaders communicate and embody the organization's vision and values?
- How does the organization respond to setbacks and challenges?

Processes and Interfaces

Effective process management, particularly the capacity to handle variety, is the key to transformation. Processes that can adapt and accommodate various workflows allow companies to promptly respond to market changes and emerging technologies. This enhances their agility and promotes innovation. Conversely, a lack of flexibility can significantly limit transformation potential. Inflexible, uniformly standardized processes do not support a variety of business approaches. This restricts the ability to adapt to new challenges and opportunities, ultimately limiting growth and adaptability and leading to stagnation. To evaluate how well your organization's processes and interfaces support the implementation of antifragile principles, consider the following:

- How do current processes facilitate or impede the exploration and support of new business opportunities?
- How effectively do interfaces between systems or departments facilitate seamless communication and collaboration across organizational functions?
- How capable are processes and interfaces of adapting quickly to changes in the organization's environment?
- How easy is it to contribute ideas and feedback regarding processes, interfaces and standards?
- How responsively and transparently does the organization deal with such ideas and feedback?

Structures and Governance

Flexible and dynamic structures and governance frameworks can greatly enhance an organization's ability to adapt and evolve. They enable swift decision-making and facilitate the flow of information, which is essential for promoting innovation and responsiveness to market trends. On the other hand, rigid structures and overly bureaucratic governance impede innovation and severely hinder transformation efforts. Closed hierarchies impede both decision-making and the exchange of information and ideas, resulting in missed opportunities and reduced market responsiveness. To initially assess the adaptability of an organization's structures and governance, consider these questions:

- How quickly and efficiently can the organization mobilize resources to take advantage of new market opportunities?
- What review cycles are in place for continually assessing and adapting the organizational structures and governance frameworks?
- What is considered responsible behaviour in the organization?
- How deeply are accountability and transparency embedded in the organizational culture?
- How are team goals being aligned with the overall purpose and strategic goals of the organization?
- What mechanisms are in place to assess the validity of decision-making?

Technology and Competencies

Technology is a catalyst for antifragile transformation, because it can radically change the way organizations operate by unleashing the vast skills and capabilities of networked value creation. Building a strong technological infrastructure, and skillfully using it, opens up new strategic pathways, especially for innovation, operational efficiency and adaptability. Alternatively, outdated technology and skills can block an organization's adaptability and transformation efforts. Without proper investment in technology and continuous skill development, organizations risk falling behind in a rapidly changing market. To initially assess this action field, consider the following:

- How does the organization facilitate seamless collaboration and information flow through technology?
- How does it use advanced technologies to better understand and meet customer needs?
- How does current technology contribute to creating shared situational awareness and inclusive decision-making?
- How does the organization support the development of tech skills and competencies among its workforce?
- How are new technologies evaluated and integrated to meet current and future needs of the organization?

Antifragile Patterns in the Case Studies

Bibliography

1. Kelly, W. (1970). "We Have Met the Enemy and He Is Us." Earth Day poster. Ohio State University Libraries. https://library.osu.edu/site/40stories/2020/01/05/we-have-met-the-enemy/.

2. Straub, R., & Kirby, J. (2020). "A Narrative for the Next Management." *Global Peter Drucker Forum*. https://www.druckerforum.org/blog/a-narrative-for-the-next-managementby-richard-straub-and-julia-kirby/.

3. Taleb, N. N. (2012). *Antifragile: Things that Gain from Disorder*. Penguin Books.

4. Drucker, P. F. (1969). *The Age of Discontinuity: Guidelines to Our Changing Society*. Harper & Row.

5. Schumpeter, J. A. (1950). *Capitalism, Socialism and Democracy*. Harper Collins.

6. Peltonen, T. (2018). *Towards Wise Management: Wisdom and Stupidity in Strategic Decision-Making*. Springer.

7. Johnson, J. & Gheorghe, A. V. (2013). "Antifragility Analysis and Measurement Framework for Systems of Systems." *International Journal of Disaster Risk Science*, 4, 159–168. https://doi.org/10.1007/s13753-013-0017-7.

8. Equihua, M., Aldama, M. E., Gershenson, C., López-Corona, O., Munguía, M., Pérez-Maqueo, O., & Ramírez-Carrillo, E. (2020). "Ecosystem Antifragility: Beyond Integrity and Resilience." *PeerJ, 8*, e8533. https://doi.org/10.7717/peerj.8533.

9. Moore, F. J. (1993). "Predators and Prey: A New Ecology of Competition." *Harvard Business Review*, 71(3), 75–86.

10. Adner, R. (2012). *The Wide Lens: A New Strategy for Innovation*. Penguin UK.

11. Power, B. (2014, August 7). "Make Your Organization Anti-Fragile." *Harvard Business Review*. https://hbr.org/2013/06/make-your-organization-anti-fr.

12. Stone, B. (2013). *The Everything Store: Jeff Bezos and the Age of Amazon*. Random House.

13. Fischer, B., Lago, U. & Liu, F. (2013). *Reinventing Giants: How Chinese Global Competitor Haier Has Changed the Way Big Companies Transform*. John Wiley & Sons.

14. Fischer, B., Lago, U. & Liu, F. (2015). "The Haier Road to Growth." Strategy+business. https://www.strategy-business.com/article/00323.

15. Backaler, J. (2010, June 17). "Haier: a Chinese Company that Innovates." *Forbes*. https://www.forbes.com/sites/china/2010/06/17/haier-a-chinese-company-that-innovates.

16. Gonzales, F. (2015). *Reinventing the Company in the Digital Age*. Turner.

17. BBVA. (2018, September 14). "BBVA and the Huge Potential for Artificial Intelligence to Support Better Digital Banking." *NEWS BBVA*. https://www.bbva.com/en/bbva-huge-potential-artificial-intelligence-support-better-digital-banking/.

18. Alfaro, E., Bressan, M., Girardin, F., Murillo, J., Someh, I., & Wixom, B. H. (2019). "BBVA's Data Monetization Journey." *MIS Quarterly Executive*, 117–128. https://doi.org/10.17705/2msqe.00011.

19. Furrer, R., Hawley, J. A. & Handschin, C. (2023). "The Molecular Athlete: Exercise Physiology from Mechanisms to Medals." *Physiological Reviews*, 103(3), 1693–1787. https://doi.org/10.1152/physrev.00017.2022.

20. Keating, G. (2012). *Netflixed: The Epic Battle for America's Eyeballs*. Penguin.

21. Pontefract, D. (2019, February 4). "The Netflix Decision Making Model Is Why They're So Successful." *Forbes*. https://www.forbes.com/sites/danpontefract/2019/02/04/the-netflix-decision-making-model-is-why-theyre-so-successful/.

22. Gottschalk, S., Egeln, J., Kinne, J., Hauer, A., Keese, D. & Oehme, M. (2017). *Die volkswirtschaftliche Bedeutung der Familienunternehmen*.

23. Stiftung Familienunternehmen. (2023). "Daten, Fakten, Zahlen zu Familienunternehmen – Stiftung Familienunternehmen." https://www.familienunternehmen.de/de/news/daten-fakten-zahlen-zu-familienunternehmen.

24. Useem, J. (2019, November 20). "The Long-Forgotten Flight That Sent Boeing Off Course." *The Atlantic.* https://www.theatlantic.com/ideas/archive/2019/11/how-boeing-lost-its-bearings/602188/.

25. Drucker, P. F. (2004, June). "What Makes an Effective Executive." *Harvard Business Review.* https://hbr.org/2004/06/what-makes-an-effective-executive.

26. Krings-Klebe, J., Heinz, J. and Schreiner, J. (2017). "Future Legends: Business in Hyper-Dynamic Markets." Tredition.

27. Iverson, K. (1997). *Plain Talk: Lessons from a Business Maverick.* John Wiley & Sons.

28. Hamel, G. & Zanini, M. (2020). *Humanocracy: Creating Organizations as Amazing as the People Inside Them.* Harvard Business Review Press.

29. Chouinard, Y. (2022, September 14). "Earth is now our only shareholder." *Patagonia.* https://www.patagonia.com/ownership/.

30. Minnaar, J. & De Morree, P. (2020). *Corporate Rebels: Make Work More Fun.* Corporate Rebels Nederland B.V.

31. Knowledge at Wharton. (2018, April 20). "For Haier's Zhang Ruimin, Success Means Creating the Future." *Knowledge at Wharton.* https://knowledge.wharton.upenn.edu/podcast/knowledge-at-wharton-podcast/haiers-zhang-ruimin-success-means-creating-the-future/.

32. De Smet, A., Steele, R., & Zhang, H. (2021). "Shattering the Status Quo: A Conversation with Haier's Zhang Ruimin." *The McKinsey Quarterly.*

33. GE Appliances (2022, August). "A Human Approach to Doing Business." Fortune, 186(1), 32–33. https:// geappliancesco.com/content/pdf/Fortune%20August%202022.pdf.

34. World Management Agility Forum. (2024, March 8). *Darrell Rigby & Kevin Nolan – The Agile Human Ecosystem (GE Appliances Case Study)* [Video]. YouTube. https://www.youtube.com/watch?v=CFdBjUA3W8E

35. Minnaar, J. (2022, September). "The EMC Contract as a Smart Coordination Mechanism." *GlobalFocus.* https://www.globalfocusmagazine.com/the-emc-contract-as-a-smart-coordination-mechanism/.

36. Jacobides, M. G., & Duke, L. (2020). "Haier's (2019) Ecosystem Revolution: From Rendanheyi 2.0 to Rendanheyi 3.0." *London Business School Case Study* CS-20-14. https://publishing.london.edu/cases/haier-s-2019-ecosystem-revolution-from-rendanheyi-2-0-to-rendanheyi-3-0.

37. Nobles, W. & Redpath, J. (1997). "Market Based Management™ - A Key to Nucor's Success." *Journal of Applied Corporate Finance*, 10(3), 104–115. https://doi.org/10.1111/j.1745-6622.1997.tb00151.x.

38. Boundaryless. (2020, May 28). *Haier CEO Zhang Ruimin Exclusive Interview on Rendanheyi, Platforms and Ecosystems [Video]. YouTube.* https://www.youtube.com/watch?v=RgQrz3EVhU0.

39. Grønning, T. (2016). "Working Without a Boss: Lattice Organization With Direct Person-to-Person Communication at W. L. Gore & Associates, Inc." In *SAGE Publications: SAGE Business Cases Originals eBooks*. https://doi.org/10.4135/9781473947542.

40. Danneels, E. (2008). "Organizational Antecedents of Second-order Competencies." *Strategic Management Journal*, 29(5), 519–543. https://doi.org/10.1002/smj.684.

41. Haleem, R. M., Salem, M. Y., Fatahallah, F. A. & Abdel-Fattah, L. (2015). "Quality in the Pharmaceutical Industry – A Literature Review." *Saudi Pharmaceutical Journal*, 23(5), 463–469. https://doi.org/10.1016/j.jsps.2013.11.004.

42. Frynas, J. G., Mol, M. J., & Mellahi, K. (2018). "Management Innovation Made in China: Haier's Rendanheyi." *California Management Review*, 61(1), 71-93. https://doi.org/10.1177/0008125618790244.

43. Koster, N. & Nandram, S. (2014). "Organizational Innovation and Integrated Care: Lessons from Buurtzorg." *Journal of Integrated Care*, 22(4), 174–184. https://doi.org/10.1108/jica-06-2014-0024.

44. Lobb, A. (2023, June 23). "This Company Lets Employees Take Charge—Even with Life and Death Decisions." *HBS Working Knowledge*. https://hbswk.hbs.edu/item/this-company-lets-employees-take-charge-buurtzorg.

45. Schein, E. H. (1972). *Organizational Psychology*. Prentice Hall.

46. Gino, F., Staats, B. R., Hall, B. J., & Chang, T. Y. (2013). "The Morning Star Company: Self-Management at Work." *Harvard Business School Case* 914-013. (Revised June 2016.)

47. Henry, A. (2021). *Platform and collective intelligence : Digital ecosystem of organizations*. John Wiley & Sons.

48. Secundo, G., Dumay, J., Schiuma, G., & Passiante, G. (2016). "Managing Intellectual Capital Through a Collective Intelligence Approach." *Journal of Intellectual Capital*, 17(2), 298-319. https://doi.org/10.1108/jic-05-2015-0046.

49. The BBVA New Headquarters Team. (2015). "New Workplaces for BBVA: Promoting a Culture of Collaborative Work." In *Reinventing the Company in the Digital Age* (S. 293–334). BBVA. https://www.bbvaopenmind.com/en/articles/new-workplaces-for-bbva-promoting-a-culture-of-collaborative-work/.

50. *BBVA in 2015 - Online Annual Report*. (2015). https://accionistaseinversores.bbva.com/microsites/bbvain2015/en/strategy/a-new-environment-for-the-financial-industry-/.

51. Bock, L. (2015). *Work rules!: Insights from Inside Google That Will Transform How You Live and Lead*. Hachette UK.

52. Smithson, N. (2023, October 7). "Google's (Alphabet's) Organizational Structure & Culture – An Analysis." *Panmore Institute*. https://panmore.com/google-organizational-structure-organizational-culture.

53. Apple and Google. (2021). "Exposure Notification Privacy-preserving Analytics (ENPA)." Retrieved March 12, 2024, from https://covid19-static.cdn-apple.com/applications/covid19/current/static/contact-tracing/pdf/ENPA_White_Paper.pdf.

54. Schein, E. H. (2016). *Organizational Culture and Leadership*. John Wiley & Sons.

55. *Euromonitor Awards | Haier*. (2023). https://corporate.haier-europe.com/press-release/haier-appointed-as-the-no-1-global-major-appliances-brand-for-the-15th-year-by-euromonitor-international/.

56. *Haier Smart Home Co., Ltd. 2023 Annual Report*. (2024). Haier Smart Home Co., Ltd. https://smart-home.haier.com/en/gpxx/iv/P020240430516036471343.pdf.

57. Torres, C., Vila. (2023). "Letter from the Chair." In *BBVA Annual Letter*. https://shareholdersandinvestors.bbva.com/microsites/bbvain2023/en/publication/contents/media/2028975.pdf.

58. *MacroTrends*. (2023). https://www.macrotrends.net/stocks/stock-comparison?s=revenue&axis=single&comp= X:NUE.

59. "Amazon Web Services Revenue 2023 | Statista." (2024, February 9). *Statista*. https://www.statista.com/statistics/233725/development-of-amazon-web-services-revenue/.

60. Hatch, M. J. (1993). "The Dynamics of Organizational Culture." *The Academy of Management Review*, 18(4), 657-693. https://doi.org/10.2307/258594.

61. Follett, M. P. (1924). *Creative Experience*. Longmans, Green and Company.

62. Cameron, K. S. & Quinn, R. E. (2011). *Diagnosing and Changing Organizational Culture: Based on the Competing Values Framework*. John Wiley & Sons.

63. Denison, D. R. (1990). *Corporate Culture and Organizational Effectiveness.* John Wiley & Sons.

64. O'Reilly, C. A., Caldwell, D. F., Chatman, J. A. & Doerr, B. (2014). "The Promise and Problems of Organizational Culture." *Group & Organization Management*, 39(6), 595–625. https://doi.org/10.1177/1059601114550713.

65. Löffler, S. (2021, January 13). "Agile Business Development at ZEISS Digital Innovation." *Zeiss.* https://blogs.zeiss.com/digital-innovation/en/agile-business-management-at-zeiss-digital-innovation/.

66. Fonstad, N. O., & Salonen, J. (2021). *Four Changes: How BBVA Generated Greater Strategic Value*. MIT Centre for Information Systems Research (CISR).

67. Krings-Klebe, J. & Schreiner, J. (2023, June 19). "How Haier's Antifragile Strategy Succeeds Amidst Disruption by Janka Krings-Klebe & Jörg Schreiner." *Global Peter Drucker Forum BLOG*. https://www.druckerforum.org/blog/how-haiers-antifragile-strategy-succeeds-amid-disruptionby-janka-krings-klebe-jorg-schreiner/.

68. Bezos, J. (2017, April 17). "2016 Letter to Amazon Shareholders." https://www.aboutamazon.com/news/company-news/2016-letter-to-shareholders.

69. BBVA. (2022, April 12). "How BBVA Uses Data to Look After Its Customers' Financial Health." *NEWS BBVA*. https://www.bbva.com/en/financial-health/how-bbva-uses-data-to-look-after-its-customers-financial-health/.

70. BBVA. (2018, January 9). "TCR: Three Letters that are Changing the Way BBVA Works." *NEWS BBVA*. https://www.bbva.com/en/tcr-three-letters-changing-way-bbva-works/.

71. Schoemaker, P. J. H. & Kuhn, J. S. (2021). "Haier: Ecosystem Leadership." *Strategy & Leadership*, 49(5), 16-22. https://doi.org/10.1108/sl-09-2021-0087.

72. Zohar, D. (2022). *Zero Distance: Management in the Quantum Age*. Springer Nature.

73. Christensen, C. (2013). *The Innovator's Dilemma: When New Technologies Cause Great Firms to Fail*. Harvard Business Review Press.

74. Hastings, R. & Meyer, E. (2020). *No Rules Rules: Netflix and the Culture of Reinvention*. Penguin.

75. Cao, Y. (2018). *The Haier Model: Reinventing a Multinational Giant in the Network Era.* LID Publishing.

76. Gao, J., He, H., Teng, D., Wan, X. & Zhao, S. (2021). "Cross-border Knowledge Search and Integration Mechanism – A Case Study of Haier Open Partnership Ecosystem (HOPE)." *Chinese Management Studies*, 15(2), 428–455. https://doi.org/10.1108/cms-05-2020-0196.

77. Catmull, E. (2008, September). "How Pixar Fosters Collective Creativity." *Harvard Business Review.* https://hbr.org/2008/09/how-pixar-fosters-collective-creativity.

78. Catmull, E. (2014). *Creativity, Inc.: An Inspiring Look at How Creativity Can - and Should - Be Harnessed for Business Success by the Founder of Pixar.* Random House.

79. Zhang, Y., Sun, Z. & Sun, M. (2022). "Unabsorbed Slack Resources and Enterprise Innovation: The Moderating Effect of Environmental Uncertainty and Managerial Ability." *Sustainability*, 14(7), 3782. https://doi.org/10.3390/su14073782.

80. Gulati, R., Ciechanover, A., & Huizinga, J. (2019). "Netflix: A Creative Approach to Culture and Agility." *Harvard Business School Case 420-055*.

81. Centobelli, P., Cerchione, R., Del Vecchio, P., Oropallo, E. & Secundo, G. (2022). "Blockchain Technology for Bridging Trust, Traceability and Transparency in Circular Supply Chain." *Information & Management*, 59(7), 103508. https://doi.org/10.1016/j.im.2021.103508.

82. EFPIA. (2022). "EFPIA Code Report 2022–2023." Retrieved from https://www.efpia.eu/media/bvppoajb/efpia-code-report-2022-20230718.pdf.

83. Henkel. (2021, September 28). "*Weltwirtschaftsforum zeichnet Henkel zum dritten Mal als Vorreiter für Industrie 4.0 aus.*" https://www.henkel.de/presse-und-medien/presseinformationen-und-pressemappen/2021-09-28-weltwirtschaftsforum-zeichnet-henkel-zum-dritten-mal-als-vorreiter-fuer-industrie-4-0-aus-1344812.

84. Henkel. (2020, January 2). "*Gut vernetzt dank digital Backbone.*" https://www.henkel.de/spotlight/2020-01-02-gut-vernetzt-dank-digital-backbone-1010690.

85. Palepu, K., Narayandas, D., Kak, R. & Tahilyani, R. (2023). "Digital Transformation at Tata Steel." *Harvard Business School Case 323-053*, January 2023. (Revised January 2024).

86. Kumar, R., Dubashi, N., Gupta, R. & Singh, K. (2021, March 8). "How a Steel Plant in India Tapped the Value of Data—and Won Global Acclaim." *McKinsey & Company*. https://www.mckinsey.com/industries/metals-and-mining/how-we-help-clients/how-a-steel-plant-in-india-tapped-the-value-of-data-and-won-global-acclaim.

87. Mani, R. N. (2022, August 30). "Tata Steel Mission 2025: Lead the Digital Steelmaking." https://www.cio.inc/tata-steel-mission-2025-lead-digital-steelmaking-a-19996.

88. Fretty, P. (2021, July 7). "Inside Tata Steel's Digital Transformation." *IndustryWeek*. https://www.industryweek.com/technology-and-iiot/article/21168392/inside-tata-steels-digital-transformation.

89. Ma, X. (2023). "Methodology for Digital Transformation." In *Management for Professionals*. https://doi.org/10.1007/978-981-19-9111-0.

90. Falcone, E. C., Kent, J. L., & Fugate, B. S. (2019). "Supply Chain Technologies, Interorganizational Network and Firm Performance." *International Journal of Physical Distribution & Logistics Management*, 50(3), 333–354. https://doi.org/10.1108/ijpdlm-08-2018-0306.

91. Alibaba. (2020, November 12). "Number of Online Orders Generated on Alibaba E-commerce Properties on Singles Day from 2013 to 2020 (in billions) [Graph]." *Statista*. https://www.statista.com/statistics/364780/number-of-orders-alibaba-singles-day/.

92. AliResearch, China Taobao Village Development Alliance, & Alibaba Research Centre for Rural Dynamics. (2020). "China Taobao Village Research Report." https://arc-quan-hangzhou.oss-accelerate.aliyuncs.com/aliresearch/2021-02-08/c2db6aad669647d3aaa8219a9aa0a96d/China%20Taobao%20Village%20Research%20Report%20(2020).pdf.

93. Zeng, M. (2018, August 21). "Alibaba and the Future of Business." *Harvard Business Review*. https://hbr.org/2018/09/alibaba-and-the-future-of-business.

94. Stone, B. (2021). *Amazon Unbound: Jeff Bezos and the Invention of a Global Empire*. Simon and Schuster.

95. LaValle, S. et al. (2010, December 21). "Big Data, Analytics and the Path From Insights to Value." *MIT Sloan Management Review*. https://sloanreview.mit.edu/article/big-data-analytics-and-the-path-from-insights-to-value/.

96. Haier. (2020, June 18). "Haier Internet of Clothing No.1 Store: It's a Store and a Butler." *Haier*. https://www.haier.com/global/haier-ecosystem/list/20201021_149584.shtml.

97. "Global Lighthouse Network: Insights from the Forefront of the Fourth Industrial Revolution." (2023, November 16). *World Economic Forum*. https://www.weforum.org/whitepapers/global-lighthouse-network-insights-from-the-forefront-of-the-fourth-industrial-revolution.

98. Bean, R. (2020, September 30). "Why Culture Is the Greatest Barrier to Data Success." *MIT Sloan Management Review*. https://sloanreview.mit.edu/article/why-culture-is-the-greatest-barrier-to-data-success/.

99. U.S. Securities and Exchange Commission. (2010). "Findings Regarding the Market Events of May 6, 2010." https://www.sec.gov/files/marketevents-report.pdf.

100. Lazer, D., Kennedy, R., King, G., & Vespignani, A. (2014). "The Parable of Google Flu: Traps in Big Data Analysis." *Science*, 343(6176), 1203–1205. https://doi.org/10.1126/science.1248506.

101. European Parliament. (2023, June 14). "EU AI Act: First Regulation on Artificial Intelligence | News | European Parliament." https://www.europarl.europa.eu/news/en/headlines/society/20230601STO93804/eu-ai-act-first-regulation-on-artificial-intelligence.

102. Amar, J., Rahimi, S., Von Bismarck, N. & Wunnava, A. (2022, November 1). "Smart Scheduling: How to Solve Workforce-planning Challenges with AI." *McKinsey & Company*. https://www.mckinsey.com/capabilities/operations/our-insights/smart-scheduling-how-to-solve-workforce-planning-challenges-with-ai.

103. De Modesti, P. H., Fernandes, E. C. & Borsato, M. (2020). "Production Planning and Scheduling Using Machine Learning and Data Science Processes." In *Advances in Transdisciplinary Engineering*. https://doi.org/10.3233/atde200153.

104. Marion, R. & Uhl-Bien, M. (2001). "Leadership in Complex Organizations." *The Leadership Quarterly*, 12(4), 389–418. https://doi.org/10.1016/s1048-9843(01)00092-3.

105. Kouzes, J. M. & Posner, B. Z. (2017). *The Leadership Challenge: How to Make Extraordinary Things Happen in Organizations*. John Wiley & Sons.

106. Nicholson, N. (2005). "Meeting the Maasai." *Journal Of Management Inquiry*, 14(3), 255–267. https://doi.org/10.1177/1056492605279095.

107. Tonn, J. C. (2008). *Mary P. Follett: Creating Democracy, Transforming Management*. Yale University Press.

108. Hamel, G. (2011, December). "First, Let's Fire All the Managers." *Harvard Business Review*. https://hbr.org/2011/12/first-lets-fire-all-the-managers.

109. ReasonTV. (2012, December 27). *I, Tomato: Morning Star's Radical Approach to Management* [Video]. YouTube. https://www.youtube.com/watch?v=qqUBdX1d3ok.

110. World Management Agility Forum. (2024, June 6). *Reimagining Management Towards Excellence* [Video]. YouTube. https://www.youtube.com/live/4rj8bSKYGSY.

111. Kirkpatrick, D. (2011). *Beyond Empowerment: The Age of the Self-Managed Organization.* Morning Star Self-Management Institute.

112. Edmondson, A. C. & Harvey, J. (2017). *Extreme Teaming: Lessons in Complex, Cross-Sector Leadership.* Emerald Group Publishing.

113. Edmondson, A. C. (2018). *The Fearless Organization: Creating Psychological Safety in the Workplace for Learning, Innovation, and Growth.* John Wiley & Sons.

114. Lowrey, Y. (2016). *The Alibaba Way: Unleashing Grass-Roots Entrepreneurship to Build the World's Most Innovative Internet Company.* McGraw Hill Professional.

115. Nie, W., Xin, K., & Zhang, L. (2009). *Made in China: Secrets of China's Dynamic Entrepreneurs.* John Wiley & Sons (Asia).

116. Tse, E. (2015). *China's Disruptors: How Alibaba, Xiaomi, Tencent, and Other Companies are Changing the Rules of Business.* Penguin.

117. Erisman, P. (2015). *Alibaba's World: How a Remarkable Chinese Company Is Changing the Face of Global Business.* Pan Macmillan.

118. Nandram, S. S. (2014). *Organizational Innovation by Integrating Simplification: Learning from Buurtzorg Nederland.* Springer.

119. Gallup, Inc. (2024). "State of the Global Workplace Report." *Gallup.com.* https://www.gallup.com/workplace/349484/state-of-the-global-workplace.aspx.

120. Quinn, R. E. & Thakor, A. V. (2018, July-August). "Creating a Purpose-Driven Organization." *Harvard Business Review.* https://hbr.org/2018/07/creating-a-purpose-driven-organization.

121. Durand, R. & Ioannou, I. (2023, November 7). "How Leaders Can Create a Purpose-Driven Culture." *Harvard Business Review.* https://hbr.org/2023/11/how-leaders-can-create-a-purpose-driven-culture.

122. Mankins, M., & Garton, E. (2017, February 9). "How Spotify Balances Employee Autonomy and Accountability." *Harvard Business Review.* https://hbr.org/2017/02/how-spotify-balances-employee-autonomy-and-accountability.

123. Bungay, S. (2011). *The Art of Action: How Leaders Close the Gaps between Plans, Actions and Results*. Hachette UK.

124. Kniberg, H. (2019, July 30). *Spotify Engineering Culture - Part 1 (aka the "Spotify Model")* [Video]. YouTube. https://www.youtube.com/watch?v=Yvfz4HGtoPc.

125. Gulati, R. (2022). *Deep Purpose: The Heart and Soul of High-Performance Companies*. HarperCollins.

126. Lee, M. Y., Koo, W. W.-Y., & Minnaar, J. (2022). *Haier: Organizing to Build a Smart Ecosystem Brand*. INSEAD.

127. Raymond, E. S. (2001). *The Cathedral & the Bazaar: Musings on Linux and Open Source by an Accidental Revolutionary*. O'Reilly Media.

128. Weber, S. (2009). *The Success of Open Source*. Harvard University Press.

129. Ashby, W. R. (1956). "An Introduction to Cybernetics." *Biodiversity Heritage Library*. https://doi.org/10.5962/bhl.title.5851.

130. Benedict, G., & Sebastian, I. M. (2024). "Designing Ecosystem Governance to Grow Value (MIT CISR Research Briefing No. XXIV-2)." *MIT Centre for Information Systems Research*. https://cisr.mit.edu/publication/2024_0201_EcosystemGovernance_BenedictSebastian.

131. Ajuntament de Barcelona. (2018). "Barcelona City Council Digital Plan." https://www.barcelona.cat/digitalstandards/en/data-management/0.1/_attachments/barcelona_data_management_0.1.en.pdf.

132. Bakıcı, T., Almirall, E. & Wareham, J. (2013). "A Smart City Initiative: The Case of Barcelona." *Journal of the Knowledge Economy*, 4(2), 135–148. https://doi.org/10.1007/s13132-012-0084-9.

133. Capdevila, I. & Zarlenga, M. I. (2015). "Smart City or Smart Citizens? The Barcelona Case." *Journal of Strategy and Management*, 8(3), 266–282. https://doi.org/10.1108/jsma-03-2015-0030.

134. Calzada, I. & Cobo, C. (2015). "Unplugging: Deconstructing the Smart City." *Journal of Urban Technology*, 22(1), 23–43. https://doi.org/10.1080/10630732.2014.971535.

135. Laursen, L. (2014, November 18). "Barcelona's Smart City Ecosystem." *MIT Technology Review*. https://www.technologyreview.com/2014/11/18/12190/barcelonas-smart-city-ecosystem/.

136. Charnock, G., Purcell, T., & Ribera-Fumaz, R. (2014). *The Limits to Capital in Spain: Crisis and Revolt in the European South*. Springer.

137. Ponzini, D. (2020). *Transnational Architecture and Urbanism: Rethinking How Cities Plan, Transform, and Learn*. Routledge.

138. Ferrer, J. (2017, June 1). "Barcelona's Smart City Vision: An Opportunity for Transformation." *Field Actions Science Reports, Special*, Issue 16, 70-75. https://journals.openedition.org/factsreports/4367.

139. Angelidou, M. (2014). "Smart City Policies: A Spatial Approach." *Cities*, 41, S3–S11. https://doi.org/10.1016/j.cities.2014.06.007.

140. Ojo, A., Curry, E., Janowski, T., & Dzhusupova, Z. (2015). "Designing Next Generation Smart City Initiatives: The SCID Framework." In *Public Administration and Information Technology* (pp. 43–67). https://doi.org/10.1007/978-3-319-03167-5_4.

141. Minnaar, J. (2018, January 31). "The World's Most Pioneering Company of Our Times." *Corporate Rebels.* https://www.corporate-rebels.com/blog/haier.

142. Hamel, G., & Zanini, M. (2018). "The End of Bureaucracy." *Harvard Business Review*, 96(6), 50-59.

143. Zhang, R. (2015). RenDanHeYi 2.0: "Building an Ecosystem to Co-create and Win Together." *Haier Group and the Economic Information Daily Of Xinhua News Agency.* http://www.druckerforum.org/retrospective/fileadmin/user_upload/2015/files/zhang_ruimin_speech.pdf

144. Mader, S., & Frankenberger, K. (2021). "Klöckner & Co SE Evaluating Digital Transformation." *(Teaching Note)*. Reference no. 321-0308-1.

145. Klöckner & Co SE. (2018). "Kloeckner & Co SE Annual Report 2017." https://www.kloeckner.com/dam/kco/files/en/publications/2018/earnings/Kloeckner_Co_Annual_Report_2017.pdf.

146. Klöckner & Co SE. (2020, February 10). "Kloeckner & Co SE Focus Call Presentation." https://www.kloeckner.com/dam/kco/files/en/presentations/2020/KloecknerCo_FocusCall_10.02.2020.pdf.

147. Goldratt, E. M., & Cox, J. (2016). *The Goal: A Process of Ongoing Improvement.* Routledge.

148. Piketty, T. (2017). *Capital in the Twenty-First Century.* Harvard University Press.

149. World Economic Forum. (2019, December 2). "Davos Manifesto 2020: The Universal Purpose of a Company in the Fourth Industrial Revolution." https://www.weforum.org/agenda/2019/12/davos-manifesto-2020-the-universal-purpose-of-a-company-in-the-fourth-industrial-revolution/.

About the Authors

Janka Krings-Klebe, holding a Dr.-Ing. in Mechanical Engineering, is a leading strategy expert in Industry 4.0, digital transformation and business ecosystems with over 20 years of international experience. In 2016, she co-founded co-shift GmbH, a company that supports organizations across all industries in digital transformation, offering executive training and coaching. Previously at Bosch, she led digital transformation initiatives, crafting corporation-wide strategies and mentoring leaders. A founding member of the Business Ecosystem Alliance and a visiting lecturer on innovation, culture and leadership, she also serves as Vice Chair of the Digitalization & IT Economy Committee of the Chamber of Industry and Commerce in Stuttgart.

Jörg Schreiner is a visionary thinker who combines systemic insights with the latest technological developments, global business trends and societal issues to cultivate a holistic understanding of digitally empowered organizations. As a trainer and senior business coach with over 20 years of experience in various industries, he is an expert in business platforms and entrepreneurial organizations. Jörg has coached digital transformation initiatives for engineering and software development companies and lectures on organizational development and business processes. As co-founder of co-shift GmbH, he enables companies to navigate digital transformation with innovative strategies.

www.ingramcontent.com/pod-product-compliance
Lightning Source LLC
Chambersburg PA
CBHW030457210326
41597CB00013B/705